The Slugs

On G. I Gurdjieff's Beelzebub's Tales to His Grandson

Christopher P. Holmes

ZERO POINT
Institute for Mystical and Spiritual Science
Box 700, 108 Clothier Street East
Kemptville, Ontario, Canada K0G 1J0
zeropoint@bell.net
(613) 258-6258
www.zeropoint.ca

Zero Point Publications 2010

© 2010 by Zero Point Publications
All rights reserved. No part of this publication may be
commercially reproduced without permission from the author.
However, the reader is free to quote passages in criticism,
reviews or other writings. Inquiries are welcome.

Cover illustration: Anita J. Mitra
Graphic Design and Prepress: Željka Županić

1st Printing - 2002

The Slugs
On G. I Gurdjieff's Beelzebub's Tales to His Grandson
Christopher P. Holmes.

ISBN 978-0-9689435-4-0

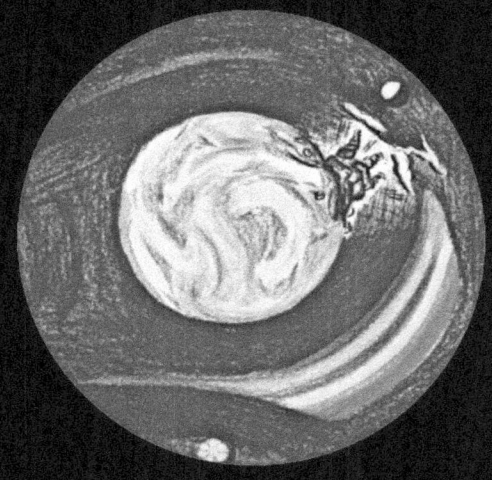

"... 'Hasnamussian science,' invented by certain pimpled beings among them, in which it is nonchalantly proved that the periodic reciprocal destruction on the Earth is very, very necessary, and that if it did not exist an intolerable overpopulation would result on the Earth, and such economic horrors would ensure that men-beings would begin to eat one another. ..."

"... every kind of data for individual manifestation have already quite ceased to be crystallized in most of these three-brained beings who have taken your fancy, particularly the contemporary ones ..."

- Beelzebub's Tales to His Grandson -
- G. I. Gurdjieff, 1950 / p.1072 -

Table of Content

VI - VII	**Preface** by a Fool at the Zero Point
	I /
2	**G. I. Gurdjieff and** **Beelzebub's Tales to His Grandson**
3	1. Background Notes
7	2. A New Language
9	3. "The Slugs"
13	4. Beelzebub's History
15	5. About the Strange Psyche of the Three-Brained Beings on Planet Earth
17	6. The Question of the Soul & the Higher Being-Bodies
20	7. Similitudes of the Whole
	II /
24	**The Strange Psyche** **& Psychopathology of Your Favorites**
25	1. The Dual Consciousness
27	2. To 'Tickle' their Numerous Weaknesses
30	3. The Heart & the Emotional Center
33	4. On Pleasure, Sperm, Sex & Abstinence
36	5. The Atrophy of the Sacred Being-Impulses of Faith, Hope & Love
39	6. The Awakening of Conscience: The remaining Sacred and Divine Being-Impulse in the Subconscious
42	7. On Education & the Automatic Reason-of-Knowledge
46	8. Human Psychopathology & the Causes of War
52	9. Notes on the Moon & the Causes of War
57	10. Hasnamuss-Individuals & the 'Naloo-osian-spectrum-of-impulses
61	11. The Hasnamussian Sciences, the 'Intelligentsia' & the 'Crats'
68	12. A Portrait of 'Man' in Quotation Marks
72	13. Being-Partkdolg-Duty: On Conscious Labors and Intentional Suffering
74	14. Remembering, Forgetting & the Inevitability of Death

	III /
78	**"Objective Science"**
79	1. The Sacred Fundamental Cosmic Laws of World-Creation and World-Maintenance
79	1a. Triamazikamno
81	1b. Heptaparaparshinokh
83	2. The Autoegocratic and the Trogoautoegocratic Systems
87	3. In the Beginning ...
91	4. The Etherokrilno & the Omnipresent Okidanokh
94	5. The Law of Falling & the Law-of-Catching-Up
96	6. Time: The 'Ideally-Unique-Subjective-Phenomena'
	IV /
100	**Science of the Soul**
101	1. An Impartial Perspective on "All the Rubbish Accumulated during the Ages in Human Mentation"
104	2. The Sacred Triamazikamno and the Three Being-Brains
107	3. The Origin and Nature of the Tetartocosmoses, and the Higher Being-Bodies
113	4. The Evolution and Involution of Exioehary
117	5. The Alchemy of the Blood
120	6. Afterlife Processes
120	6a. The Sacred Rascooarnos
122	6b. The Choot-God-Litanical period
123	6c. The Holy Planet Purgatory
124	6c. The Fate of Hasnamuss-individuals
127	7. Gradients of being-Reason, Objective or Divine Reason
131	8. Striving for Self-Perfection
	V /
138	**A Particle of all that Exists**
139	1. A Particle of all that Exists
142	**The Author**
144	**Bibliography**
146	**ZP Publications**

Preface

by a Fool at the Zero Point

Unfortunately, there are no commentaries on Gurdjieff's ultrafantastic *Beelzebub's Tales to His Grandson* within the existing literature of humankind, which I know of, that do more than scratch the surface of this masterpiece story. *The Slugs* focuses primarily upon three areas of inquiry. The first concerns the general psychopathology of humankind—*"your favorites"* in the terminology of Beelzebub. Gurdjieff provides a remarkable teaching of psychology with extensive commentaries upon the strange psyches of those three-brained beings breeding on planet Earth, and particularly concerning their horrific processes of reciprocal destruction, or war, which periodically occurs on that planet. Secondly, *The Slugs* articulates the main principles of *"Objective Science"* according to Beelzebub—including materials on the Sacred primordial Cosmic Laws, the processes of creation—*in the beginning*, the nature of the ethers and the mechanisms of evolution and involution which occur within Cosmoses. Thirdly, this work elaborates a profound *"science of the soul"* outlined by Beelzebub—detailing the processes of the formation of the higher being-bodies and the attainment of Objective Reason. On all of these subjects, Gurdjieff's teachings present an absolutely astonishing viewpoint—unlike anything otherwise offered within contemporary psychology, science, religion and philosophy. *The Tales* soars above almost anything else as an "ultrafantastic book" —examining the *"great inscrutable mysteries of Nature."*

Hopefully, this writing will help to fill the void in the scant existing literature on Gurdjieff's masterpiece *Tales*. *The Slugs* certainly does not simply *"pour-from-the-empty-into-the-void,"* as do so many contemporary 'learned beings' in their 'wiseacring' about the human condition or other people's writings and ideas. Instead, it captures essential qualities and teachings of the magical *Tales,* and a shocking perspective on the current state of humankind sinking into an all time low.

Gurdjieff's grand *Tales* are so difficult and sweeping in scope that no writer has made the effort to tackle this epic work. Being a slug myself, but oh what a slug, I should have had a better sense than to take on such a project. However, casting aside these doubts, my deeper essence-feeling is that *The Slugs* captures some of the essential themes and teachings of *Beelzebub's Tales* and provides a shocking perspective on the state of humankind, the mysteries of creation and the possibilities for human transformation, if we can avoid the Hasnamussian sciences.

Over time, I hope to expand upon this presentation, as every time that I read *Beelzebub's Tales*, I discover so many things new or anew, Gurdjieff's humour is ever deeper and strange, and the meaning of everything takes on a further significance. Upon preparing this newest edition of *The Slugs*, I was astonished to reread Beelzebub's remarks about the causes of war, the role of Hasnamuss individuals, societies and science, so-called, and such. In the precarious times in which we live, Beelzebub's insights into the Hasnamusses, the stock jugglers and the power-possessing and important peoples, provide a shock to highlight the current *archcriminal* state of the human race controlled and concocted by such psychopaths and special societies—terrestrial nullities as Beelzebub calls them.

Gurdjieff's masterful *Tales* can be read and reread and always discloses new meanings and allows for a deeper comprehension—as only a true mystery and master story can do. Beelzebub's depiction of the life and psychopathology of humankind, his accounts of ancient history and of aliens within the life of the solar system, his travels and observations of humankind are a treasury of tragic-comic humour, blended with cosmic wisdom and spiritual teaching.

On an individual level: I would like to thank Anita J. Mitra for her cover illustration and other prints within *The Slugs*, as well as for her love and support through twenty years of our studies of such things as these and reading *The Tales*; James Moffatt, a life long friend and fellow seeker after truth, editor and contributor to my work; Karen T. Hale, who suffered through those periods of my absorption and preoccupations with such other-worldly things while all around us a world gone mad, ruled by Hasnamusses and the periodic psychoses of strange three brained beings, and who yet helped to see this book through to its completion; and finally, Zeljka Zupanic, from Croatia, a gifted designer and sincere soul, who has contributed so significantly in bringing this work to fruition in such a splendid fashion. Love to you all, special nuts like myself, if you know what I mean.

Sincerely,
Christopher P. Holmes, Ph. D.
October 2010

Zero Point
Institute for Mystical and Spiritual Science
Box 700, Kemptville, Ontario, Canada

"… in everything under the
care of Mother Nature
the possibility is foreseen for
beings to acquire
the kernel of their essence,
that is to say, their own 'I.'"

- 1950 -

Gurdjieff

I /
G. I. Gurdjieff and Beelzebub's Tales to His Grandson

1. Background Notes

At the turn of the century, G. I. Gurdjieff (1872-1949) and a group of individuals, who called themselves the *"seekers after truth,"* attempted to piece together a system of ancient, esoteric knowledge about the origins, nature and purpose of life on Earth. As a result of his search, Gurdjieff came into contact with the fourth way, an esoteric teaching which he dates to *pre-Egyptian times.* Gurdjieff once responded to a student's inquiry concerning the origins of the fourth way by stating that: *"if you like, this is esoteric Christianity."* (1949, p. 102) However, Gurdjieff then explained that Christian forms of worship and teachings were themselves borrowed from earlier pre-Egyptian times: *"... only not from the Egypt that we know but from one which we do not know. This Egypt was in the same place as the other but it existed much earlier. Only small bits of it survived in historical times, and these bits have been preserved in secret and so well that we do not even know where they have been preserved."* (1949, p. 02)[1]

When introducing the *enneagram*, the mystical symbol unique to the fourth way, Gurdjieff claimed that: *"The teaching whose theory is being here set out is completely self-supporting and independent of other lines and it has been completely unknown up to the present time."* (1949) Gurdjieff claimed that the fourth way had appeared and disappeared several times in the course of human history. As its latest emissary, his mission appears to have been that of introducing this extraordinary system of ideas, practices and disciplines to the western world. Although Gurdjieff suggested that he maintained contact with his teachers, who and where these were, remained hidden in secrecy.[2] On one occasion, Gurdjieff offered the rather cryptic remark: *"I am a small man compared to those who sent me."* (Patterson, 1998, p. 180)

Although the fourth way contains elements similar to other esoteric traditions, it clearly stands on its own merits. As a system of psychological, mystical, metaphysical and cosmological knowledge, it offers a unique and integrative perspective on the nature of the human condition, our psychological possibilities and deep relationships to the larger Universe, and as concerns the mysteries of creation. The fourth way is an ancient and lost teaching—of largely unknown origins, although varied hints are given within *The Tales* as to the unknown history of humanity and the role played by certain secret brotherhoods. There are many enigmas and mysteries surrounding Mr. Gurdjieff and his masterpiece story of *Beelzebub's Tales to His Grandson.*

Georges Ivanovitch Gurdjieff was an extraordinarily complex, enigmatic, charismatic, outrageous and profound human being. He was once described in *Time* magazine (1952) as *"a remarkable blend of P.T. Barnum, Rasputin, Freud, Groucho Marx and everybody's grandfather."* On a superficial level, that description captures something of Gurdjieff's unique and colourful presence. It seems unlikely

---

[1] A recent news item, reported by *The Associated Press,* announced *"Archaeologists discover 2,500-year-old lost cities."* The report states that archaeologists had found *"an intact city"* submerged in water only six to nine metres deep off the northern coast of Egypt. The ruins are theorized to have been build during the waning days of the pharaohs in the 7th or 6th century B.C.. The secretary general of the Supreme Council of Antiquities, Egypt's top archaeology body, describes the find as *"the most exciting find in the history of marine archaeology."* (Ottawa Citizen, 2001)

[2] John Bennett (1973) states that one student of Gurdjieff, Miss Merton, was *"confident that he remained in touch with the schools in Turkistan,"* and further, that others with him in Paris on various occasions thought that he had travelled to Asia under the guise of visiting Germany. Gurdjieff is known to have corresponded with friends in Asia up until the end of his life.

that anyone can fully come to grips with what Gurdjieff was doing—even those who were closest to him and his most senior pupils. There was always an air of great mystery surrounding this remarkable man. Therefore, while an outline of Gurdjieff's life provides some useful information about his formative experiences and influences, that which remains unknown about him is likely much more significant than that which we do know.

Gurdjieff was born in the 1870's in the city of Alexandropol in the Caucasus region of Asia Minor, which has since annexed by Russia and is now part of Armenia. His father was of Greek origin and his mother Armenian. Growing up in the town of Kars, he was recognized as being an especially precocious youngster. Consequently, his father and the dean of the local Russian military academy paid him special attention, tutoring him in the study of science, medicine and philosophy. As a boy, Gurdjieff witnessed varied unusual psychic and paranormal phenomena. However, when he sought explanations for these strange occurrences, the answers that adults offered were clearly lacking in substance. Rather than simply accepting the existence of the unexplained, such experiences whetted Gurdjieff's appetite for knowledge. He questioned the completeness of the scientific theories and set about searching for esoteric or hidden knowledge about human nature and the deeper purposes of life on earth. Gurdjieff describes these youthful influences as forming in him:

> ... an "irrepressible striving" to understand clearly the precise significance, in general, of the life process on earth of all the outward forms of breathing creatures and, in particular, of the aim of human life in the light of this interpretation. (1933, p.13)

Joining forces with other like-minded individuals, *"the seekers after truth,"* Gurdjieff traveled widely for over twenty years throughout the near and far East, living in monasteries and religious communities, and studying various religious and mystical ideas, disciplines and practices.

By 1915, Gurdjieff was in Moscow where he worked with small groups of select students. Foremost amongst these Russian pupils was P. D. Ouspensky (1878-1947), a noted journalist, mathematician and scholar of esoteric thought and mysticism. Like Gurdjieff, Ouspensky had traveled through the East in search of ancient knowledge. However, until he met Gurdjieff in Russia, Ouspensky had been frustrated by his failure to find a genuine esoteric teaching or to come under the influence of a true master. Once he began to study with Gurdjieff, Ouspensky became convinced that "G." was a real teacher and that the fourth way embodied a profound ancient knowledge of humankind and the Universe.

Although Gurdjieff had planned to establish his work in Moscow and St. Petersburg, the outbreak of the Russian revolution in 1917 forced him to alter his plans. Amidst the chaos wrought by the revolution, he moved a small band of students and their families through Russia and the Caucasus, to locate first in Tiflis, then Constantinople and later in Germany, before eventually settling in the outskirts of Paris, at Fontainebleau. Here, Gurdjieff established the *"Institute for the Harmonious Development of Man"* in 1922. Over the next years, he accepted an assorted group of professionals, artists, intellectuals, writers, dancers, musicians and adventurers, as students at the Institute–in addition to extended family members living within his small community.

P.D. Ouspensky is generally acknowledged as the most renowned and eloquent spokesman for the fourth way teaching. In his brilliant book, *In Search of the Miraculous: Fragments of an unknown teaching* (1949), Ouspensky recounts his times with Gurdjieff from 1915 to 1921 and recalls verbatim accounts of G.'s lectures on the fourth way teaching. Although he ended his contact with Gurdjieff in

1924 for reasons largely unknown, Ouspensky continued to teach the fourth way system–working with groups of students firstly in England and later in America. His books, *The Fourth Way* (1957) and *The Psychology of Man's Possible Evolution* (1950), include his explanations of the Gurdjieff teaching and question-answer sessions with pupils. The Ouspensky version of the Gurdjieff teaching, with its particular language and systematic presentation of ideas, is generally more widely known than the language later invented or coined by Gurdjieff for his own writings on *Beelzebub's Tales*.

Unfortunately, the program at the Institute was largely cut short after Gurdjieff suffered a nearly fatal automobile accident in July of 1924. During his extended period of recovery, Gurdjieff was unable to maintain the active program at the Institute, had few remaining funds and was abandoned by some of his friends and students, while he sent others away. At this time, Gurdjieff had to reassess how best to carry forward the teachings of the fourth way for the future benefit of humankind and thus he turned his attention to writing. From December of 1924 until April of 1935, this was the primary focus of Gurdjieff's activity, although he always continued to see people on an individual basis. During this period, Gurdjieff completed *Beelzebub's Tales to His Grandson: An objectively impartial criticism of the life of man*, *Meetings with Remarkable Men*–his autobiographic writing, and *Life is Real Only Then, When 'I Am'*—a work based on lectures given to students in New York in 1930 and 1931 and which remains incomplete. In addition, Gurdjieff composed over a hundred pieces of Eastern and religious music between 1925 and 1927.

As Gurdjieff was recovering from his accident, he began by dictating *Beelzebub's Tales to his Grandson* in Russian to Madame Olga DeHartmann. Soon afterwards, when he began to write himself, it was in Armenian–his mother's language. These notes were subsequently translated by his Armenian students into Russian and then into English. Overtime, Gurdjieff did most of his writing away from the Institute, sometimes at the Grand Café in Paris, his 'Paris Office,' or within other such *"kindred 'temples' of contemporary morality,"* or during car trips–described as somewhat madcap escapades–through the French countryside or into the Alps.

Although Gurdjieff had intended initially to publish *The Tales* in 1928, his public readings of sample chapters demonstrated that listeners were unable to grasp his meanings as the writings were so obscure. This led in 1927 to a period of despair, when Gurdjieff realized that everything had to be rewritten in order to make it more accessible to his students. Eventually, he was able to complete this over an eighteen month period, although the revisions of some chapters, particularly that on *Purgatory*, were reworked in the ensuing years. Although small numbers of the *Tales* were printed through the 1930's, the final version was not published for more widespread circulation until 1950–the year after Gurdjieff's death.

Having completing *The Tales* and closing his Institute in 1933, Mr. G. moved into a small flat in Paris where he lived through the Second World War, while continuing his work in a clandestine fashion with French pupils. After the war, students from England and America again sought out Mr. G. in Paris. Evening festivities at G's flat included readings from *Beelzebub's Tales*, memorable 'toasts to the idiots' and feasts–all supervised in Gurdjieff's highly idiosyncratic and colorful fashion. He continued to receive and teach pupils until his death on October 22 of 1949.

The primary result of Gurdjieff's writing efforts was the highly unusual and thoroughly misunderstood masterpiece, *Beelzebub's Tales to His Grandson: An objectively impartial criticism of the life of man.* (1950) Gurdjieff himself referred to the *Tales* as an *"ultrafantastic book."* The *Tales* are written in an extremely strange and challenging fashion–a remarkable work that defies easy reading, classification or understanding. Even the setting of the *Tales* is out of the ordinary as the story is told from a cosmic, extraterrestrial perspective—as befits a work of such otherworldly aspirations and dimensions. The central figure and narrator, Beelzebub, is traveling through the cosmos on the spaceship Karnak. To pass the time and to fulfill his *"being obligations"* to his grandson Hassein, Beelzebub takes the opportunity to educate Hassein concerning the laws of the cosmos and the strange psyche of the three-brained beings on planet Earth– all while recounting his six visits to the planet earth. In particular, Beelzebub explains the abnormalities of its inhabitants, those strange *"three-brained beings on planet Earth,"* while portraying in great detail the peculiarities of the human psyche and the history of their ill-fated solar system *"Ors."*

The resulting allegoric and epic tale, which Beelzebub recounts, provides a most unusual view of the life of humanity and our role within the larger cosmic drama. An indication of just how far it stands apart from popular literature is found in Gurdjieff's statement about the aim of his series of writings, *All and Everything*:

> ... to destroy in people everything which, in their false representations, as it were, exists in reality, or in other words "to corrode without mercy all the rubbish accumulated during the ages in human mentation." (p. 1184)

The extent to which Gurdjieff realizes this grandiose aim testifies to how much *Beelzebub's Tales*, book one of the larger *All and Everything* series, is unlike any other popular work of fiction or non-fiction. It is indeed, as G. describes, *an ultrafantastic Tale.*

Those willing to make the special effort necessary to decipher *Beelzebub's Tales* are rewarded with one of the most provocative and astonishing commentaries on the human condition ever penned. Gurdjieff's account of humanity's strange history and his analysis of the unique psychopathology which afflicts the strange and peculiar psyche of those *"three-brained beings"* on planet Earth, is both merciless and wonderfully insightful. With an objectivity that only an alien intelligence is capable of providing, Beelzebub paints a searing portrait of life on planet Earth. He portrays the follies and foibles which beset human beings and keeping them throughout the ages in a state of terrifying unconsciousness. Gurdjieff's assault on the strange three-brained beings' vanity and self-love, presented with great comic effect, is so thoroughly deflating as to leave any intelligent reader with an entirely different feeling about what it means to be called a *"man,"* or what Gurdjieff refers to as *"a man in quotation marks." Beelzebub's Tales* clearly stands as one of the most unique works of literature, art and social commentary of modern times. It also contains innumerable deep mystical and cosmic truths about Objective Science and about the science of the soul.

2. A New Language

It is ample testimony to the sleepwalking state of humanity, that Gurdjieff's masterpiece story is so largely unknown within modern literary, philosophical and scientific circles. It also testifies to the difficult and otherworldly nature of the *Tales* that so few interpretive works have been offered. As an allegorical exposition of an esoteric teaching, *Beelzebub's Tales* contains deep meanings which are not immediately obvious to the reader, but are hidden and encrypted in a unique syntax of language, symbols, myths, tales and sly humour. In its mode of presentation, vision and substance, *Beelzebub's Tales* reveal Gurdjieff to have been a highly enigmatic man of some unusual stature. Furthermore, the *Tales* actually do live up to Gurdjieff's stated objective: *"To destroy, mercilessly ... the beliefs and views, by centuries rooted in him, about everything existing in the world."* Gurdjieff exposes what he labels *"all the rubbish accumulated in human mentation"* and offers an profoundly alternative cosmic view of the strangeness of the human psyche, the nature of reality and a science of the higher faculties of the human soul.

Gurdjieff intentionally made *Beelzebub's Tales* difficult to understand in order to make the reader work consciously at uncovering its meaning. According to Mr. Gurdjieff, contemporary literature has degenerated into *"word prostitution."* People write books unconsciously and mechanically, and people read books mechanically and unconsciously. Hence, rather than presenting his Tale in a fluid and easily accessible fashion, which he refers to derisively as the *"bon ton"* literary approach, Gurdjieff adopts a highly unconventional style. By doing so, he disrupts the reader's usual mechanical associations-disorienting and bewildering him-thereby forcing one to consciously work at making sense of what the author is intending to portray. The book also has an effect on a subconscious level and over time, deeper and deeper levels of meaning can be uncovered as one grasps the cosmic humour and obscure secrets of the *Tales*. As an introduction to the book, Gurdjieff offers some *"friendly advice"*-which is to read the book three times. Firstly, read it as you are *"mechanized"* to read contemporary works; secondly, as if you were reading aloud to another person; and thirdly while trying to *"fathom the gist of my writings."* Even after three readings, one is likely to feel that they are just beginning to comprehend the *Tales*.

In *Beelzebub's Tales*, Gurdjieff introduces a new language, markedly different from that used in his earlier talks as recorded by Ouspensky and other students. He talks of the Most, Most, Holy Sun Absolute, HIS ENDLESSNESS, the Common Father, Mother Nature, and introduces other Angels, Archangels, Sacred Messengers and cosmic characters and historical figures. There are also scientific and/or cosmological principles and laws introduced-all with unusual and foreign sounding names-such as the Autoegocratic and the Trogoautoegocratic systems, the Sacred Fundamental Cosmic Laws of Triamazikamno and Heptaparaparshinokh, the Foolasnitamnian and Itoklanos principles-in addition to invented names for such obscure cosmic substances as the Etherokrilno, Askokin vibrations, the Omnipresent Okidanokh and much more. Beelzebub has a language full of such neologisms-eccentric and otherworldly terms used even to depict mundane objects and phenomena. Even familiar objects are sometimes assigned one of the over two hundred invented words used within *The Tales*: a telescope becomes a 'teskooano,' water is 'sakiakooriap,' and time is the Merciless Heropass. Many of these terms have roots in the Armenian, Russian, Turkish or Greek languages, while other are more fortuitous.

Gurdjieff also has some particular practices as far as punctuation and grammar are concerned. He often uses single quotation marks to emphasize words and he will join a series of words with hyphens—in a sense defining an object or process for which we have no singular word. He talks of 'pouring-from-the-empty-into-the-void,' of time as the 'ideally-unique-subjective-phenomena,' of 'being-Partkdolg-duty' and the 'being-obligolnian-strivings,' and so on and on. Some phrases are repeated enough times that one becomes increasingly familiar with the basic terms and concepts: for example, the phrase 'your favorites' which refers to those 'three-brained beings' on planet Earth.

For those students familiar with P. Ouspensky's presentations of Gurdjieff's psychology, cosmology and metaphysics, they will find new twists and turns provided throughout Beelzebub's explanations of the nature of things. This includes new elements to the formulations of the sacred cosmic laws, the "being-centers," "being-foods" and the "higher being-bodies," and explanations of other obscure substances—such as the Askokin vibrations, the Etherokrilno and the Omnipresent Okidanokh. Particularly important are Beelzebub's secrets about the nature of the higher being-bodies, how these can be coated for the life of the soul and what the soul might attain. As Beelzebub, Gurdjieff elaborates on how a human being can embody the universe, as a microcosm of the macrocosm—or *"a particle of all that exists."* Beelzebub even provides a creation scenario dealing with how it all came about—*in the beginning.*

With time, patience and effort, the reader begins to learn a new language with very ancient roots and meanings. In fact, Gurdjieff's masterpiece can be read many times and always reveals new things full of significance. The reading and study of *The Tales* in fact can serve for individual enlightenment and realization and acts even on the subconscious level. Most importantly, it is the result of impartial mentation and it provides an objective view of the life of *"your favorites."*

3. The "Slugs"

The *"slugs"* is a term used on only a few occasions within *The Tales*. The first occasion is in a short two-page chapter entitled *"The Impudent Brat Hassein, Beelzebub's Grandson, Dares to Call Men "Slugs."*" Beelzebub's grandson Hassein is attempting to refer back to those *"three brained beings"* on that planet Earth which have been the subject of Beelzebub's stories. Hassein is not sure of their name and unknowingly refers to them as "slugs." This is the story line in this excerpt which gives a background setting to the larger *Tales*:

> Hassein immediately sat down at Beelzebub's feet and coaxingly said:
>
> "... Dear and kind Grandfather, tell me then something about those ... how? ... those ... I forget ... yes, about those 'slugs.'"
>
> "What? About what slugs?" asked Beelzebub, not understanding the boy's question.
>
> "Don't you remember, Grandfather, that a little while ago, when you spoke about the three-centered beings breeding on the various planets of that solar system where you existed for such a long time, you happened to say that on one planet–I forget how you called it–that on that planet exist three-centered beings who, on the whole, are like us, but whose skin is a little slimier than ours."
>
> "Ah!" laughed Beelzebub. "You are surely asking about those beings who breed on the planet Earth and who call themselves 'men.'"
>
> "Yes, Grandfather, yes, just that. Tell me about those 'men-beings,' a little more in detail. I should like to know more about them," concluded Hassein.
>
> Then Beelzebub said: "About them I could tell you a great deal, for I often visited that planet and existed among them for a long time and even made friends with many of those terrestrial three-brained beings.
>
> "Indeed, you will find it very interesting to know more about these beings, for they are very peculiar.
>
> "There are many things among them which you would not see among any other beings of any other planet of our Universe.
>
> "I know them very well, because their arising, their further development, and their existence during many, many centuries, by their time calculations, have occurred before my eyes.

> "And not only their own arising occurred before my eyes, but even the accomplished formation of the planet itself on which they arise and exist.
>
> "When we first arrived on that solar system and settled on the planet Mars, nothing yet existed on that planet Earth, which had not yet even had time to cool off completely after its concentration.
>
> "From the very beginning, this same planet has been the cause of many serious troubles to our ENDLESSNESS.
>
> "If you wish I will tell you first of all about the events of general cosmic character connected with this planet ..." (pp. 79-80)

Thus, in the *Tales*, Beelzebub is a cosmic character who has been living on Mars within the solar system of "Ors" even before the Earth was completely cooled and consolidated. He later visited the planet on six occasions during different periods of human history. The first visit is during the time of Atlantis, then in Babylon and Egypt, later in India and Tibet, and elsewhere. The final visit of Beelzebub was to Germany, Russia, France and America in the period of the early nineteenth and twentieth century—Gurdjieff's own era and the period of his visits to these countries.

The term *"slugs"* was a term used in an offhanded way by Hassein in conversation with his Grandfather to refer to those *"men-beings"* on that planet Earth, who cause such problems for the greater cosmic harmony. Its inhabitants are, according to Beelzebub, most peculiar and strange, and manifest in ways so unnatural, as to be unknown in the larger Universe. During his visits to Earth, Beelzebub studies humankind while in disguise and living among them. Although Beelzebub was able to pass himself off as a human, this was only because he had *"lost his horns"* when he had been exiled from his home planet within a distant solar system. Furthermore, he had to hide his tail while living among the "men-beings." One reason why Beelzebub visited the Earth was to report to a High Commission on the problems of those three-brained beings breeding on that ill-fated planet. This is a basic background to the wonderful, humorous and enchanting *Tales*.

A second reference to "slugs" occurs when Beelzebub is elaborating upon the evolution of life on Earth. The first living beings to arise were *"Similitudes-of-the-Whole"* or *"microcosmoses"*–or cells. These then aggregated together to produce two forms of vegetation called *"Oduristelnian"* and *"Polormedekhric."* The microcosmoses also grouped together to form the more complex *"Tetartocosmoses"* –the three-brained beings. *"And among these latter there then first arose just those biped "Tetartocosmoses" whom you a while ago called "slugs."* (p. 86)

Beelzebub explains further that those "men-beings" on planet Earth:

> "... had in them in the beginning the same possibilities for perfecting the functions for the acquisition of being-Reason as have all other forms of 'Tetartocosmoses' arising throughout the whole Universe." (p. 86)

Humankind have latent faculties for attaining different levels of being-Reason, as well as for refining "higher being-bodies" for the life of the soul—just as do all other three-brained Tetartocosmoses within other solar systems.

Unfortunately, *"a misfortune"* occurred. Beelzebub relates:

> "But afterwards, just in the period when they also, as it proceeds on other similar planets of our great Universe, were beginning gradually to be spiritualized by what is called 'being-instinct,' just then, unfortunately for them, there befell a misfortune which was unforeseen from Above and most grievous for them." (p. 86)

Under normal conditions, human beings would have become *"spiritualized"* by *"being-instinct,"* but a series of misfortunes and miscalculations, to be recounted by Beelzebub, resulted in other peculiarities forming within the human psyche–properties unknown within the larger Universe.

On a third occasion, Beelzebub uses the term *"slugs"* in order to elaborate upon the strangeness of the human psyche. In this instance, he explains to Hassein what would be done to him if those three-brained beings living on Earth happened to hear that Hassein had used such a derogatory word as 'slugs' to describe them:

> "Now let us return to those three-brained beings arising on the planet Earth, who have interested you most of all and whom you have called 'slugs.'
>
> "I shall begin by saying how glad I am that you happened to be a long way from those three-centered beings whom you called by a word so 'insulting to their dignity' and that they are not likely ever to hear of it.
>
> "Do you know, you poor thing, you small boy not yet aware of himself, what they would do to you, particularly the contemporary beings there, if they should hear what you called them?
>
> "What they would have done to you if you had been there and if they got hold of you–I am seized with horror at the very mention of it.
>
> "At best they would have thrashed you so ...."
>
> ... "You must know that during the time of my observations of them from the planet Mars and during the periods of my existence among them, I studied the psyche of these strange three-brained beings very thoroughly, and so I already know very well what they would do to anybody who dared to give them such a nickname. (p. 94)

Beelzebub then elucidates the strange psyche of humankind to Hassein in a fanciful characterization of human social life, the practices of 'solemn councils' and their intellectual nullity:

> "Provoked by such an incident as your thus insulting them, if everything was rather 'dull' with them at the given moment, owing to the absence of any other similar absurd interest, they would arrange somewhere in a previously chosen place, with previously invited people, all of course dressed in costumes specially designed for such occasions, what is called a 'solemn council.' (pp. 95-96)

Beelzebub goes on to explain how this *solemn council* would select a *'president'* and proceed with their *'trial,'* where they would *"'pick you to pieces,' and not only you, but your father, your grandfather, and perhaps even all the way back to Adam."* If Hassein is found guilty, he would then be sentenced *"according to the indications of a code of laws collated on the basis of former similar 'puppet plays' by beings called 'old fossils.'"* Beelzebub carries on the tale, with the three-brained beings *"pouring from the empty into the void,"* all in efforts to *"anathematize"* poor Hassein for calling them *slugs*. In this case:

> "The most 'important' beings will decree to all the other beings that in all their appointed establishments, such as what are called 'churches,' 'chapels,' 'synagogues,' 'town-halls,' and so on, special officials shall on special occasions with appointed ceremonies wish for you in thought something like the following:
>
> "That you should lose your horns, or that your hair should turn prematurely grey, or that the food in your stomach should be turned into coffin nails, or that your future wife's tongue should be three times its size, or that whenever you take a bite of your pet pie it should be turned into 'soap,' and so on and so forth in the same strain.
>
> "Do you understand to what dangers you exposed yourself when you called these remote three-brained freaks 'slugs'?"
>
> Having finished thus, Beelzebub looked with a smile on his favorite. (p. 97)

Beelzebub finished with a smile on his face, as might have Mr. Gurdjieff himself, after telling such a fanciful Tale to his grandson, Hassein.

In a final reference to 'slugs,' Beelzebub mentions that at particular periods on planet Earth, *"the birth rate of what are called 'slugs,' 'snails,' 'lice,' 'mole crickets,' and many other similar parasites who destroy everything good, each time always increases more and more."* (p. 630) This reference to 'slugs' occurs during Beelzebub's sixth visit to planet earth, when he is in Russia amidst a period of revolution and chaos. 'Slugs' are parasites who destroy everything good and their numbers increase. Although Beelzebub seldom refers to *'slugs,'* those three-brained beings on planet Earth are most worthy of being so described, according to the *Tales* which elaborate upon humankind's unknown history. Beelzebub explains that in truth, those strange three-brained beings *"know nothing about long-past events on their planet."* (p. 631) Instead, among the contemporary beings, "the slugs," it has *"become quite proper to their nature to see only unreality."* (p. 85)

Another term used repeatedly by Beelzebub in his stories to Hassein–to refer to those three-brained beings on planet Earth–is that of *"your favorites."* As Hassein loves to hear his grandfather's stories, particularly about his visits to Earth, Beelzebub repeatedly refers back to *"your favorites"*–those men-beings who Hassein dared to call "slugs."

4. Beelzebub's History

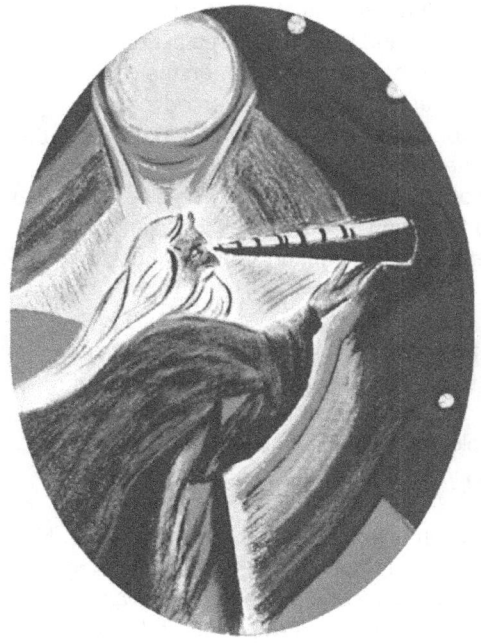

The Tales are recounted as Beelzebub, Hassein and Ahoon are on the upper deck of the *"transspace ship"* Karnak, under a large *"glass bell."* From here, they can observe the boundless spaces of the universe—which serve as an appropriate setting for such an extra-terrestrial story. *The Tales* include Beelzebub's narrations of his six visits to the Earth and his critiques of the life of humankind—all interspersed with his esoteric descriptions of 'Objective science.'

The story opens in *"the year 1921 after the birth of Christ"* by human calculation, or the year 223 after the creation of the World—according to *"objective time-calculation."* Beelzebub, his grandson Hassein, his servant Ahoon, and other kinsmen and attendants are travelling through the *"spaces of the 'Milky Way,'"* or *"Assooparatsata."* Beelzebub has left his home planet of Karatas and is traveling to the solar system of the Pole Star in order to attend a conference. Beelzebub has only recently returned to his home planet Karatas from our solar system of "Ors," where he had been banished for many years of his life under conditions quite foreign to his nature.

"Long, long before," as a youth on his home planet of Karatas, Beelzebub had an *"extraordinarily resourceful intelligence"* and was taken into service on the *"Sun Absolute"* as an attendant upon *"HIS ENDLESSNESS."* Unfortunately, because of a certain misunderstanding –due to his youth and impetuous mentation–Beelzebub *"saw in the government of the World"* something which seemed *"illogical"* to him. He gained support for his views among some comrades, also youthful and not yet fully formed, and then *"interfered in what was none of his business."* This almost brought about a revolution within the central kingdom of the Megalocosmos.

Despite the "All-lovingness" and "All-forgiveness" of HIS ENDLESSNESS, Beelzebub was banished to *"one of the remote corners of the Universe"*–which happened to be our solar system, *Ors*. He was assigned to live on the planet Mars. At that time, the Earth had still to cool off after its "concentration" and no life existed upon the planet. During his time in exile, Beelzebub set up living quarters and an observatory with a telescope on Mars, from where he could observe the Earth and other *"remote points of the Universe."* Others from his assembly re-located from Mars to exist on other planets of the solar system, including the Earth.

Like a character from another dimension of time, Beelzebub drops in on the Earth at various periods in human history in order to study the strange psyche of those "three brained beings" which arose there, or to carry out certain assignments. Having an extremely long life–by Earth standards, Beelzebub had been witness to the early cosmic catastrophes which occurred and the abnormal events which subsequently transpired on Earth through the course of human history.

Beelzebub's first visit was at the time of Atlantis. A kinsman living on Earth had become involved in a very unfortunate matter involving finances and the affairs of state. Beelzebub's council was requested in order to resolve the difficulties. Beelzebub's second visit was eleven centuries later–after the submerging of Atlantis. At that time, the survivors of Atlantis and kinsmen of Beelzebub who had known ahead of time of the impending catastrophe were re-established either on the continent of Africa (or Grabontzi) or in three areas of Ashhark (Asia). These groups had 'invented' peculiar religions involving animal sacrifice. These abnormal practices became so widespread that the deaths (or Rascooarnos) of such large numbers of beings threatened the cosmic harmony of the solar system. Beelzebub was asked by an Archangel on behalf of a High Commission to visit the Earth and try to eradicate such awful practices. The transspace ship Occasion landed on the Caspian Sea and Beelzebub carried out his mission in Tikliamish–one of the three newly arisen 'centers of culture' in Ashhark.

Beelzebub returns briefly to Mars before returning for his third visit–again to uproot the practices of sacrificial offerings. This time, he visits the city of Gob, the center of culture in Maralpleicie, and Kaimon, the major city of the third group on the continent of Asia. During this visit, Beelzebub's travels take him to India (called Pearl-land) and Tibet. Upon completing his mission, Beelzebub returned to Mars and for a long time simply observed the Earth and its inhabitants through his telescope.

Beelzebub's fourth brief visit to the Earth was to bring back some 'apes' for study–in order to resolve issues of their origins. He visits Thebes in Nilia (or Egypt), where his kinsmen are living and then Cairo, where an observatory was being built–the pyramids started by one of the Pharaohs and by initiates of the learned society Akhaldan, who originated from Atlantis. He stays briefly in Cairo, returns to Thebes, captures some apes in South Africa and again returns to Mars.

It is centuries again before Beelzebub's fifth visit. During this time, further major changes had taken place on Earth. Great winds had worn down elevated areas of the Earth and filled in depressions, covering parts of Egypt, northern Africa and Asia with sands. Earlier civilizations had dispersed and a "great transmigration of races" had followed. This time, Beelzebub visits the Earth in order to understand the causes of the terrible processes of reciprocal destruction–war, and he settles in the new 'Center of Culture'–Babylon. This was at the time when the *"burning issue of the day"* concerned the existence of the human soul.

Beelzebub's sixth and final visit to the Earth was again to elucidate the strangeness of the human psyche and the causes of war. This visit was the longest– lasting over three centuries. Beelzebub set up a base of operation in Turkistan, and traveled widely through Egypt, Asia, Europe and to America. Beelzebub's last excursions–to Russia, France, Germany and America were during the late nineteenth and early twentieth century; Gurdjieff's own time period living in these lands.

Beelzebub also recounts to Hassein the role of various Sacred Messengers or individuals *"actualized from above"* sent to the planet Earth through the history of humankind in order to regulate the conditions of "being-existence" established there. These included such figures as Lord Buddha, Saint Lama, Jesus Christ, Saint Mohammed and others–particularly, Ashiata Shiemash.

As Beelzebub had fulfilled a certain role for the mission of Ashiata Shiemash, when the latter returned to the Sun Absolute, he requested of HIS ENDLESSNESS, that Beelzebub, who was now very old, might be pardoned from exile and return to his home planet. It was upon his return to Karatas, that Beelzebub met his grandson Hassein and took an instant liking to him. He assumed a role in educating his grandson and so is now taking him along for his trip to the solar system of the Pole Star, where he has been invited to attend a conference on events happening within another solar system. During the course of these travels, Beelzebub takes the opportunity to participate in the education of his grandson Hassein. He elaborates upon the history of the solar system *Ors*, the misfortunes which occurred on Earth and how the strangeness of the three brained-beings there had come about.

5. About the Strange Psyche of the Three-Brained Beings on Planet Earth

According to *Beelzebub's Tales*, the early harmony of the solar system *"Ors"* was disrupted by a cosmic catastrophe. A comet collided with the earth and broke off two fragments which became the Moon and a secondary satellite, Anulios—unknown to modern science. This catastrophe threatened to disrupt the broader Cosmic Harmony, until the moons were stabilized in their new orbits. A second catastrophe then occurred when the Earth's *"center-of-gravity"* shifted—as an aftereffect of Moon being ejected and later falling back into orbit. This caused the submerging of the continent Atlantis and the rising of other land masses. Later catastrophes, the great winds, were also byproducts of adjustments involving the Moon and its atmosphere, in conjunction with the Earth. One of the cosmic adjustments instituted required that a certain *"sacred vibration," "askokin vibrations,"* be produced by the Earth in order to maintain the moons. Such energies are produced by organic life on earth and by the existence of humankind–the Tetartocosmoses. Beelzebub states: *"... by their existence they ... maintain the detached fragments of their planet."*

Unfortunately, other unforeseen cosmic misfortune occurred when certain archangels on a Most Holy Commission implanted a special organ called the *Kundabuffer* in humankind, at the base of the spine. The purpose of this intervention was to prevent humans from becoming aware of their enslavement to the moon and thus rebelling in order to escape their fate. The properties of this special organ are most peculiar in their effects upon humankind. The Kundabuffer causes humans firstly to *"perceive reality topsy-turvy"* and secondly, to be conditioned by *"sensations of 'pleasure' and 'enjoyment.'"*

Beelzebub describes this *"topsy-turvy"* process as taking the *"ephemeral for the real,"* as contemporary three-brained beings have *"mechanized themselves to see nothing real."* One aspect of this peculiarity of the human psyche is the tendency to *"depend exclusively only upon what others say about (any) given question"*–that is, the qualities of suggestibility and gullibility. The three-brained beings' knowledge of reality is no longer based upon their own being-experience, the fulfilling of their being obligations and *"being-Partkdolg-duty,"* nor is it based upon their own *"sane or active deliberations,"* nor upon the *"instinctual sensing of reality."* Instead, Beelzebub describes people as ready to believe any old tale, simply recording what is heard or what one is told or reads, in a 'formatory' way.[3] People then imagine that they understand themselves and all those things about which they talk, profess and write their books. Gurdjieff refers distastefully to *"the scientists of new formation"* with their invented sciences and philosophies, and the *"disease of lying,"* by which people imagine that they know all kinds of things–none of which they have directly experienced or arrived at through their own *'sane deliberations.'* The first effect of the organ Kundabuffer was that the three-brained beings breeding on planet earth no longer *"instinctually sense reality"* but came to perceive reality *"topsy-turvy."*

The second major effect of the organ Kundabuffer is also quite odd, as explained by Beelzebub: *"that every repeated impression from outside should crystallize in them data which would engender factors for evoking in them sensations of 'pleasure' and 'enjoyment."* (p. 88) The Kundabuffer causes humankind to become conditioned by sense pleasure and enjoyment. Beelzebub consistently describes the laziness and self indulgence of human beings, their imaginary concerns, vanity and egoism, and multiform sexual vices. He portrays humans as continually misusing their sexual substances, *"only for the satisfaction of the said impulse"*–of pleasure. Humans do not understand the role that these sacred sexual substances play in the psychology of their possible evolution and the coating of the *"higher being-bodies."*

The Kundabuffer organ was eventually removed from human beings–again by a higher Commission– when the moons were apparently no longer a threat to the larger cosmic harmony. However, the effects of the Kundabuffer on the human psyche had become crystallized in humans' presences and were maintained by the abnormal conditions of being-existence which had become established. The properties of the Kundabuffer thus passed from generation to generation even in the absence of the organ itself. In various stories to his grandson, Beelzebub provides humorous insights into the peculiarities and deficiencies of the strange human psyche–all explained in reference to a background of cosmic occurrences.

Over time, the strangeness of the human psyches increased and, according to Beelzebub, *"the quality of their radiations went steadily from bad to worse."* (p. 106) These 'radiations,' or *'Askokin vibrations,'* are ordinarily released at the destruction of beings and are required for the maintenance and evolution of the Moons and the Earth–but not in such vast quantities. Great Nature thus increased the numbers of the three-brained beings on Earth in order to accommodate the atrophy of the human psyche and the degeneration of the Askokin vibrations. However, other adverse effects were then produced–including decreasing age expectancies, from centuries to seventy years or so; various illnesses; animal sacrifice and slaughter; and the worst *"horror of the situation,"* human warfare–the *"process of reciprocal destruction."* These pathological symptoms of the degradation of the human psyche continue to disrupt the larger cosmic harmony, because the deaths (or Rascooarnos) of such large numbers of beings produces surpluses of poor 'Askokin vibrations.'

---

[3] The formatory mind or apparatus is described by Ouspensky as the mechanical portion of the intellectual center–which simply tape-records or memorizes what is put into it. This is regarded as the lowest form of intellectual activity.

Beelzebub's tales also describe the roles of various Sacred Individuals who visited the earth trying to bring sanity back to those disturbed three-brained beings breeding there, mainly through the awakening of various *sacred being-impulses* which are still dormant in the unconscious. Unfortunately, the 'spiritual part' of humans has passed into their subconscious and a *'false consciousness'* system has been formed and maintained by the Kundabuffer and its properties crystallized in their presences, and by the abnormal conditions of being-existence established on Earth.

Beelzebub's tales are rich in surrealistic humour and portray most vividly the horror of the situation and the strangeness of the human psyche evident on that ill-fated planet Earth. Serious undesirable qualities have became crystallized in humans, who are no longer capable of sincere and active mentation or the instinctual sensing of reality, but are controlled by their 'egoism,' the reflexes of the stomach, material interests, sexual vices, self-calming and other 'Hasnamussian' traits. As Beelzebub suggests, the only serious thing for a "slug" is to awaken and overcome the strangeness of their psyche.

6. The Question of the Soul & the Higher Being-Bodies

Within *The Tales*, Beelzebub elaborates upon the issues of the soul and the *"higher being- bodies,"* which can be *"coated"* for the life of the soul. One story told by Beelzebub concerns the events surrounding his fifth visit to the earth during the time of Babylon. This tale is recounted in the typical Gurdjieff manner:

"The learned beings collected ... there in the city of Babylon from almost the whole of the planet used often to meet together and of course to discuss among themselves, as it is proper to the learned beings of the planet Earth, questions which were either immeasurably beyond their comprehension, or about which they could never elucidate anything useful whatsoever, either for themselves or for ordinary beings there.

"Well, it was just during these meetings and discussions that there arose among them, as it is in general proper to arise among learned beings there, what is called 'a-burning-question-of-the-day,' a question which in some way or other indeed interested them at that time to, as they say, 'their very marrow.'

"The question which chanced to become the-burning-question-of-the-day so vitally touched the whole being of every one of them, that they even 'climbed down' from their what are called 'pedestals' and began discussing it not only with the learned like themselves, but also here, there and everywhere with anyone they chanced to come across. ...

"It was talked about and discussed by the young and old, by men and women, and even by the Babylonian butchers. Exceedingly anxious were they, particularly the learned, to know about this question.

"Before our arrival there, many of the beings existing in Babylon had ultimately even lost their reason on account of this question, and many were already candidates for losing theirs.

"This burning-question-of-the-day was that both the 'sorry-learned' and also the ordinary beings of the city of Babylon were very anxious to know whether they had a 'soul.'

"Every possible kind of fantastic theory existed in Babylon upon this question; and more and more theories were being freshly cooked up; and every, as it is said there, 'catchy theory' had, of course, its followers.

"Although whole hosts of these various theories existed there, nevertheless they were one and all based upon only two, but two quite opposite assumptions.

"One of these was called the 'atheistic' and the other the 'idealistic' or 'dualistic.'

"All the dualistic theories maintained the existence of the soul, and of course its 'immortality' and every possible kind of 'perturbation' to it after the death of the being 'man.'

"And all the atheistic theories maintained just the opposite.

"In short, my boy, when we arrived in the city of Babylon there was then proceeding what is called the 'Building-of-the-Tower-of-Babel.' ...

"And it was precisely these two teachings which began to pass from generation to generation, and to confuse their 'being-sane-mentation' which had already been confused enough without them. ...

"One of these two teachings which then had many adherents in Babylon was just the 'dualistic' and the other, the 'atheistic;' so that in one of them it was proved in beings there is the soul, and in the other, quite the opposite, namely, that they have nothing of the kind." (pp. 329-331, p. 339)

Gurdjieff writes with a profound sense of humour and cosmic insight, depicting what happened in ancient Babylon when the issue of the soul became the "burning-question-of-the-day."
Mr. G. elaborates the dualistic teaching in relationship to the issue of the soul:

> "In the dualist or idealist teaching, it was said that within the course body of the being-man, there is a fine and invisible body, which is just the soul. This 'fine body' of man is immortal, that is to say, it is never destroyed. ... Every man, already at birth, consists of these two bodies, namely, the physical body and the soul." (p. 389)

Beelzebub's view of the soul is neither atheistic nor dualistic, but somewhere in between. A human can attain a certain immortality of the soul, within certain limits, but this is not truly present in the individual unless it is acquired or achieved. In response to Hassein's question about the three brained-beings on planet Earth, Beelzebub explains:

> "Yes ... on almost all the planets of that solar system also, three-brained beings dwell, and in almost all of them higher being-bodies can be coated. Higher being-bodies, or as they are called on some planets of that solar system, 'souls' arise in the three-brained beings." (pp. 60-1)

Higher being-bodies need to be coated or crystallized for the life of the soul. Beelzebub provides a fascinating explanation of how such processes occur, what the higher being-bodies are, and how the immortality of the soul might be attained.

These themes were evident in Gurdjieff's teaching during his period in Russia and while in France. In a lecture at the Institute, in 1921, Gurdjieff remarked:

> "A soul is a luxury. No one has yet been born with a fully developed soul. ... A soul may disintegrate immediately after death, or it may do so after a certain time. For example, a soul may be crystallized within the limits of the earth and may remain there, yet not be crystallized for the sun." (1975, p. 87)

Similarly, John Bennett (1977) explains:

> Gurdjieff intends the doctrine of higher being bodies to be taken literally and with it the immortality of the soul. There is, however, the one all-important distinction from ordinary doctrines of immortality, namely that the soul is not present in man until it is acquired. Moreover, he constantly reiterated that a soul is a rare and most precious possession, to which only those few can attain who are able and willing to pay the price. (p. 107)

Bennett illustrates this teaching with verses from the Gospels: *"For many are called but few are chosen,"* and *"Every tree that bringeth not forth good fruit is hewn down and cast into the fire."* Gurdjieff gives such teaching a twist and suggests that human beings can *"die like dog,"* or perhaps we might say, a slug.

The life of the soul is associated with the crystallization and perfection of the higher being-bodies. The atheist view of ancient Babylon (and of modern psychology and science) is too simplistic in viewing a human being as having only one body, or simply a body and a mind. So also, the theistic views are dualistic, arguing for a body and a soul. Gurdjieff's more complex teaching about the higher being-bodies does not fall into either dualistic viewpoint. Instead, there is an inner hierarchy of subtle being-bodies which can be coated and become vehicles for experience and action for the life of the soul.

7. Similitudes of the Whole

According to Beelzebub, the three-brained beings on planet Earth are potentially *"similitudes of the Whole"*–microcosmoses embodying the macrocosm. As such, they have the possibility of not only serving local cosmic purposes, feeding the earth and moon as part of organic life, but also of attaining various levels of Objective Reason and individuality–and even of *"blending again with the infinite."* (p. 945) As a microcosm of the macrocosm, a human being can potentially coat higher being-bodies for the life of the soul, instinctually sense cosmic truths and phenomena, and maintain his or her existence within the subtle realms of being after death while achieving different levels of immortality. Unfortunately, humans came to perceive reality topsy-turvy, to be conditioned by pleasure and self-love, and to squander their sacred sexual substances. They no longer remember or realize their deeper cosmic purposes, duties and possibilities.

Gurdjieff describes two principles by which a human can live and die, giving them the unlikely, invented names of *Foolasnitamnian* and *Itoklanoz*. In the eccentric and seemingly bizarre language of Beelzebub, the first principle *Foolasnitamnian* is described as proper to the existence of all three-brained beings arising on any other planet of the Universe. According to this principle, three-brained beings *"have all possibilities ... for the perfecting in them of both higher-being-bodies."* (p.775) In addition to serving Cosmic purposes, an individual can coat or crystallize higher being-bodies which allow for the continued evolution of the soul.

However, because of a series of cosmic catastrophes, these strange three brained beings formed in ways quite unbecoming for such beings:

> "... they began to exist already excessively abnormally, that is to say, quite unbecomingly for three-brained beings, and when in consequence of this they had on the one hand ceased to emanate the vibrations required by Nature for the maintenance of the separated fragments of their planet, and, on the other hand, had begun, owing to the chief peculiarity of their strange psyche, to destroy beings of ... their planet ... then Nature Herself was compelled gradually to actualize the presences of these three-brained beings, according to the second principle, namely the principle "Itoklanoz," that is, to actualize them in the same way in which She actualizes one-brained and two-brained beings ... . (p. 131)

> "... there are transmuted through them the cosmic substances required not for purposes of a common-cosmic character, but only for that solar system or even only for that planet alone, in which and upon which these one-brained and two-brained beings arise. (p. 130)

Beelzebub's Tales describes how human beings became so abnormal in their functioning. They no longer have normal sensations of cosmic phenomena; they are oblivious of the need to fulfill their sacred being-obligations and duties; their true consciousness passes into the subconscious, and a false consciousness system becomes crystallized in their presences. The terror of the situation is that such people *"die like dog"* according to the Itoklanoz principle, and serve Nature's purposes by becoming nothing more than fertilizer. Beelzebub explains that the majority of contemporary beings *"remain with presences consisting of the planetary body alone, and thus are, for themselves, destroyed forever."*

According to Gurdjieff, being a real human is only a possibility—which is generally unrealized. Living in sleep and ignorance, people serve only the purposes of Mother Nature and become fertilizer—that is, food for the earth and moon. However, self knowledge and the struggle to awaken can enable a three-brained being to serve higher and sacred purposes, even to attain real "I" and become *"immortal within the limits of the solar system."* All of these possibilities depend on the chemistry and alchemy of the soul. Although Common Mother Nature provides for the possibility for attaining the soul, this is not guaranteed. It depends upon the individual's conscious efforts to awaken and to fulfill their being obligations and duties. Through awakening and knowing Self, three-brained beings can serve larger cosmic purposes. Gurdjieff provides a remarkable teaching for the awakening of humanity—but a dismal view of human psychopathology.

Beelzebub explains to his grandson Hassein that the phrase *"We are the images of God,"* is *"one of the only 'cosmic truths'"* expressed by the three brained beings on planet earth, although they have no understanding of what it truly means. Then, in his humorous and insightful manner, Beelzebub elaborates upon how those *"unfortunates,"* humankind on earth, have taken this deep truth:

> "'Good ... if we are "images of God" ... that means ... means ... "God" is like us and has an appearance also like us ... and that means, our "God" has the same moustache, beard, nose, as we have, and he dresses also as we do. ... almost with a comb sticking out of his left vest pocket ...
>
> "... those 'learned' beings ... assembled in the city of Babylon ... began to invent various maleficent fictions concerning their 'God,' which were afterward by chance widely spread everywhere on that ill-fated planet. ... it was said ... that that famous 'God' of theirs had, as it were, the appearance of a very old man, just with a heavy beard." (pp. 776-7)

In order to understand how a three-brained being could embody the whole of the "Megalocosmos," we will have to consider the creation processes elaborated by Beelzebub, the fundamental principles of world-creation and world-maintenance, and assorted esoteric teachings about the lost science and knowledge of the soul.

Beelzebub refers to three-brained beings as potentially *"a particle of all that exists."* (p. 162) On another occasion, Beelzebub talks of his efforts to fulfill his being obligations and duties in order to be worthy of *"becoming a particle though an independent one, of everything existing in the Great Universe."* (p. 183) Elsewhere, he describes humans, *"as beings having in their presences every possibility for becoming particles of a part of Divinity ...."* (p. 452)

A soul is not given to a human being but must be acquired. Unfortunately, the cosmic catastrophes which occurred to the earth and the miscalculations regarding the organ Kundabuffer led to the emergence of a strange breed on that planet. According to Beelzebub, they are willing to believe any old tale and have innumerable other unnatural and unbecoming traits and characteristics formed in their presences. Humans are lulled into sleep, convinced they are eagles and magicians, and that they will never be turned to fertilizer. Humans thus miss the mark and do not establish their own inner triangle or sevenfold nature—thus failing to complete the inner cosmic octave in order to blend again with the Most Most Holy Sun Absolute.

Human beings are potentially similitudes of the whole—particles of the Great Universe—with deep hidden roots within vaster dimensions of being and non-being. Behind essence is real I, behind real I, is God, or at least the Most Most Holy Sun Absolute. Beelzebub's tales to his grandson, Hassein, provide strange and highly provocative insights into the nature of the peculiar three-brained beings breeding on the planet Earth.

"But as for the sacred data for genuine being–consciousness put into them by Great Nature–which consciousness ought to be possessed by them from the very beginning of their preparation for responsible existence together with the properties inherent in them which engender in them the genuine sacred being-impulses of 'faith,' 'hope,' 'love,' and 'conscience'— these data, ... come to be regarded as what is called the 'subconsciousness.'"

II /
The Strange Psyche & the Psychopathology of "Your Favorites"

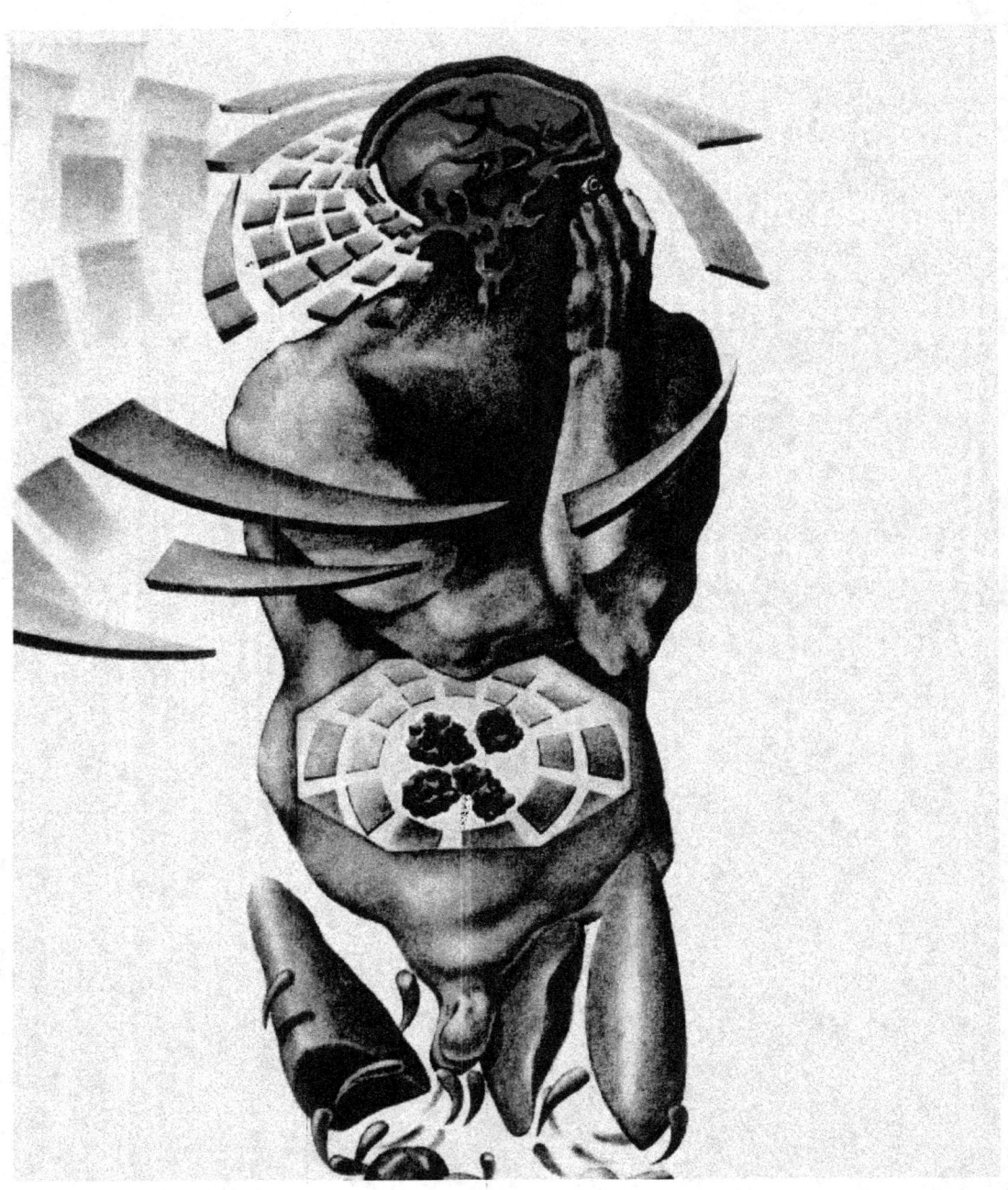

1. The Dual Consciousness

Remarkably, Gurdjieff presents his teachings within *Beelzebub's Tales* in an almost totally new language and format than that used in his earlier more formal lectures recorded by Ouspensky and other students. It is unfortunate that many of the Gurdjieff study groups focus primarily upon Ouspensky's presentations rather than upon the more obscure and difficult *Tales*.

With reference to consciousness, Beelzebub explains that the *"genuine being-consciousness"* of those strange three-brained beings on planet Earth has passed into their *"subconsciousness."* In consequence, a *"fictitious consciousness"* system has become dominant. The distinction between the *"genuine being-consciousness"* and the false consciousness system is between consciousness rooted within the essence of the individual and that structured around the false personality–acquired through the processes of conditioning, education and the like.

While elaborating upon the phenomenon of hypnosis, Beelzebub explains to his grandson, how a *"two-system-Zoostat"* or *"two independent consciousnesses"* formed within the strange psyches of those three-centered beings. Beelzebub emphasizes the destructive roles of education and socialization in forming this false consciousness system:

> "... ensuing from the abnormal conditions of the being-existence of your favourites ... from the beginning of the arising of their offspring, they intentionally try by every kind of means, for the purpose of making them respond to these abnormal conditions round them, to fix in their 'logicnestarian-localizations' as many impressions as possible obtained again due to the results of their abnormal existence–which maleficent action of theirs towards their offspring they call 'education'–then the totality of all such artificial perceptions gradually segregates itself in their common presences and acquires its own independent functioning, connected only as much with the functioning of their planetary body as is necessary merely for its automatic manifestation, and the totality of these artificial perceptions is then perceived by them, owing to their naiveté, as their real 'consciousness.'" (p. 565)

Education and socialization impresses *"artificial perceptions"* upon the centers (the logicnestarian-localizations), which come to dominate within the false personality. This system is based upon the formation of habit structures which allow for the automatic functioning of the individual. This artificial, fictitious or "false" consciousness is then unknowingly taken to be the real consciousness of the individual! Certainly, this would be a sad state of affairs.

The fictitious consciousness is formed from the perception of accidental and mechanical impressions and the sounds of words which are described as *"empty,"* having meanings not connected to genuine being data, direct experience or to sane deliberations. Mr. G. describes the formation of this false consciousness:

> "... when these children grow up and become responsible beings, they already automatically produce their manifestations and their acts; just as during their formation they were 'taught,' just as they were 'suggested to,' and just as they were 'wound up;' in a word, just as they were 'educated.'" (p. 378)

Beelzebub explains what happens to the consciousness based on essence, which should be the predominant system:

> "But as for the sacred data for genuine being–consciousness put into them by Great Nature–which consciousness ought to be possessed by them from the very beginning of their preparation for responsible existence together with the properties inherent in them which engender in them the genuine sacred being-impulses of 'faith,' 'hope,' 'love,' and 'conscience'–these data, becoming gradually also isolated and being left to themselves, evolve independently of the intentions of the responsible beings, and of course also independently of the bearers of them themselves, and come to be regarded as what is called the 'subconsciousness.'" (p. 565)

Hence all the *"sacred data"* inherent within humans, which could allow for responsible life, become isolated from their general functioning and remain in a primitive state; while the *"false consciousness"* predominates in their automatic functioning. This is how Beelzebub explains to Hassein the formation of the strange psyches of those three-brained beings breeding on planet Earth, who perceive reality topsy-turvy and are so conditioned by egotism, the impulses of pleasure, the wandering of nerves and the sexual organs.

In recounting his work as a hypnotist while visiting the Earth, Beelzebub explains that the functioning of these two consciousness systems is related to differences in the blood flow within the human organism. In particular, he explains that the *"centre-of-gravity-of-the-blood-pressure"* in their presences will sometimes predominate within one part of the general system of blood vessels, and at other times within another part of the blood vessels. These differences are related to differences between the waking and sleeping states and used to explain the phenomena of hypnosis. Beelzebub functioned as a hypnotist putting humans into such a state by altering the particularities of their blood flow, primarily through the use of his own Handbledzoin (or blood of the Kesdjan, or astral body)– which he labels as "animal magnetism," in accord with the terminology of Mesmer's day. However, Beelzebub explains that even the ordinary waking existence of humans flows under the influence of such a hypnotic state.

Humans subsequently no longer instinctually sense reality and cosmic truths, nor acquire genuine being-Reason, as is proper to three-centered beings, nor do they experience the sacred being-impulses. A false "egoism" has been formed and is the root of many other peculiar being impulses– which Beelzebub describes as *"existing under the names of 'cunning,' 'envy,' 'hate,' 'hypocrisy,' 'contempt,' 'haughtiness,' 'servility,' 'slyness,' 'ambition,' 'double-facedness,' and so on and so forth."* (p. 379) Beelzebub emphasizes that those "slugs" are really not at all what they imagine themselves to be:

> "With such an already quite 'automated consciousness,' and completely 'nonsensical feelings,' they feel themselves to be immeasurably superior to what they really are." (p. 513)

II / **The Strange Psyche & the Psychopathology of "Your Favorites"**

The true consciousness, now in the subconscious, requires for its growth, the fulfilment of individual *"being-partkdolg duty,"* of *conscious labours* and *intentional suffering*, which would help to accumulate the data necessary for the development of the faculties of genuine being-Reason and to accumulate the substances required for the coating of the higher being-bodies.

Beelzebub describes the activities of various sacred individuals or messengers who visited the Earth attempting to awaken the genuine being impulses within humankind—as these are still latent within the so-called *"subconscious."* Particularly, Beelzebub emphasizes the importance of the awakening of objective conscience, which from a person's early life, has been *"driven-back-within."* The lot of humankind, the slugs on that ill-fated planet Earth, has been to become crystallized within a false consciousness system. One of the few sources of hope for humanity still lies in the awakening to the deeper dimensions of self latent within the subconscious, in the deeper emotional nature.[4]

2. To 'Tickle' their Numerous Weaknesses

The falsity of humans is portrayed in a shocking manner by Beelzebub to his grandson Hassein, when he explains what *"pity"* he felt for them after meeting some of their infamous actors and artists, so-called*" adepts of contemporary art,"* with their *"exaggerated, inner, abnormal, what is called 'being-self-appreciation.'"* Beelzebub suggests that in reality, *"every one of them really being in respect of genuine essence almost what is called a non-entity."*

On one occasion, Ahoon, Beelzebub's attendant, takes the initiative to explain to Beelzebub's grandson an important lesson about getting along with human beings and what he must and must not do if he ever happens to visit the planet Earth. This selection exemplifies Gurdjieff's surrealistic humour and deep insights into human nature:

> "Well then, dear Hassein, ... my advice to you is that if you should indeed have to exist among the beings of that planet Earth and have dealings with these representatives of contemporary art, then you must first of all know that you must never tell the truth to their face.
>
> "Let Fate spare you this!
>
> "Any kind of truth makes them extremely indignant, and their animosity towards others almost always begins from such indignation.
>
> "To such terrestrial types you must always say to their face only such things as may 'tickle' those consequences of the properties of the organ Kundabuffer unfailingly crystallized

---

[4] In the terminology of the Ouspensky version of the fourth way teaching, the only hope is through the dissolution of the false personality and the attainment of true self-consciousness, based upon the growth of the essence and the awakening of the higher emotional center.

in them and which I have already enumerated, namely, 'envy,' 'pride,' 'self-love,' 'vanity,' 'lying,' and so on.

"And the means of tickling which infallibly act on the psyche of these unfortunate favourites of yours are, as I noticed during my stay there, the following:

"Suppose that the face of one of these representatives of art resembles the face of a crocodile, then be sure to tell him that he is the image of a bird of paradise.

"If one of them is as stupid as a cork, say that he has the mind of Pythagoras.

"If his conduct in some business is obviously 'super idiotic' tell him that even the great cunning Lucifer could not have thought out anything better.

"Suppose that on his features you see signs that he has several terrestrial diseases from which he is progressively rotting day by day, then with an expression of astonishment on your face ask him:

"Do, please, tell me, what is your secret for always looking so fresh, like "peaches and cream," and so on. Only remember one thing ... never tell the truth. (pp. 515-6)

Such were Ahoon's insights into the imaginary self-importance and "nonsensical feelings" which dominate the automated consciousness so characteristic of the strange three-brained beings on planet Earth.

On another occasion, Beelzebub refers back to Ahoon's description of how to 'tickle' those strange three-brained beings with their artificial consciousness system:

> "At that time, our dear Ahoon, bearing in mind their numerous weaknesses, such as their self-love, pride, vanity, and still many others, indicated to you in which cases just which of these specific properties of theirs it was necessary, as he expressed it, to 'tickle.' ... if on each occasion you 'tickle' these particular properties of theirs, they will indeed 'worship' you and in everything always behave towards you not worse than those who were called there Asklaian slaves.' (p. 1074)

Beelzebub explains to Hassein that it would however be inconvenient for him to have to always remember *"all these numerous particularities and each time to stop and think on which occasion which of these numerous weaknesses of theirs must be 'tickled.'"* Beelzebub then takes the opportunity to reveal another great 'secret' of their strange psyches:

> " I wish to point out to you one great 'secret' of their psyche, namely, I wish to point out to you only one particularity of theirs which, if you know how to profit by it, might create in each one of them the same effect in their manifestations about which Ahoon spoke.
>
> "If you will act upon them through this same particularity, then you will not only be on very good terms with them all, but even, if you wish, you will be able, knowing this

'secret' of their psyche, fully to ensure your tranquil and happy existence there both as regards 'money' necessarily required there, as well as other conveniences, the taste and blissful significance of which out dear Teacher expressed by the words 'Roses, Roses.'

" You, no doubt, my boy, have already guessed that by this secret of their psyche I refer just to this same, as I called it, 'psycho-organic-need' of theirs to 'teach others sense' and 'to put them on the right road.'

"This special property formed in their psyche, thanks of course also always to the same abnormally established conditions of ordinary being-existence, becomes as it were— when each one of them already becomes a responsible being—an obligatory part of his presence.

"Everyone there without exception has this 'psycho-organic need'; old and young, men and women and even those whom they call 'prematurely born.'

"The mentioned 'particular need' of theirs arises in them, in its turn, thanks to another particular property of theirs which is that form the very moment when each of them acquires the capacity of distinguishing between 'wet' and 'dry,' then, carried away by this attainment, he ceases forever to see and observe his own abnormalities and defects, but sees and observes those same abnormalities and defects in others.

"It has already become customary there at the present time that all your favorites always teach others like themselves even things the notion of which they have not even dreamed of, and the joke of it is that if these others do not learn from him, or at least, do not pretend that they wish to learn, then they are not only offended, but even always inwardly very sincerely indignant; and on the contrary, if one of these others should learn 'sense' from them or at least pretend that he is very anxious to learn it, then these beings will not only 'love' and 'respect' him but will feel fully satisfied and greatly delighted.

"It must be remarked here that only in these circumstances can your favorites speak about others without malice and without criticism.

"And so, my boy …

"I strongly advise you that if for any reason you have to exist among them, always pretend that you wish to learn something from them. Act in the same way towards their children and then you will not only be on excellent terms with them all, but the whole family will even look on you as the honoured friend of the house. (pp. 1075-6)

And so, through the Tales, Beelzebub portrays the falsity of the men-beings, with an automated consciousness system formed around the effects of the organ Kundabuffer—such as their self-love and vanity, imagined self-importance, envy, pride and so on, and on.

3. The Heart & the Emotional Center

Beelzebub most frequently refers to humans as *"your favorites"* and as those *three-brained* or *three-centered beings* breeding upon planet Earth:

> "... they, like every other three-brained being of the whole of our Great Universe, have three separately independent spiritualized parts, each of which has, as a central place for the concentration of all its functioning, a localization of its own which they themselves call a 'brain' ...." (p. 480)

Humans are three-brained beings and impressions arising from within or without will be perceived independently by these three aspects of a person's presence. Each brain will experience according to the nature of the impressions, and the independent associations or responses evoked. Gurdjieff refers to these three localizations as: *"thinking center, feeling center and moving-motor center."* (p. 1172) On other occasions, the *moving-motor center* is referred to as the *moving-instinctual center*. This triune distinction is most important to understand. Humans experience and function mentally, emotionally and physically–enabling thinking, feeling and sensation/action.

Beelzebub identifies each brain or center with different anatomical structures where it is localized. The intellectual or thinking center is associated with *"the head of each one of them,"* or *"as the terrestrial learned call them, the 'cells-of-the-head-brain.'"* The second brain–the moving-instinctual center–is identified with the *"vertebral column,"* the spinal cord and in particular with the *"'brain notes' of their spinal marrow."* (p. 779)

The emotional or feeling center is a third independent brain. In his *Tales*, Beelzebub tells an unusual tale about the fall of those three-brained beings on planet Earth and how the center of their emotional life changed:

> "... in the beginning these three-brained beings of the planet Earth ... had this concentration (the emotional center), similarly to us, in the form of an independent brain localized in the region of their what is called 'breast.'
>
> "But from the time when the process of their ordinary being-existence began particularly sharply to change for the worse, then Nature ... was compelled, without destroying the functioning itself of this brain of theirs, to change the system of its localization.
>
> "That is to say, she gradually dispersed the localization of this organ, which had its concentration in one place in them, into small localizations over the whole of their common presence, but chiefly in the region of what is called the 'pit of the stomach.' The totality of these small localizations in this region they themselves at the present time call the solar plexus or the 'complex of the nodes of the sympathetic nervous system.'"
> (pp. 779-780)

Beelzebub in fact does not explicitly state that *the heart* is this independent brain in the region of the breast. What this brain is, is not commented upon further, at least explicitly. However, we can draw the inference, which seems fairly straightforward, that the heart was the original center of the emotional life.

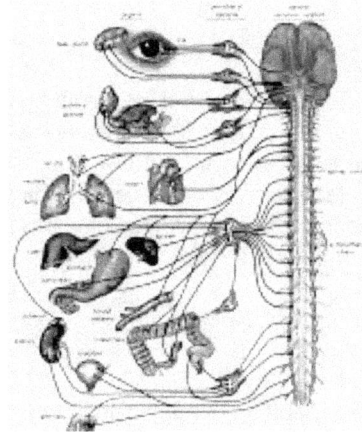

However, among the three-brained men-beings on planet Earth, the heart is no longer the center of the emotional life and the emotional reactivity has been dispersed to the solar plexus and other nerves of the sympathetic system. Beelzebub is thus suggesting that humans ordinarily are not properly centered within the heart and the emotional center, but that the solar plexus and *"pit of the stomach"* became the primary localizations for emotional reactivity.[5]

In describing the strange psyche of those three brained beings on planet Earth to his grandson Hassein, Beelzebub, explains how self-love, vanity, egoism, vanity, cunning and so forth, came to be crystallized in the beings' presences, so that they were no longer capable of experiencing the sacred being-impulses, especially Love. Instead, the person is typically imprisoned by narcissism in its varied forms. So-called love is based on self-love, centered more in the solar plexus or genitals, than in that *"independent brain localized in the region of their what is called 'breast.'"* (p. 780)

Beelzebub characterizes what is taken as 'love' among those strange three-brained *"men-beings:"*

> "... in none of the ordinary beings-men here has there ever been, for a long time, any sensation of the sacred being-impulse of genuine Love. And without this "taste" they cannot even vaguely describe that most beatific sacred being-impulse .... Here, in these times, if one of those three-brained beings "loves" somebody or other, then he loves him either because the latter always encourages and undeservingly flatters him; or because his nose is much like the nose of that female or male, with whom thanks to the cosmic law of "polarity" or "type," a relation has been established which has not yet been broken; or finally, he loves him only because the latter's uncle is in a big way of business and may one day give him a boost, and so on and so forth. But never do beings-men here love with genuine, impartial and non-egoistic love." (pp. 357-358)

Understanding this shift of the emotional center is of profound importance to understand the degradation of the human psyche and why humans no longer experience the *"sacred being-impulses."* Beelzebub, like all other Tetartacosmoses within the Universe, has the center of his emotional life within this *"independent brain"* in the region of *"the breast,"* but unfortunately, the

---

[5] The sympathetic nervous system consists of two nerve tracts that extend from the base of the skull and run parallel to the vertebral column but outside of it. The nerve tracts branch to different plexuses such as the solar, cardiac and hypogastric plexuses, and then to different organs of the body. The illustration depicts the autonomic nervous system composed of the complementary sympathetic and the para-sympathetic nerves. The sympathetic system is active during the fight and flight syndrome of arousal, while the para-sympathetic system is dominant during the relaxation response. The autonomic nervous system exerts a widespread influence on the organs (smooth muscles) and glands of the body, the breath and the heartbeat. The solar plexus is the largest of the autonomic nerve plexus and a particularly important center for emotional reactivity, related to the organs of the viscera (i.e., the stomach and intestines) and the adrenal glands.

emotional life of humankind has been dispersed into the "pit of the stomach" and other nerve nodes within the autonomic system.[6]

Unfortunately, according to Beelzebub, modern educators and parents, and other maleficent influences within historic and contemporary culture, encourage the formation of *"egoism"* in these strange three-brained beings. This 'egoism' is then the basis for a whole array of other abnormal and unbecoming 'being-impulses:'

> "From the time when the said egoism had become completely 'inoculated' in the presences of your favorites, this particular being-property became, in its turn, the fundamental contributory factor in the gradual crystallization in their general psyche of the data for the arising of still several other quite exclusively-particular being-impulses now existing there under the names of 'cunning,' 'envy,' 'hate,' 'hypocrisy,' 'contempt,' 'haughtiness,' 'servility,' 'slyness,' 'ambition,' 'double-facedness' and so on and so forth." (p. 379)

These are some of all those negative emotions and being-impulses which so dominate the life of those strange three-brained beings on planet Earth.

Beelzebub explains a profoundly important principle underlying the degeneration of humankind and the dispersal of the emotional center–from the independent brain in the region of 'the breast.'   This concerns how this 'egoism' became so crystallized in those strange three-brained beings, that it maintains a false consciousness system and usurps the role of real 'I.' He states: *"... this said 'Unique-property' egoism usurped the place of the 'Unique-All-Autocratic-Ruler' in their general organization."* (p. 380)

---

[6] Dr. Holmes' (2010) series, *Within-Without from Zero Points*, offers extensive elaborations of "the heart doctrine." Book I, *The Heart Doctrine: Mystical Views of the Origins and Nature of Human Consciousness*, examines the physical, spiritual and divine dimensions of the human heart while drawing from diverse mystical, spiritual and esoteric teachings. In light of the complexity of 'the heart doctrine,' we can understand why Gurdjieff as Beelzebub did not actually name this "independent brain" as being the heart, which people would then imagine that they understood as simply referring to a physical organ.   Gurdjieff, in *Views from the Real World* (1975), notes: *"There do exist inquiring minds, which long for the truth of the heart, seek it, strive to solve the problems set by life, try to penetrate to the essence of things and phenomena and to penetrate into themselves."* (p. 43)

4. On Pleasure, Sperm, Sex & Abstinence

In the *Tales*, Beelzebub explains the unfortunate events which happened on planet Earth, the cosmic disruptions that led to the implanting and removal of the organ Kundabuffer and how these events brought about the degeneration of the human psyche:

> "... when various consequences of the properties of the organ Kundabuffer had already begun to be crystallized in their presences, a being impulse began to be formed in them which later became predominant.
>
> "This impulse is now called 'pleasure'; and in order to satisfy it they had already begun to exist in a way unbecoming to three-centered beings, namely, most of them gradually began to remove this same sacred being-substance from themselves only for the satisfaction of the said impulse. ... most of them ceased to utilize this sacred substance consciously for coating their higher being-bodies ... ." (p. 276)

The three-centered beings squander their *"sacred being-substance"*–of sperm and comparable substances in women–simply to satisfy the impulses of pleasure. Further, they know nothing of the importance of these substances for their own evolution and the crystallizing of the higher being-bodies.

Beelzebub explains to Hassein that the three-brained beings do know of the *"being-Exioehary,"* which they call sperm, but they perform all kinds of *"manipulations"* with it–wasting and squandering it whenever possible. Beelzebub describes such misuse of sexual energies as the *"chief vice of contemporary three-brained beings"*–part of the *"phenomenal depravity"* which began during Greek and Roman times with the invention of orgies, varied *'sexual turns'* and the *"passion-for-depravity."* However, such practices were imitated by others and passed from generation to generation through to contemporary European and American life. The pervasive misuse and squandering of sexual energies is a chief abnormality characterizing the life of humanity and this serves the further degradation of the human psyche.

Beelzebub explains that because of the *"perverted function"* that sexuality became, then:

> "... all the impulses arising in them, in the sense of striving for evolution are already automatically paralyzed at their very roots, and which they themselves call 'sexuality.'" (p. 534)

The three-centered beings on planet Earth, through the wastage of their sacred sexual substances, would paralyse even the impulses to strive towards their own self-perfection.

Beelzebub also depicts some of the pathologies that results *"when they do not remove it from themselves."* In this case, they will experience the sensation of *"Sirklinianmen"* or what *"your favorites"* would call being *"out of sorts"*–likely grumpy and irritable at the best of times. At the worst of times, when several of their years pass without beings of the opposite sex, Beelzebub describes the men-beings as turning to *"onanism"* (masturbation) and *"pederasty."* The history of the church and other 'sexual psychopaths' certainly verifies the difficulties arising when the slugs do not consciously transform the sacred sexual substances and are dominated by the crystallization of the properties of the organ Kundabuffer. Beelzebub describes onanism one of humans' means of *self calming*—of putting oneself to sleep and maintaining the life of a slug.

Beelzebub offers very interesting teachings about the role of sexual energies in the process of acquiring a soul. The transmutation of these sexual energies is an essential part of the inner alchemy by which the *Kesdjan body* and the highest being-bodies are crystallized:

> "This sacred substance which arises in the presences of beings of every kind is almost everywhere else called 'Exioehary'; but your favourites on the planet Earth call it 'sperm.'"

> "... this sacred substance arises in the presences of all beings without distinction of brain system and exterior coating, chiefly in order that by its means they might, consciously or automatically, fulfill that part of their being-duty which consists in the continuation of the species; but in the presences of three-brained beings it arises also in order that it might be consciously transformed in their common presences for coating their highest being-bodies for their own Being." (p. 276)

Contemporary *"men-beings"* still have no idea of how the inner alchemy of being is dependent upon the refinement of these sacred sexual substances.

Further, because *your favorites* do not actualize their 'being-Partkdolg-duty,' these sexual substances begin to *"involve back ... towards those crystallizations from which their evolution began."* This involution of the sexual substances tends to *"'deperfect' their previously established essence-individuality,"* leading to innumerable *"illnesses"* and diminishing the *"thirst for Being."* (pp. 793-794) And so, the slugs do not use the substances of the 'Exioehary' for their own self-perfection, to coat and perfect the higher being-bodies, or even to *consciously reproduce* themselves. Without such an inner alchemy, the beings are described as *"strongly sensing the emptiness of their existence."*

Beelzebub explains that the knowledge of the origin and significance of the *"being-Exioehary'* was known among some of the inhabitants of Atlantis and afterwards among various groups of genuine initiates. However, after periods of war and other catastrophes, this ancient knowledge was lost. Fragments of such knowledge survived but without any precise understanding of what was involved. This led some of the three-brained beings to strive for self-perfection by *"abstaining from the ejection from oneself in the customary manner of these substances formed in them called sperm ...."* (p. 807) Unfortunately, the beings did not understand the necessity of fulfilling of their being-Partkdolg-duty, if this abstinence was to have its desired effect–in terms of quenching the thirst for being.

Instead, they began *"to imitate"* the practices of the genuine initiates and began to organize themselves in various groups and sects, putting this abstinence into effect. Thus, *"monasteries"* were established and various *"monks"* began to refrain from the ejection of sperm, but little was ever achieved as the brothers did not understand the importance of fulfilling one's being obligations, or of *"intentionally absorbing"* the second and third being-foods. These practices led to varied pathologies and perversions according to Beelzebub.

II / **The Strange Psyche & the Psychopathology of "Your Favorites"**

Beelzebub elaborates upon two ill-effects of such ill-advised abstinence—characterizing humankind in his surrealistic and humorous fashion:

> "The first kind of action of this definite substance consists in this, that it promotes the depositing of superfluous what is called 'Karatsiag,' or, as they call it there "fat." And its second kind of action promotes the arising and the dispersing over the whole planetary body of what are called 'Poisonioonoskirian-vibrations.'
>
> "... one indeed meets among them these fat monks specimens with such an abundant deposit of fat, that they could give many points to that form of being there which they expressly fatten in order to increase this same fat in their planetary bodies, and this form of being they call there 'pig.'
>
> "And in the second case, on the contrary, these abstaining monks become, as it also usually said there, 'meagre-thin'; and the action of the 'Poisonioonoskirian-vibrations' which penetrate through them is chiefly evident in their general psyche which becomes sharply dual and the manifestations of which are divided into two diametrically opposite kinds—the outer, visible and for show, sensed by everyone around them, and the inner and hidden, which the ordinary beings there, especially the contemporary, are entirely incapable of ascertaining or perceiving—namely, in their outer visible manifestations, these 'Poisonioonoskirian-monks' appear to what your favorites would express as 'bigots' of a high degree; and in their hidden inner manifestations, not shown to others, what your favorites would call 'expert cynics,' also of a high degree.
>
> "As regards the causes why 'Poisonioonoskirian-vibrations' are obtained among certain of the abstaining monks from the involutionary process of the Exioehary instead of the deposit of fat, there even exists one detailed theory ... that this proceeds because in the first year of their existence these same 'thin monks' very zealously occupied themselves with that occupation from which 'pimples'—known even to medicine there—generally appear on the faces of young beings there." (pp. 808-810)

Beelzebub is referring to masturbation as that activity which gives youth pimples and which predisposes the monk to either the accumulation of fat or the formation of their bigotry and cynicism. Beelzebub offers shocking portraits of humankind—the misuse and squandering of the sacred sexual energies and the involution of these substances into poisons. The lack of being-partkdolg-duty and the striving towards self-perfection, and the failure to consciously absorb all three being-foods, leads to various forms of the degeneracy common among *"your favorites."*

5. The Atrophy of the Sacred Being-Impulses: Faith, Hope & Love

During Beelzebub's fifth visit on the spaceship *"Occasion"* to the Earth from the planet Mars, he visits the *"Center-of-Culture"* of the time–the majestic city of Babylon. Beelzebub was attempting to elucidate for himself and a High Commission, the factors which were contributing to the *"acceleration of the rate of the degeneration of their 'psychic-organization."* Beelzebub explains to Hassein that the beings no longer had a *"real being-psyche"* and there had been an *"atrophy"* within them of the three sacred *"being-impulses"* –of Faith, Hope and Love. (p. 321)

Beelzebub recounts various stories about Sacred Individuals who visited the Earth or who were *"intentionally actualized from Above."* The Tales include materials on Saint Krishnatkharna, Saint Buddha, Saint Lama, Saint Mohammed, Saint Jesus Christ and Saint Moses. These Sacred Individuals had attempted to help humankind through one of the three *"sacred ways for self-perfecting,"* namely based on the arousing of the three sacred being-impulses of *faith, hope and love.* During his fifth visit to Earth, Beelzebub reads from a *"legominism"* or statement by another Sacred Individual, the *"Very Saintly Ashiata Shiemash,"* entitled *"The Terror-of-the-Situation."* Ashiata Shiemash had similarly been *actualized from Above* and intended to influence the course of events through the means of the traditional sacred ways for self-perfecting. However, his observations and experiences on the planet Earth raised grave *"essence-doubt"* about the possibility of doing so, because of *"the consequences of the properties of the Kundabuffer ... (which had) crystallized in their presences."* These ill-effects formed an artificial *"second nature"* within the three-brained beings and each of the sacred being-impulses had degenerated within their strange psyches.

Ashiata Shiemash, after a period of meditation, realized that it was *"already too late"* to save the contemporary beings by the three traditional ways. Each of the sacred being-impulses had passed into the subconscious and atrophied into new peculiarities within the human psyche. Properties of the organ Kundabuffer, which resembled the sacred being-impulses, had become mixed with them. Ashiata Shiemash explained:

> "The contemporary three-centered beings here do at times, believe, love, and hope with their Reason as well as with their feelings; but how they believe, how they love, and how they hope–ah, it is exactly in this that all the peculiarity of these three being-properties lies!" (pp. 355-6)

Firstly, these sacred being impulses no longer arise or function "independently," as they do in other three-brained beings in the Universe, but instead they always depend upon some consequence of the organ Kundabuffer–*"as for instance, ... "vanity," "self-love," "pride," "self-conceit," and so forth. ... "swagger," "imagination," "bragging," "arrogance," and so on."* (p. 356)

Faith has degenerated into a willingness to *"believe-any-old-tale,"* if it evokes these characteristics within the men-beings. Similarly, the genuine being-impulse of love is confused with sexual sense, pity, desire for submission, a craze for outer things and so on. Ashiata Shiemash elaborates on the nature of Love as a sacred being-impulse:

> "... that most beatific sacred being-impulse in the presence of every three-centered being of the whole Universe, which, in accordance with the divine foresight of Great Nature, forms those data in us, from the result of the experiencing of which we can blissfully rest from the meritorious labors actualized by us for the purpose of self-perfection." (p. 357)

Of course, other three-brained beings in the Universe, as well as Beelzebub and Hassein, have as the center of their emotional life, *"an independent brain localized in the region of their what is called 'breast'"*—instead of a center dispersed through the body in the nodes of the sympathetic nervous system, but most primarily in the 'pit of the stomach' and the solar plexus. (pp. 779-780)

Similarly, the sacred-being impulse of Hope has atrophied into a *"newly-formed-abnormal hope,"* where they *"always hope in something."* The hope of the slugs has become a hope for tomorrow, for better things and it is fed by self-love and imagination. This so-called hope leads to *"possibilities ... being paralysed in them."*

At various points within the *Tales*, Beelzebub provides brief depictions of the atrophied forms of the sacred being-impulses and their true forms. Generally, he depicts the slugs as *"always believing, always loving, and always hoping in everything newly perceived."* (p. 567) In contrast, the true being-impulse of faith is depicted:

> "... owing to faith alone does there appear in a being, the intensity of being-self-consciousness necessary for every being, and also the valuation of personal Being as a particle of Everything Existing in the Universe." (pp. 191-2)

The intensification of being self-consciousness brings about an awareness of self as a particle of everything existing and a faith in God, the Endlessness, as the ultimate life source. According to Beelzebub, three brained beings can *"instinctually sense reality"* and this should be the basis of Faith, not the wishing for tomorrow or for something new. Faith arises, like love and hope, as a result of sensing the reality of one's being and not from imagination or outward things.

Love, according to Beelzebub, *"should predominate always and in everything during the inner and the outer functioning evoked by one's consciousness,"* but such a love is only in the presences of those who are *"formed in the lawful parts of every whole"*—requiring an awakening to the realities of self. (p. 310) Elsewhere, Beelzebub explains that the *"being-property of sensing the inner feeling of similar beings in relations to oneself"* is another property which *"must infallibly exist in all beings of our Great Universe,"* but this again has atrophied among the men-beings of planet Earth. Beelzebub depicts experiences which are generally unknown among the contemporary beings. However,

> "... occasionally, one of those favourites of yours perfects himself firstly to the degree of sensing with all his spiritualized parts that every being or, as is said, 'every breathing creature' is equally near and dear to our COMMON FATHER ...." (p. 878)

Higher emotions or the sacred being-impulses are experienced only when a man-being becomes spiritualized in his parts and attains a certain *"totality-of-self-awareness."*

Nott (1969), a student of Gurdjieff, describes moments of awakening to such a state of self-consciousness. His account illustrates a taste of the sacred being-impulses:

> It was during this summer that I had the first deep and vivid experience of higher consciousness. The three previous experiences of this unexpected impact of higher forces were a taste of real consciousness of self. The present one was different. One hot day I was walking from the house across the fields to bathe in the Wisconsin river. About half way a strange and wonderful force began to enter into me and permeate my whole being, and filled me with light and power. I stopped and stood still and let the force flow. Although I was aware of my surroundings–the forest and fields and the hot sun, they were only a background to the inner experience; all anxieties and cares of ordinary life dropped away; at the same time I saw myself and my relations with people quite clearly; I saw the patterns of my life, my organism moving as it were along its appointed path. There was time no longer, and an understanding of the whole of life seemed possible for me. It was as if for a few moments I had entered into my real life; and the outer life, which had seemed so important and took up all my time, was not the real life but something ephemeral, a sort of cinema film with which I was identified. Only the inner something was eternal-I, the real self of me. I AM. (p.154)

Moments of self-consciousness enable one to penetrate the hidden dimensions of being and self. Experiences involve the transformation of the sense of time, illumination of the patterns of one's life, realization of one's interconnectedness with nature and the larger cosmos, and experiences of objective emotions–including the sacred being-impulses of faith, hope and love. The experience of self-consciousness involves a quantum shift in the experience of I–awakening to one nature as a particle of the living and sacred whole.

Higher emotions do not come about through the refinement or intensification of typical personal emotions. Real emotions require the dissolution of the false consciousness system, based upon self-love and self-feeling, attachments and identifications, *"swagger"* and *"cunning."* Such personal emotions are based on the complex of nerve nodes within the sympathetic system, particularly in the *"pit of the stomach"* and not within the original center of emotions, related by Beelzebub to a independent brain in the area of *"the breast."* All esoteric mystical paths teach the importance of transcending personal elements in the emotional life and the awakening of the Heart.

Unfortunately, for *your favorites*, humankind on planet Earth, the sacred being-impulses have atrophied contributing further to the degradation of the human psyche.

6. The Awakening of Conscience: the remaining Sacred and Divine Being-Impulse in the Subconscious

Gurdjieff explains that a human's soul is given by Mother Nature but only as a possibility for growth. The awakening of conscience is ascribed a central role in determining a human's fate. Gurdjieff elaborates:

"Nature only give possibility for soul, not give soul. Must acquire soul through work. But, unlike tree, man have many possibilities. As man now exist he have also possibility grow by accident—grow wrong way. Man can become many things, not just fertilizer, not just real man: can become what you call 'good' or 'evil,' not proper things for man. Real man not good or evil—real man only conscious, only wish acquire soul for proper development."

... "Think of good and evil like right hand and left hand. Man always have two hands-two sides of self-good and evil. One can destroy other. Must have aim to make both hands work together, must acquire third thing: thing that make peace between two hands, between impulse for good and impulse for evil. Man who all 'good' or man who all 'bad' is not whole man, is one-sided. Third thing is conscience; possibility to acquire conscience is already in man when born; this possibility given-free-by Nature. But is only possibility. Real conscience can only be acquired by work, by learning to understand self first. ... (Peters, 1964, pp.42-3)

Gurdjieff assigns a central role to the awakening of conscience in the alchemy of transformation. Conscience is a state in which a human *"feels all at once everything that he in general feels and can feel."* (Ouspensky, 1949) This form of feeling together serves to unify an individual's presence, overcoming the inner inconsistencies and contradictions which are usually maintained by "buffers" or defences. Buffers prevent an individual from realizing their falsities and their "nullity." The impact of the organ Kundabuffer and its crystallized ill-effects has been to isolate the true conscience within the subconscious.

A particularly important role is assigned by Beelzebub throughout his tales to the *awakening of conscience* as a route to overcoming the abnormalities established within the strange psyche of the three-brained beings on planet Earth. This theme is tied into the history of humanity, to the catastrophes that occurred on that ill-fated planet Earth and to the historic roles of various Sacred Messengers and Divine Teachers—such as Saint Buddha, Jesus Christ, Mohammad and particularly, Ashiata Shiemash. These Sacred Messengers have intervened in attempts to normalize the strange psyches of those peculiar three-brained beings breeding on planet Earth, whose actions threaten the larger common cosmic harmony.

In *The Tales*, Beelzebub describes conscience as a *"fundamental Divine impulse."* Unfortunately, he explains that there is *"... a total absence of the participation of the impulse of sacred conscience in their waking-consciousness."* Humankind came instead to *"strive to arrange their welfare during the process of their ordinary existence, exclusively for themselves."* Beelzebub provides shocking insights into how mechanical human beings usually deal with what he calls, so humorously, the arising of *the prick of conscience*:

> "... these favourites of yours (humankind), particularly the contemporary ones, become ideally expert in not allowing this inner impulse of theirs, called Remorse-of-Conscience, to linger long in their common presences.
>
> "No sooner do they begin to sense the beginning, or even only, so to say, the 'prick' of the arising of the functioning in them of such a being-impulse, than they immediately, as it is said 'squash' it, whereupon this impulse, not quite formed in them, at once calms down.
>
> "For this 'squashing' of the beginning of any Remorse-of-Conscience in themselves, they have even invented some very efficient special means, which now exist there under the names of 'alcoholism,' 'cocainism,' 'morphinism,' 'nicotinism,' 'onanism,' 'monkism,' 'Athenianism,' and others with names also ending in 'ism.'" (p. 382)

Gurdjieff's writing is full of subtle and rich humour, portraying so simply the follies, weakness and stupidities of humankind. There are many ways of squashing the pricks of conscience, all part of what Beelzebub labels the Evil God of *"self calming."* It is because of this egoism and the evil god *"self-calming"* used to squash any *prick* of conscience—manifest in such "isms"–that the sacred being impulse of conscience remains within the subconscious. However, this sacred being impulse did not simply disappear. Beelzebub explains:

> "... in that consciousness of theirs, which they call their subconsciousness, even in the beings of the present time, the said data for the acquisition in their presences of this fundamental Divine impulse conscience does indeed still continue to be crystallized and, hence, to be present during the whole of their existence." (p. 381)

According to Beelzebub, the awakening of conscience is one of the few avenues remaining to change the sorry state of those unfortunate three-brained beings. The data necessary for the awakening of the sacred being impulse conscience have not undergone the more complete *"degeneration to which all the other sacred being-impulses were subject"*–those sacred impulses of *Faith, Love and Hope*.

The need for the awakening of conscience is a primary theme of *Beelzebub's Tales*, especially given the horrors of the situation, with humankind engaging in the process of reciprocal destruction, war and animal slaughter, and producing an increasingly inferior quality of Askokin vibrations. Whereas human beings asleep are governed by the push and pulls of the good and bad, *"real man only conscious"* –and he has acquired *"conscience."* Gurdjieff states that this real conscience has to be acquired by work and the fulfilling of one's being duties and obligations.

The awakening of conscience brings about a form of conscious suffering, compared to the unconscious sufferings based on desires and attachments of the planetary body. Beelzebub provides a cosmic perspective of the origins of the sacred being impulses of conscience:

> "The factors for the being-impulse conscience arise in the presences of the three-brained beings from the localization of the particles of the "emanations-of-the-sorrow" of our OMNI-LOVING AND LONG-SUFFERING-ENDLESS-CREATOR; that is why the source of the manifestation of genuine conscience in three-centered beings is sometimes called the REPRESENTATIVE OF THE CREATOR." (p. 372)

Beelzebub explains that human beings can actually assume a role in bearing the *"Sorrow of our Endlessness,"* through the awakening of conscience.

Morality, as humans commonly understand it, is very different from the moral sense awakened with conscience and the development of consciousness. Ordinary *"subjective morality"* is an accidental thing based on conditioning, imitation and rote learning, indoctrination, education, external rewards and punishment. Subjective morality differs from one individual, time and country to another. In contrast, *"objective morality"* is the same everywhere and involves a consciousness of the objective nature of self and the realities of life and the cosmos. Objective morality and conscience are based upon a deeper consciousness than people ordinarily know and the *"instinctual sensing of reality"* and cosmic truths.

Beelzebub explains that humans can work in order to have the Divine function of conscience in their consciousness by *"transubstantiating"* in themselves the five *"being-obligolnian- strivings"*–being obligations or duties. These being obligations are elements of an objective morality:

> "The first striving: to have in their ordinary being-existence everything satisfying and really necessary for their planetary body.
>
> "The second striving: to have a constant and unflagging instinctive need for self-perfection in the sense of being.
>
> "The third: the conscious striving to know ever more and more concerning the laws of World-creation and World-maintenance.
>
> "The fourth: the striving from the beginning of their existence to pay for their arising and their individuality as quickly as possible, in order afterwards to be free to lighten as much as possible the Sorrow of our COMMON FATHER.
>
> "And the fifth: the striving always to assist the most rapid perfecting of other beings, both those similar to oneself and those of other forms, up to the degree of the sacred 'Martfotai,' that is, up to the degree of self-individuality.   (p.386)

The first being-obligation refers to maintaining the physical body and not being overly indulgent and conditioned by physical desires, the stomach and sex organs. The second involves striving for one's self-perfection, the attainment of real "I," one's individuality. The third involves seeking after truth about self and the nature of the world, while striving to understand the fundamental cosmic laws which create and sustain life. The fourth involves paying for our arising in order to help lighten the Sorrow of our Common Father, overcoming egoism and striving to lessen the suffering and unhappiness within the world. The final striving, or being obligation, is to help others towards their self-perfection, to attaining real "I."

Beelzebub, in *The Tales*, explains that if it were not for the cosmic catastrophes which occurred, it would be natural for humankind as three-centered beings to strive in these directions. The degradation of humankind has led humans to forget their sacred *being-Partkdolg-duties* and their *'being-obligolnian-strivings,'* and to strive instead only for their own welfare–their own pleasuring, egoism, self-love and vanity, all through insincerity and cunning. The sacred being obligations and duties form an "objective morality" serving to connect humans to deeper cosmic processes, the sacred and divine.

Beelzebub describes humans *"as beings bearing in themselves particles of the emanation of the Sorrow of our COMMON FATHER CREATOR."* (p. 385) The awakening of conscience is thus a profoundly important stage in the transformation of the emotional life, leading to the awakening of the higher emotional center and connection with the life of the Common Father.

The possibility for remorse of conscience also prevents the *"final degradation"* in humankind of the other sacred being impulses of *"Faith, Love, and Hope."* The experience of remorse and the bearing of the sorrow of the Common Father are steps to awakening and transformation. Fortunately, the data are still present within human beings for such *"sacred being impulses,"* although they have passed into the subconscious. Meanwhile, humans invent ever new mean for their self-calming. The nature of true conscience has to be understood in terms of much deeper cosmic processes than slugs would ever imagine.

7. On Education & the Automatic Reason-of-Knowledge

Beelzebub regards methods of contemporary so-called 'education' as another factor contributing to the diminishing faculties of the three-brained beings breeding on planet Earth. Although each individual has *"three separate independent spiritual parts,"* each with its own 'brain,' modern education consists primarily of filling up the head-brain with the useless fictions and invented theories of humankind–all the rubbish accumulated through the centuries and 'empty' words–all learned by rote. Beelzebub refers to such, as the *"fantastic-informations-learned-by-them-parrotlike by compulsion."* Education among the three-brained beings on Earth undermines sane and active mentation, and hinders Nature from bringing about the spiritualization of the three being-centers. It also neglects consideration of the 'subconscious,' the awakening of the sacred being-impulses and objective knowledge or morality. Instead, education cultivates forms of artificiality, deceit and an inflated egoism.

Beelzebub explains that a human being has three 'brains'–enabling us to function mentally, emotionally and physically. Each brain allows *"for the perception and accumulation of all kinds of impressions, as well as of the results of conscious being-awareness ...."* We can perceive mentally, emotionally and physically, and 'impressions' accumulate in the memories of each of these being-centers. Beelzebub describes the brains in the newly born as *"quite pure and of maximum perceptivity,"* but then as being *'dirtied'* with false or imaginary ideas, impressions and influences. Ideally, education should cultivate *"conscious being-awareness"* within the realms of the three being-brains and help to enable the formation of a *'completed presence.'*

However, from Beelzebub's perspective, contemporary education is peculiarly strange:

> "... Thanks to their maleficent usage 'to educate,' they fill and drive into what are called the ... 'brains' of these newly born beings, all kinds of their ephemerally fantastic ideas .... As a result of all this, ... firstly, the general functioning, present in their whole being ... little by little adapts itself to respond only to the sum of these false and fantastic ideas; and, secondly, the whole presence of each one of them gradually accustoms itself to perceive all subsequent new external impressions ... also only according to these previously introduced false and fantastic ideas present in them. ...

> "... when these contemporary favorites of yours already become responsible beings, everything newly seen and newly heard is perceived by them of its own accord automatically without the participation of any effort whatsoever on the part of their essence-functions, and without at all evoking in them, as I have already said, the being-need itself of sensing and understanding everything proceeding within them as well as without.

> "In a word, they are satisfied with that alone, which someone once consciously or unconsciously put into them. (pp. 686-7)

Children are taught by rote and imitation and then respond to new impressions increasingly on the basis of what has already been *"put into them."* Such education proceeds without effort *"on the part of their essence-functions."*

An individual has to cultivate real *"conscious being-awareness"* and not simply assimilate new impressions according to what has previously been *"put into them"*–especially when what has been put in are *"false and fantastic ideas."* It is thanks to the prevailing form of education, or *'Oskiano,'* that the three-brained beings attain only *"automatic Reason,"* the lowest form of being reasoning.

Beelzebub explains to Hassein that the 'conscious Reason' of those three-brained beings on planet Earth consists mainly of the *'Reason-of-knowing,'* whereas that of other three-brained beings in general, is the *'Reason-of-understanding.'* There are profound differences between these two forms of reason. Beelzebub defines the 'Reason-of-knowing:'

> "... every kind of new impression perceived through this Reason, and likewise every kind of intentionally or simply automatically obtained result from formerly perceived impressions is only a temporary part of the being, and might result in them exclusively only in certain surrounding circumstances, and on the definite condition that the information which constitutes all his foundation and entirety should without fail be from time to times so to say 'freshened' or 'repeated'; otherwise these formerly perceived impressions change of themselves, or even entirely, so to say, 'evaporate' out of the common presence of the three-brained being." (p. 1167)

The Reason of knowing has only 'temporary' conditioning effects upon the psyche and is elicited only in situations corresponding to the learning environment. Such knowledge has to be refreshed in order to be maintained or else it will 'evaporate.' It forms only in an individual's outer personality and is not assimilated into their being or into their essence.

> "The conscious Reason-of-understanding, which in general it is proper for three-brained beings to have, is a 'something' which blends with their common presence, and therefore information of every kind perceived with this Reason becomes forever their inseparable part.
>
> "The information perceived with this Reason, or results obtained thanks to being-contemplation of the totality of formerly perceived information–however a being himself may change and whatever changes may proceed in the spheres around him–will be forever a part of his essence." (p. 1166)

Everything learned through the Reason-of-knowing remains simply as information *"without any cognizance by the whole of their being."* Beelzebub also describes such knowledge as having *"no significance at all for the welfare of their own subsequent existence."* This provides a dismal view of contemporary educational processes and the superficiality of rote memorization and the repetition of contemporary rubbish and wiseacring.[7]

At one point, Hassein asks his grandfather Beelzebub to explain why those three-brained beings *"take the 'ephemeral' for the Real,"* and why in human's reason *"fantasy may be perceived as reality."* Beelzebub then explains that *"this particularity in their psyche"* arose because their *"predominant part"* allowed the other parts of their presence to *"perceive every new impression without ... 'being-Partkdolg-duty' but just merely as, in general, such impressions are perceived by the separate independent localizations."* This describes the predominant part–the false personality or crystallized egoism, functioning separately automatically, without the active participation of the other being-centers. Humans are described as then no longer capable of *"conscious active manifestation."*

One of the effects of this is that the *"subjective being-convictions"* formed in people are not based upon their own *"logical deliberations"* and life experiences, but only upon *"what others say about the given question."* (p. 104) Beelzebub depicts this:

> "In general, any new understanding is crystallized in the presence of these strange beings only if Smith speaks of somebody or something in a certain way; and then if Brown says the same, the hearer is quite convinced it is just so and couldn't possibly be otherwise. ... This strange trait of their general psyche, namely, of being satisfied with just what Smith or Brown says, without trying to know more, became rooted in them already long ago and now they no longer strive at all to know anything cognizable by their own active deliberations alone." (pp. 103-4)

People do not form their *"own subjective being-convictions"* based on their logical and active deliberations. This is an aspect of being-Partkdolg-duty and of true education. Instead, the strange

---

[7] The Reason-of-understanding develops only as a person engages in their own *"being-logical confrontation"* with impressions and data, and maintains an active *"striving towards the manifestation of one's own individuality."* Reason-of-understanding thus requires a certain 'self-remembering' or 'being self awareness' at the reception of impressions, and a completed presence–the results of individual being–partkdolg duty.

three-brained beings simply record things heard and repeat them as one's own. The faculties for sane and logical deliberation eventually atrophied among the majority of your favorites.

Beelzebub outlines other maleficent side effects of education and how it effects the emotional nature of children:

> "To teach and to suggest to their children how to be insincere with others and deceitful in everything, has become so ingrained in the beings of the planet Earth of the present time, that it has even become their conception of their duty towards their children; and this kind of conduct towards their children they call by the famous word 'education.'
>
> "They 'educate' their children never to be able and never to dare to do as the 'conscience' present in them instinctually directs, but only that which is prescribed in the manuals of 'bon ton' usually drawn up there by various candidates for 'Hasnamusses.'
>
> "And of course when these children grow up and become responsible beings, they already automatically produce their manifestations and their acts; just as during their formation they were 'taught,' just as they were 'suggested to,' and just as they were 'wound up'; in a word, just as they were 'educated.' (p. 378)

Beelzebub is describing the effects of both parents and educators in cultivating insincerity and deceit, all according to the good manners, or bon ton of Hasnamuss influences. Further, the child does not learn to act in accordance with their own conscience, which is 'driven back inside' along with the other sacred being-impulses. Further, modern educators and parents, like other maleficent influences within contemporary culture, all encourage the formation of *"egoism"* in these strange three-brained beings. This 'egoism' is then the basis for a whole array of other abnormal and unbecoming 'being-impulses,' and constitutes a false consciousness system.

Meanwhile, the *"sacred data for genuine being-consciousness"* and for the genuine 'being-impulses'– of faith, hope, love and conscience, become *"gradually isolated and ... evolve independently of the intentions of the responsible beings ...."* (p. 565)   Education among your favorites is not at all what it should be, in order to foster the *"preparation for responsible existence."* Education in the proper sense of the term has to address the individual at both conscious and subconscious levels, and cultivate awareness of the deeper emotional nature, genuine being-consciousness and objective being-reason. In fact, these are just those things which Beelzebub himself is encouraging throughout his strange and ultrafantastic *Tales*, as he takes the opportunity of his travels to 'educate' his grandson Hassein.

But how far is this from that 'education' of contemporary humankind? Beelzebub explains that the main consequences of the abnormal education, established amidst the abnormal conditions of being-existence upon the Earth, are such that the beings become the *"possessors of only 'automatic-Reason,'"* rather than *"genuine objective being-Reason."* Through education, the *"'still-innocent-in-everything' newly arising beings"* do not develop at all as they should in order to become responsible beings. Their *"essence-center-of-gravity"* becomes only *"that strange totality of automatically perceived artificial even deceptive impressions,"* which has "*nothing in common with the localization of their spiritualized being-parts."* (p. 816) Further, this false consciousness system becomes so established that *"the whole process of their existence flows automatically."* (p. 816)

8. Human Psychopathology & the Causes of War

> "... on that strange planet alone in the whole of the Universe does that horrible process occur among three-brained beings which is called the 'process of reciprocal destruction of each other's existence,' or, as it is called on that ill-fated planet, 'war.'" (p.107)

> "... it was possible sometimes to observe very strange manifestations of theirs, that is, from time to time they did something which was never done by three-brained beings on other planets, namely, they would suddenly, without rhyme or reason, begin destroying one another's existence. ... from this horrible process of theirs their numbers rapidly diminished ... ." (p. 91)

In a sense, Beelzebub and Gurdjieff are characters from a higher dimension and time, and provide a shocking portrayal of human insanity from a cosmic perspective. Gurdjieff's mastery of language empowers Beelzebub to depict most succinctly and vividly the strangeness of the psyche of those three-brained beings on planet Earth and the horrors of warfare.

At various times, Beelzebub discusses the *"process of reciprocal destruction"* and attempts to explain its causes, to a somewhat disbelieving Hassein who simply cannot image such terrors:

> "I understood at the end of my investigations ... that this abnormality there proceeds exclusively owing only to one remarkable aspect of the chief particularity of their strange psyche, namely that particularity which has become completely crystallized and is an inseparable part of their common presences and which serves as a factor for the periodic arising in them of what is called the 'urgent need to destroy everything outside of themselves.' ... (and) when they begin to carry out on some part of the surface of their planet the process of reciprocal destruction, then, at the same time, without any deliberate aim, and even without what is called 'organic need,' they also destroy everything which chances to come within the sphere of the perception of their organ of sight. During the periods of this 'phenomenal psychopathic apogee,' they destroy also all the objects in the given place ...." (pp. 312-3)

Beelzebub depicts human madness so succinctly. He quotes also from the saintly Ashiata Shiemash, who refers to the *"degree of that psychosis of theirs called the 'destruction-of-everything-existing-within-the-sphere-of-the-perception-of-visibility,"* which usually accompanies their process of reciprocal destruction. (p. 519) Beelzebub describes such processes as *"such an unimaginable horror and such a hideousness that no name can even be found for it."* (p. 1057)

On another occasion, while Beelzebub was observing the Earth from the planet Mars, he noticed something which led to his sixth visit. He recounts:

> "... I saw this time that, without moving from their place, they did with a certain thing something which resulted in a tiny puff of smoke, whereupon a being from the opposite

side immediately fell down either totally destroyed or with one or other part of his planetary body mutilated or destroyed forever. ...

"Such a means of reciprocal destruction I had never seen before ..." (pp. 525-526)

Of course, Beelzebub is describing the invention of fire-arms, but he takes them out of a familiar context and shows the horror of it all–that someone over here does a little something and a man over there falls down dead or mutilated.

On another occasion, Beelzebub explains to Hassein how in the contemporary community of England, the beings had become *"expert in inventing and distributing to the beings existing over the whole surface of your planet, vast quantities of every kind of metalwares called there locks, razors, mousetraps, revolvers, scythes, machine guns, saucepans, hinges, guns, penknives, cartridges, pens, mines, needles and many other things of the same kind."* And of course, these talents for inventing and distributing 'metalwares' were very handy for them, as they enabled the processes of reciprocal destruction to proceed much more easily. Beelzebub explains:

> "The beings of that contemporary community have been the benefactors of the other contemporary beings of your planet, offering them, as they say there, 'philanthropic aid,' especially as regards their first being-duty, namely, the duty of carrying out from time to time the process of 'reciprocal destruction.'
>
> "Thanks to them, the discharge of that being-duty of theirs has gradually become for your contemporary favorites, the 'merest trifle.'
>
> "In the absence of those inventions it used to be exceedingly arduous for these poor favorites of yours to fulfill that being-duty, because they were formerly forced to spend a great deal of sweat for it.
>
> "But thanks to the adaptations of every kind invented by those contemporary beings, it is now as again our esteemed Mullah Nassr Eddin says, 'just roses, roses.'
>
> "The contemporary beings now scarcely need to make any effort whatsoever in order to destroy completely the existence of beings like themselves.
>
> "Sometimes sitting quietly in what they call their 'smoking rooms' they can destroy, just as a pastime, as it were, ten and sometimes even hundreds of others like themselves. (p. 433)

Imagine what Beelzebub would think of modern warfare with its arsenals of weapons for remote mass murder all at the hands of the 'power-possessing beings' among us, who so periodically feel such "urgent needs" to destroy other breathing creatures by one means or another.

Beelzebub wanted to understand how those men-beings' *"essence is gradually brought to such a phenomenal being-ableness to destroy, for no rhyme or reason, the existence of other beings similar to themselves."* (p. 526) He concludes that this *"terrifying periodic being-need"* to destroy each others' existence had been acquired over centuries due to the abnormal conditions of existence established there by past generations, through the falsity of the human's educational system, as well as due to cowardice and fear: *"... he begins from a natural feeling of self-preservation to strive with all his Being to destroy as many as possible of the existences of the beings of the enemy side in order to have the greater chance of saving his own existence."* (p. 527) In modern times, this same sentiment motivates the arch-cunning Lucifer with his 'special societies' to seek population reduction and to maintain the world under the aristocratic and financial control of certain 'important' and 'power-possessing beings.'

On hearing of the horrors of war from his grandfather, Hassein is shocked that this *"need for periodically occupying themselves with the destruction of each other's existence"* ran *"like a crimson thread through all your tales."* (pp. 1055-6) Hassein wonders:

> "Don't they really see that these processes of theirs are the most terrible of all the horrors which can possibly exist in the whole of the Universe, and don't they ever ponder on this matter, so that they might become aware of this horror and find a means of eradicating it? (p. 1056)

Beelzebub answers Hassein by elaborating upon why nothing is ever accomplished either by individuals or through their 'special societies.' Beelzebub explains that partly nothing is ever attained due to *"the absence there, as is usual, of one common-planetary organization for a single line of action."* (p. 1056) Beelzebub then characterizes the psychological development of those *"power possessing beings,"* who might assume a role in eradicating such horrific processes of reciprocal destruction and the nature of the 'special societies' which they form. Beelzebub draws this portrait of the power possessing beings among your favorites:

> "... I must tell you that thanks to the abnormally established conditions of being-existence there, the 'waking psyche' as it is expressed there, of each one of them gradually becomes from the very beginning of responsible existence such that he can 'think sincerely' and see things in the true light exclusively only if his stomach is so full of the first being-food that it is impossible for what are called 'wandering nerves' in it to move, or, as they themselves say, he is 'stuffed quite full;' and besides, all his needs already inherent in him which are unbecoming to three-brained beings and which had become the dominant factors for the whole of his presence, are fully satisfied, of course, only for that given moment. ...

> "When these three-brained beings of your planet, particularly of the present time, who have the means of gorging to satiety and of fully satisfying all their other needs and who perhaps could do something for the struggle against this phenomenal evil prevailing on their planet, are satiated, and their mentioned needs are satisfied, and they are seated on what are called their 'soft English divans' in order, as is said there, 'to digest it all'–they do not profit, even during this time so suitable for sincere thinking ... but indulge instead in the maleficent self-calming. ...

> "For instance, when after gorging and satisfying themselves these important and power-possessing beings of the Earth are seated on their said divans, the associative thoughts which ought inevitably to flow in them receives shocks from the reflexes of their stomach and sex organs and wander freely in all directions, as they say there, 'to

their hearts content,' and so pleasantly free and easy, as if they, that is these thoughts of theirs, were 'strolling of an evening in Paris along the Boulevard des Capucinus.'

"When these power-possessing beings of your planet are seated on their soft divans, subjects like the following a-think in them.

"For instance, how to get his revenge on that acquaintance of his, John Smith, who a few days before looked at a woman he 'liked,' not with his right eye but with his left.

"Or this 'digesting' terrestrial power-possessing or important being thinks: 'Why did not my horse come in first yesterday at the races as I expected, but some other?'

"Or, 'Why do those stocks which are in fact quite worthless, go up every day on the market, higher and higher?'

"Or, finally, he thinks something of this kind: 'If I were in John Smith's shoes who invented a new method of breeding flies for making ivory from their skeletons, then from the profits obtained I would do this, that, and the other, and not as that fool, who, like a dog in the manger, will neither himself eat nor let others eat,' and so on in the same strain.

"Still, it does occasionally happen there, that some power-possessing or important being of the Earth suddenly chances to think not under the influences of the reflexes of his stomach and sex organs, but thinks sincerely and quite seriously about these or other questions, with particular regard to this terrifying terrestrial question.
(pp. 1057-61)

This vignette illustrates how when such 'power possessing beings' ponder on such issues, *"their thoughts flow in all directions without any intentional exertion of any part whatsoever of their presence."* The next step in this cosmic tragedy is the complete degradation of the objectives of these individual as they find their way back to their own self interest or greed: Beelzebub continues:

"… no sooner do the stomachs of these sincere agitated beings become empty or no sooner do they recover a little from these externally arisen impressions which had dejected them, than they not only instantly forget their vow, but even they themselves again begin consciously and unconsciously to do precisely everything which is generally the cause of the outbreak of these processes between communities. …

"Such a monstrous need arises in their abnormal psyche because they expect certain egoistic profits from these processes … and with their degenerated mentation they even hope that the greater the scale of the next process, the greater the extent of the said profits to be obtained, either personally for themselves or for their nearest.

"It even happens there, my boy, that certain of the power-possessing and important beings among your favourites unite and form a special society with the aim of jointly finding out and actualizing in practice some possible means for the abolition of this archcriminal property of theirs. (pp. 1061-2)

Power-possessing and important beings have united at times to form "special societies" for the eradication of warfare. Beelzebub summarizes the results of one such historical society:

> "But owing to their various personal egoistic and vain-glorious aims, the ordinary terrestrial important and power-possessing beings who had then assembled, very soon quarrelled among themselves and went their ways home without accomplishing anything." (p. 1063)

Beelzebub reports to Hassein that during his last visit to Earth, such a new society was being talked of, called the 'League of Nations' (the precursor to United Nations). According to Beelzebub, the problem is that *"the beings with objective Reason do not happen to be in these societies,"* because they are not *'important.'* And what does it mean to be 'important'? Beelzebub explains that it means one *"who either has a great deal of money or who becomes what is called 'famous' among the beings there."* (p. 1069) Furthermore, Beelzebub explains:

> "And since especially during recent times only those beings can become famous and important among them in whom the mentioned sacred function, namely 'being-conscience,' is entirely absent, then in consequence of the fact that this sacred function in the presences of beings is in general always associated with everything that represents and is Objective Reason, then, of course, those three-brained beings with Objective Reason always have conscience as well, and consequently such a being with conscience, will never be 'important' among the other beings. (p. 1069)

No one with Objective Reason or 'conscience' would ever be 'important' among the other power possessing beings on that ill-fated planet, and hence, they would have no chance of ever taking part in such 'special societies.' Instead, Beelzebub characterizes the emotional development of the power possessing beings, who *"in respect of Being are only perfected to the degree ... defined by the notion expressed in the following words: 'Look! Look! He already begins to distinguish mama from papa."* (p. 1066)

In reference to the meetings of the League of Nations, Beelzebub predicts that *"nothing effective will come of it."* Instead, he suggests that the members of the society:

> "... will achieve personally for themselves by this new contrivance of theirs one 'most formidable' and 'most useful' result, namely, thanks to this 'official society' of theirs, they will have still another as it is said very plausible excuse for drawing wool over the eyes of their what are called 'proprietresses,' who are for these terrestrial contemporary power-possessing beings either their 'wife,' 'mistress,' 'mother-in-law,' or finally, the 'assistant' in some large store, and so on.

> "Whereupon, thanks to this new official society of theirs, they will have the opportunity of passing the time tranquilly among their friends, important and power-possessing beings like themselves, and at these official 'five o'clocks' which without doubt will be very often arranged ostensibly for affairs connected as it were with the aims of this important official society of theirs, they will be able to pass the time without the silent though terrifying glances and watchfulness on the part of their 'proprietresses.' (pp. 1066-1067)

In addition to escaping the watchful eye of their proprietresses, enjoying 'five o'clocks' and *'Don-Quixoting,'* and the advantages of being with other power possessing beings, Beelzebub suggests that the society also offer other advantages:

> "From this contrivance of your contemporary favorites some advantage might be derived, even quite a great one, but only for their inevitable newspaper, for drawing-room conversations, and, of course, for the various Hasnamussian manipulations of the terrestrial as they are called 'stock-jugglers.' (p. 1070)

Beelzebub explains that such societies may begin with some individual who actually do feel some 'resurrected conscience' over previous wars, when they happen to have suffered personal loses, but then very soon, the society has to involve new members, who:

> "… join only because, according to all those same abnormally established conditions of ordinary being-existence, they, being important and power possessing, must as a matter of course be members of and participate in every 'important' society.
>
> "When these other terrestrial important and power-possessing beings enter such societies and also begin to participate in their affairs, then they, with their personal egoistic and vainglorious aims, as a rule not only very soon send all the tasks of the society and everything that has been done by the beings with 'resurrected consciences' as is said 'flying up the chimney,' but as a rule, they also very soon, as it is also said there, 'put genuine spokes into the wheels of the first founders of these societies.'
>
> "And therefore, these societies of beings which are formed there for common-planetary welfare always quickly die—and die, as I already told you, even without 'death agony.' (p. 1068)

Beelzebub's tales are rich in such surrealistic humour and portray most vividly the horror of the situation and the strangeness of the human psyche as evident on that ill-fated planet Earth. Serious undesirable qualities have become crystallized in humans, who are no longer capable of sincere and active mentation but controlled by the reflexes of the stomach, sexual itching, self calming and greed. Gurdjieff, as Beelzebub, provides a dismal view of the psychopathology of humankind, the causes of war and your favorites inability to stop it. Beelzebub explains that any three-brained being, who had attained Objective Reason and a conscience, *"will never be 'important' among the other beings."* [8]

---

[8] In modern times, the United Nations was first proposed as such a special society to eradicate war and restore world order, but it was controlled from the outset by Hasnamusses, stock jugglers and important 'power-possessing' beings, emboldened with their "Hasnamussian sciences" and seeking world domination and control. The UN produces good press and fancy words, but no results and does nothing even to expose all the lies and deceits upon which the wars are based.

9. Notes on the Moon & the Causes of War

"... the destiny of beings arising on this planet of yours is chiefly to elaborate–by means of the process of their existence–the vibrations required by Nature for the maintenance of those former parts now called Moon and Anulios ...." (p. 1105)

In *Beelzebub's Tales*, many of the woes which have befallen humanity relate to the early cosmic catastrophe which occurred when a comet collided with the earth and broke off two fragments, the moon and a secondary moon *Anulios*, unknown to us. After this, the *sacred vibrations Askokin* were required to be sent to the moons in order to maintain their stable orbits. However, as humans developed, the possibility arose that they might attain *Objective Reason*, as usually occurs among three-brained beings within other solar systems. In this case, men-beings would realize the *"stupendous terror"* of their position–that by their existence, their lives and death, they are simply maintaining the moon. If humans realized the horror of the situation and their slavery to the moon, they might *"be unwilling to continue their existence and would on principle destroy themselves."* (p. 88) It was for this reason, that the accursed organ Kundabuffer was implanted in humans–so that they would *perceive reality topsy-turvy* and be simply conditioned by *sensations of pleasure and enjoyment.*

Although the Kundabuffer was eventually removed, its effects on the human psyche had become crystallized in humans' presences and then maintained by the abnormal conditions of being-existence and education which had been established. The effects of the organ Kundabuffer thus passed from generation to generation, even in the absence of the organ itself. Over time, the strangeness of the human psyches increased and *"the quality of their radiations went steadily from bad to worse."* (p. 106) Although Great Nature increased the numbers of the three-brained beings in order to accommodate the degeneration of the human psyche, other strange phenomena were produced. These included decreasing age expectancies, increases in the birth rate, illnesses and influenzas, animal sacrifice and slaughter, and the worst phenomenally abnormal manifestation–the process of *reciprocal destruction,* or war.

Beelzebub views war as the most insane and pathological sign of humans' mechanical and unconscious life, the primary symptom of the degeneration of their radiations and strange psyches. Warfare and animal sacrifice disrupt even the larger cosmic harmony by producing a surplus of low quality Askokin vibrations. Wars threaten not only the evolution of the Earth and Moon and their atmospheres, but also, the broader harmony of the solar system 'Ors.'

Beelzebub then explains to Hassein why these terrible process of reciprocal destruction *"must already almost inevitably proceed"* on the planet Earth, and how *"Nature ... adapts itself so that its results should correspondingly blend with the harmony of this most great cosmic law"* (of the common-cosmic Trogoautoegocrat). This is elaborated with reference to another ancient society, with the motto, *"The-Earth-Is-Equally-Free-for-All"* which met in Asia with the objective of eradicating war, and which for a time had major successes. *"The-Council-of-the-Elders"* was formed from among *"the oldest and most deservedly honourable beings"* and soon the wars and civil wars on the continent of Asia *"began to diminish." "But something just then happened which began the breakup also of this society of effective men-beings of that unparalleled planet."* (p. 1093) This 'something' involved the *"very famous philosopher Atarnakh"* and his treatise entitled *"Why do Wars Occur on the Earth,"* which ends up 'confounding' the members of the society, leading to division and the eventual dissolution of the society itself.

The philosopher Atarnakh, a Kurd, had an ancient *'Sumerian manuscript'* which *"by some means there fell into his hands."* This manuscript stated: *"In all probability there exists in the World some law of the reciprocal maintenance of everything existing"* (p. 1094), which served as the basis for Atarnakh's formulation:

> In this theory of the philosopher Atarnakh it was very definitely proved that there exists in the world, without any doubt, a law of the 'reciprocal-maintenance-of-everything-that-exists' and that for this reciprocal maintenance certain chemical substances also serve, with the help of which the process of the spiritualization of beings, that is to say 'Life,' is carried out, and these chemical substances serve for the maintenance of all that exists only after the given life ceases, that is, when a being dies. ...
>
> ... at certain periods there must infallibly proceed on the Earth such a definite quantity of deaths as in their totality will yield vibrations of a 'definite degree of power.' (p. 1094)

When Atarnakh very eloquently expounded this theory before the assembly, it created *'great confusion and agitation,'* which lead to the formation of a sub-committee to investigate this theory and report back to the general assembly. Instead of unifying their disputes, there was more bewilderment and two opposite convictions formed, as to whether or not *"there must necessarily proceed 'wars' and 'civil wars' on the Earth quite independently of the personal consciousness of men."* (p. 1097) The second conviction was that was *"that which all the members of the society already previously had, namely, that if they succeeded in carrying out the program which their society had set itself, this evil also which proceeded on their planet might be destroyed root and branch, and everything might proceed in a desirable way."* (pp. 1097-8)

Once again, 'discussion, quarrels, and disturbances' arouse among members of the society and then spread to the citizens of the city, *"inflaming their abnormal psyche."* After calming down and electing Atarnakh as chief director of a new subcommittee, they concluded:

> "According to the laws of Nature, there must periodically always proceed on the Earth, independently of the will of men, 'wars' and 'civil wars'; and this is because during certain periods there is required by Nature a greater quantity of deaths. In view of this we are all, with much grief but with inevitable inner resignation, compelled to agree that by no mental decisions of man is it possible to abolish the shedding of blood between states and within states themselves; and we therefore unanimously resolve to wind up current affairs and everything done by our society and perforce disperse for home and there to drag out our inescapable 'burden of life.' (pp. 1098-9)

Beelzebub's Tales then has all the members of that 'serious society' deciding that day to carry out the *"complete liquidation of all their affairs,"* until the *"proud and self-loving Kurd Atarnakh"* again took the podium. Atarnakh was 'sincerely grieved' that he had unintentionally brought about "the dissolution of the great philanthropic undertaking," over which they had "labored unceasingly for years." He then however shared his *"final conclusion"* that: *"If the universal laws I have discovered are opposed to the means you expected ... then, however strange it may seem to you at first glance, if only these same laws be employed otherwise."* Atarnakh brilliant conclusion is that if Nature requires a certain number of deaths, it is indifferent as to whose deaths these are — *"whether the deaths of people themselves or deaths of the lives of other forms of beings."* He concludes by encouraging members to *"revive upon the Earth on a larger scale than before the ancient custom among men of offering sacrifices to their gods and saints by destroying the lives other forms."* (p. 1100)

Once again these comments set off astonishment and further days and night of *"a continuous rumble of discussion and deliberation"* before they decided in support of Atarnakh's thesis. The motto of the society was changed into "*The-Earth-Free-Only-for-Men*" and members dispersed to their countries to strengthen the idea of the people *"'making themselves agreeable' to their gods and idols by killing beings of different forms ... various weak and stupid one-brained and two-brained beings there."* (p. 1101) The result of this all was that very soon *"there on the continent of Asia, blood again 'flowed like a river."* Subsequently, there was a reduction in those terrible processes of reciprocal destruction, or at least they proceeded *"less often and on a smaller scale."* It was these events which had led to some of Beelzebub's visits to the Earth to eradicate the practices of animal sacrifice.

However, the 'mortality' of the men-beings did not improve, as instead, there was a *"progressive deterioration of their being-existence"* and of the quality of the radiative vibrations of their presences in the process of their existence required from them by Nature" and there was an increase in their 'birth rate'. (p. 1103) In the next twist in Beelzebub's long tale, considerably shortened here, a famous Assadulla Ibrahim Ogly, a Persian dervish perceived the "horrible injustice" of animal sacrifice and spread a contrary teaching through his order, which indeed, year by year, brought about a diminishing of these sacrificial offering. However, Beelzebub explains that *"the result of all the activity of this 'good' Persian dervish was precisely the latest great process of reciprocal destruction, or, as your favorites call it, 'The Great World War.'"* (p. 1104)

Beelzebub comes then to explain what the 'uncommon learned Kurd Atarnakh' had failed to understand that was most important:

> "... that the vibrations required by Nature, which have to be formed from the radiations issuing from beings both during their existence as well as from the process of their Rascooarno, have no significance quantitatively, but only qualitatively. (p. 1104)

The radiations issuing from the three-brained beings on planet Earth need to be *"yielding vibrations more akin to the vibrations required"* from them by Nature for the common-cosmic Trogoautoegocratic process and as required for the maintenance of the Moon and Anulios. However, it is not simply the quantity of such vibrations released by the Rascooarno process (of death), but the 'quality.' If the required quality of vibrations were being produced by those strange three brained beings, then animal sacrifice, war and civil war, would not be required by Nature or the moons.

Beelzebub recounts to Hassein his conversation with the then Angel, now Archangel, Looisos, who informed him that the former parts of the Earth, the Moon and Anulios, were now finally regulated within the general harmony of the solar system. Further, some "Most High, Most Sacred Individuals" had actualized on the planet the conditions required for the Sacred Askokin substance to *"continuously issue from that planet."* This cosmic substance exists in general in the Universe, blended with the two other sacred substances of 'Abrustonis' and 'Helkdonis.' However, in order for the sacred Askokin to "become vivifying" for the maintenance of the moons, it must be freed from these latter substance, hence be released.

We come then to the crux of the matter and one of Beelzebub's remarkable teachings to his Grandson. These same substances, *"Abrustdonis"* and *"Helkdonis,"* are in fact those by which the Kesdjan (or astral) body and the highest being-body are formed and perfected in a three-centred being. Further, these sacred substances are only separated through the individual fulfilling of one's *being-Parktdolg-duty* which consists of *conscious labors* and *intentional sufferings*. These individual efforts towards one's *"being self-perfecting"* are actually the means by which individuals can *"transubstantiate the sacred substances ... in themselves for the forming and perfecting of their higher bodies."*

Finally, Beelzebub comes to his central point to Hassein, as to the causes of war:

> "And so, my dear Hassein, when it appeared that the instinctive need for conscious labor and intentional suffering in order to be able to take in and transmute in themselves the sacred substances Abrustdonis and Helkdonis and thereby to liberate the sacred Askokin for the maintenance of the Moon and Anulios had finally disappeared from the psyche of your favorites, then Great Nature Herself was constrained to adapt Herself to extract this sacred substance by other means, one of which is precisely that periodic terrifying process there of reciprocal destruction." (p. 1107)

It is the strangeness of the human psyche that these unfortunate beings no longer fulfill such being obligations or strive towards self-perfection, and hence, Nature still has *"to 'puff' and 'blow' in order to adapt Herself to remain within the cosmic harmony."* (p. 1107) And so, woe to humanity, the men-beings described as slugs—engage in the processes of reciprocal destruction and lunacy—with the poor souls and strange psyches produce low quality Askokin vibrations to maintain the moons.[9]

And so, the causes of war, of population increases and decreases, plagues, animal sacrifices and much more including earth disruptions are all interrelated to maintain an overall harmony and balance in the exchanges of matters and energies within the cosmos. Beelzebub recounts another example with illustrates such dynamics:

> "In order that you may represent to yourself and understand well in what way unfortunate Nature there so adapts Herself that there should be attained what is called the 'equilibrium of vibrations,' required from this planet for the common-cosmic harmony, I shall explain to you only about one fact which is just now being actualized there, that is to say, subsequent to that process of theirs which they called the 'World War."

---

[9] The contemporary heart master Adi Da (1995), in his autobiography *The Knee of Listening*, recounts his experiences of the lunar realm: *"There were also times when I saw and learned the workings of psychic planes and subtler worlds. I remember once for a period of days I was aware of a world that appeared to survive in our moon. It was a superphysical world or astral world where beings were sent off to birth on the earth or other worlds, and then their bodies were enjoyed cannibalistically by the older generation on the moon, or they were forced to work as physical and mental slaves."* (p. 108) Adi Da's remarks are clearly in keeping with Beelzebub's and Gurdjieff's claims about the lunar world and its feeding off energies released by the death of organic life forms.

> "It was plainly owing to the fact that during the said process what is called 'poison gas' was invented by beings called 'Germans,' and what are called special 'rapid-fire machine guns' by beings called 'Englishmen,' that the amount of Rascooarnos or deaths unforeseen by Nature took place on this occasion and in a far greater quantity than was then required by Her, or, as the candidates for Hasnamuss there, namely, the commercial businessmen, would say, 'overproduction' occurred in respect of the deaths of the three-brained beings required there.
>
> "In consequence, Nature there had again to begin from that moment to 'puff and blow,' and, as is said there, 'jump out of Her skin' in order to correct this unforeseeingness and adapt Herself once again in a corresponding manner. (p. 1115)

In Beelzebub's view, life on Earth involves different cosmic substances and energies, emanations and radiations, and these compose the substances of the planetary, Kesdjan and highest being-bodies. The inner cosmos of a human being is connected with the subtle ethers which pervade space and to larger solar system and Universe, all within the ENDLESSNESS. One means of escaping the pathological state of humankind is through the performance of one's being-Partkdolg-duties—of conscious labors and intentional suffering. This process allows the release of the sacred Askokin for the stability, growth and evolution of the Moon, and further liberates the substances—the Sacred Abrustdonis and Helkdonis—necessary for coating of the higher being-bodies, as well as for attaining Divine Reason and awakening other latent faculties of the soul. Otherwise, the increasing strangeness of their psyche and their horrific process of war will cause Nature herself to 'huff and blow' and to jump out of her skin, as she has also through the history of the solar system Ors.

Beelzebub is not hopeful for humankind to eradicate this terrible process from their planet due to the ongoing degradation of their psyche and the poor quality of their vibrations. Further, the artificial educational system and culture propagate the same falsities and rubbish. At the end of the chapter, on *Beelzebub's Opinion of War*, Beelzebub concludes:

> "We can now only repeat the same in regard to this terrible property of theirs, of which we have just been speaking, namely, their periodic processes of the destruction of each other's existence.
>
> "We can only say now, that if this property of terrestrial beings is to disappear from that unfortunate planet, then it will be with Time alone, thanks either to the guidance of a certain Being with very high Reason or to certain exceptional cosmic events."
>
> Having said this, Beelzebub again began to look at Hassein with that same strange look. (p. 1118)

If conditions on planet Earth were not so disturbed, it would now be possible for the men-being there to naturally produce the Sacred Askokin vibrations required to maintain the moons, as well as to coat and perfect their higher being bodies, and to eliminate such archcriminal processes of reciprocal destruction. Of course, Beelzebub himself has been providing such guidance as a being of "very high Reason." However, aside from the guidance of a Being of high Reason or exceptional cosmic events, the situation of humankind does not look hopeful. Especially so, when we consider next the *Hasnamusses,* the power-possessing beings and their 'special societies' there on that ill-fated planet, which further insure the perpetuation of such horrors.

10. Hasnamuss-Individuals & the *'Naloo-osnian-spectrum-of-impulses'*

Throughout *The Tales*, Beelzebub uses the term *Hasnamuss* to refer in a negative way to certain classes of people whose actions, manifestations and impulses represent the worst psychopathology of humankind, and who cause the worst sufferings, falsity and misunderstanding among the three-brained beings on Earth. On one occasion, Hassein turns to Beelzebub and says:

> "My dear Grandfather, during your tales you have already many times used the expression Hasnamuss. I have until now understood only from the intonation of your voice and from the consonance of the word itself, that by this expression you defined those three-brained beings whom you always set apart from others as if they deserved 'Objective-Contempt.'
>
> "Be so kind as always and explain to me the real meaning and exact sense of this word." (pp. 234-5)

And so Beelzebub explains that the word refers to *"already 'definitized' common presences ... in which for some reason or other, data have not been crystallized for the Divine impulse of 'Objective Conscience,'"* (p. 235) A 'definitized' presence suggests that a *"something"* has become formed or crystallized in an individual—as a relatively fixed characterological complex which dominates their 'common presence.' The fact that data for the Divine impulse of Objective Conscience are not crystallized in them suggests that a false consciousness system is in full sway and the real consciousness has passed into the subconscious. Such individuals are primarily egotistical and care little how much suffering and misfortune they cause others.[10]

Beelzebub describes seven *"Naloo-osnian-spectrum-of-impulses"* which form a *"certain something"* within the Hasnamuss-individuals. There are various kinds of Hasnamusses, according to which of the seven impulses they are most subject. These include:

1. Every kind of depravity, conscious as well as unconscious
2. The feeling of self-satisfaction from leading others astray
3. The irresistible inclination to destroy the existence of other breathing creatures
4. The urge to become free from the necessity of actualizing the being-efforts demanded by Nature
5. The attempt by every kind of artificiality to conceal from others what in their opinion are one's physical defects
6. The calm self-contentment in the use of what is not personally deserved
7. The striving to be not what one is. (p. 406)

Certainly, Beelzebub does not outline a very charming list of impulses. *The Tales* are full of stories where individuals embody such Hasnamussian characteristics and qualities. Such impulses are

---

[10] Ouspensky (1957) defined the Hasnamuss individual: *"... he never hesitates to sacrifice people or to create an enormous amount of suffering, just for his own personal ambitions."* (p. 300)

formed within the crystallized "egoism," so prominent among the strange psyches of those three-brained beings on planet Earth. The Hasnamuss individual no longer experiences the impulses of *"being-self-shame"* or of Objective Conscience, and the history of humanity testifies to the horrors caused by these *"terrestrial nullities."*

However, different Hasnamuss-Individuals embody different elements from the spectrum of different Naloo-osnian-impulses and we will consider various examples of these types. The third 'Naloo-osnian impulse'—the *'irresistible inclination to destroy the existence of other breathing creatures'* and the first impulse–towards every kind of depravity are most clearly embodied by those who bring about the processes of reciprocal destruction–wars, including conquering, domination and other forms of destructiveness and violence, including animal sacrifice and slaughterhouses. Recall that on hearing of the horrors of war from his grandfather, Hassein was shocked–as this *"need for periodically occupying themselves with the destruction of each other's existence"* ran *"like a crimson thread through all your tales."* (pp. 1055-6) Beelzebub describes their phenomenally strange behaviours, unknown elsewhere in the Universe, where: *" ... they would suddenly, without rhyme or reason, begin destroying one another's existence."* Elsewhere, he similarly describes *"the periodic arising in them of what is called the 'urgent need to destroy everything outside of themselves.'* Beelzebub's observations of the Earth from Mars and his visits to the Earth were partly to understand how such atrocities could be possible. What happened within these men-beings such that their *"essence is gradually brought to such a phenomenal being-ableness to destroy, for no rhyme or reason, the existence of other beings similar to themselves."*? (p. 526) Hasnamuss-individuals have also destroyed and persecuted various sacred Messengers and their followers–obscuring the more conscious teachings which might have changed human history and brought more normal conditions of being-existence to the planet.

Beelzebub's uses the term Hasnamuss several times in quite different ways–in his impartial observations of the community of France and in his comments upon the fashion world of Paris. Writing in the 1920's in Paris and Southern France, Gurdjieff provides an amusing critique of the culture and society around him. In the *Tales*, it is during his sixth and final visit to the Earth that Beelzebub visited France, *"the contemporary 'chief-center-of-culture' for the whole of that ill-fated planet."* (p. 688) Beelzebub explains to Hassein how those beings who *"rush and flock from the whole planet"* to Paris the center of culture were particularly those who had:

> "... completely given themselves up to the 'evil-God' reigning there already without limit inside each of them, namely to that 'evil-God' who became their Ideal, and the conception of whom is very well expressed in the words: to-attain-to-a-complete-absence-of-the-need-for-being-effort-and-for-every-essence-anxiety-of-whatever-kind-it-might-be"; and coming to France, they must of course have, consciously or unconsciously, a corresponding harmful influence on the beings of the whole community. ... when beings from the whole planet ... flock to this chief center of culture, then these beings ... occupy themselves with 'new-forms-of-manifestations-of-their-Hasnamussianing,' or as is said there, with 'new fashions,' and spread them from there over the whole of the planet. (p. 688)

These beings who flock to Paris manifest the fourth Naloo-osnian-impulse: *"The urge to be free from the necessity of actualizing the being-efforts demanded by Nature."* They have given themselves over to what Beelzebub calls the 'evil-God,' which he explains is 'self-calming.' Elsewhere, Beelzebub explains how those beings avoid Remorse of Conscience and maintain their 'self-calming'–for which *"they have even invented some very efficient special means, which now exist there under the names of 'alcoholism,' 'cocainism,' 'morphinism,' 'nicotinism,' 'onanism,' 'monkism,' 'Athenianism,' and others with names also ending in 'ism.'"* (p. 382) Anyway, such Hasnamussian-individuals flocked to Paris, as today to Hollywood, and fashions became one of their chief occupations.

Beelzebub defines 'fashion' as consisting in this: *"... the beings devise various new means of being-manifestation in ordinary existence, and means for changing and disguising the reality of one's appearance."* (p. 689)

> "... These said contemporary customs or fashions of theirs are, firstly, only temporary and thus serve for the satisfaction only of the personal insignificant aims of these present and future Hasnamusses, which become phenomenally abnormal and trivially egoistic; and secondly, they are neither more nor less than the results of automatic Reason based on that relative understanding ..."

The fifth Naloo-osnian-impulse, to artificially conceal from others one's defects and the seventh, the *"striving to be not what one is,"* are both illustrated in Beelzebub's depictions of the fashion world in particular and of modern culture more generally. Beelzebub defines fashion as: *"This maleficent custom for them is that they periodically change the external form of what is called 'the-covering-of-their-nullity.'"* (p. 501)

Beelzebub also portrays the Hasnamussian characteristics of artists and actors—with their *" 'illusorily inflated' maleficent idea of their famous art."* Beelzebub describes actors and artists among 'your favorites:'

> "Every one of them really being in respect of genuine essence almost what is called a nonentity, that is, something utterly empty but enveloped in a certain visibility, they have gradually acquired such an opinion of themselves, by means of favorite exclamations always and everywhere repeated by them themselves like 'genius,' 'talent,' 'gift,' and still a number of other words empty also like themselves, that it is as if, among similar beings around them, only they have 'divine origin,' only *they* are almost 'God.'" (p. 514)

Beelzebub portrays the "terrestrial nullities" as concealing their inner emptiness and appearing as something that they are not. Modern culture, the arts and sciences, are portrayed as based upon the imaginary qualities of such Hasnamussian-individuals. Beelzebub describes them as having *"an already quite automatized 'consciousness,' and completely 'nonsensical feelings,'"* and further, *"they feel themselves to be immeasurably superior to what they really are."* (p. 513) Any observation of an evening of contemporary television, movies or dramas, among your favorites, would convince any impartial, alien intelligence of the nullity of modern culture with its infamous artists and actors.

The second 'Naloo-osnian-impulse,' of *'the feeling of self-satisfaction from leading others astray'* is illustrated in several of Beelzebub's stories. Through human history, various Hasnamuss individuals have distorted true religious teachings for their own purposes or invented theistic philosophies with fantastic fictions, which lead to mass confusion and the further degeneration of *"sane mentation"* among their followers. The 'wiseacring' of Hasnamusses obscured the teachings and messages of the Sacred Individuals 'actualized from above.' The philosopher Atarnakh, was such a Hasnamuss, who led the councils astray with false teachings and misunderstanding. Many of such Hasnamusses came to be employed with the media and academia of modern times, and especially within the think-tanks and round tables of the power-possessing beings, deceiving the human race as to the true causes of historic events and their machinations.

Beelzebub explains to Hassein that through the history of humankind, there have been two basic types of religious-teachings. The first were founded upon the teachings and instructions of various *"sacred Messengers from Above,"* as sent by attendants of the Common Father to help destroy the effects of the properties of the organ Kundabuffer, which effects had become 'crystallized' in the presences of humankind. The second type of religious-teaching was invented by Hasnamusses, who began to change everything that the sacred Messengers had taught. Beelzebub talks about this in relationship to the alchemists, to Saint Buddha, Saint Mohammed and particularly Ashiata Shiemash.

Beelzebub describes the arising of "their peculiar" religions, based upon the "inventions" of certain individuals—with the germs of Hasnamussian traits already acquired in their presences:

> "... such beings began, as is proper to them for their egoistic aims, to invent for the 'confusion' of surrounding beings similar to themselves, various fictions, among which were also every kind of fantastic, what are called 'religious teachings' ..." (p. 694)

'Your favorites' thus *"lost their 'sane mentation'"* and a large number of 'Havatvernoni' or 'religions' arose having *"nothing in common with each other."* Particularly, the *"maleficent idea"* of *"Good"* and *"Evil"* was introduced leading to further 'dilution' of their psyches.

At the time of ancient Babylon, when the issue of the day was whether or not man had a soul, another one of the *"terrestrial Hasnamussian candidates of that time"* propounded the *"atheistic teachings of that period."* Beelzebub explains that according to this teaching:

> "... it was stated that there is no God in the world, and moreover no soul in man, and hence that all those talks and discussions about the soul are nothing more than the deliriums of sick visionaries.
>
> "It was further maintained that there exists in the World only one special law of mechanics, according to which everything that exists passes from one form into another .... Man also is therefore only a consequence of some preceding cause and in his turn must, as a result, be a cause of certain consequences.
>
> "Further, it was said that even what are called 'super-natural phenomena' really perceptible to most people are all nothing but these same result ensuing from the mentioned special law of mechanics. (pp. 343-4)

Such Hasnamussian theories are the mainstay of modern psychology, philosophy and science—which deny the soul in man, the validity of all 'super-natural phenomena' and the existence of God or Divinity in the World. Instead, everything is conceived to have followed mechanically from earlier causes, such as evolution by fortunate random mutations and happenstance.

Beelzebub recounts that when these ideas caught on in Babylon and due to *"their collective wiseacrings,"* it was gradually transformed into *"a veritable mill of nonsense."* The three-brained beings thus had *"a further mass of data for Hasnamussian manifestations"* and when they returned to their homelands, they began to *"propagate like contagious bacilli"* all the wrong notions about the soul and the World. These false teachings, along with all the false religious doctrines, ultimately destroyed the last remnants of the holy labors of Saintly Ashiata Shiemash, as has been done with the teachings of other Sacred Individuals actualized from Above.

Beelzebub offers a remarkable view of Hasnamusses and the spectrum of their perverse impulses. The Hasnamuss-individuals have the most disturbed and crystallized forms of false personality, some kind of special 'something' in their character and human history is littered with their names and stained with their blood crimes. Unfortunately, contemporary society and culture are today dominated by their influences and egotistic values, or lack thereof, and their invented theories and religions. Today as throughout history, there is indeed a wide spectrum of Hasnamusses, without objective conscience, power-possessing beings, media shrills, masters of war and 'stock jugglers,' with 'special societies' for 'important' people. The Hasnamusses promote every type of depravity, sexual obsession, random and fortuitous violence, perversion and superficiality.

11. The Hasnamussian Sciences, the 'Intelligentsia' & the 'Crats'

> "And that is just as it is everywhere on Earth: donkeys are alike, they are only differently called." **Mullah Nassr Eddin** (quoted by Beelzebub, p. 1090)

When discussing the League of Nations, Beelzebub expresses his opinion that nothing will likely become of such a 'common-planetary society' mainly because *"impartial Reason, proper to the presence of all three-brained beings who have already attained responsible age, is absent in them (its members)...."* (p. 1071) Beelzebub explains that their 'maleficent' education is particularly adapted to those young beings who will latter as a rule become 'power-possessing.' The capacities for 'sincere thinking,' the 'sensing of reality' and 'logical reflection' indeed *"become a very rare luxury on this planet ...."* Instead, their so-called 'education' mainly teaches them how best to *"give oneself up to what is called 'self-calming' ..."* and encourages such ignoble traits as *"'egoism,' 'partiality,' 'vanity,' 'self-love,' and so on."* (p. 1059)

Beelzebub explains to Hassein that the inherency towards the processes of reciprocal destruction has now become *"fixed in their psyche during hundreds of centuries"* and that it *"can never be decrystallized in the course of a few decades."* He suggests that such 'important' beings as might sincerely aim to eliminate warfare would best direct their energies towards *"the eradication of the conviction ... of the virtue of two notions they have."* The first of these concern,

> "... the practice of exalting certain of the participants in these processes to what are called 'heroes' and rewarding them with honors and what are called 'orders'...."
> (pp. 1071-2)

Beelzebub explains that such hero worship becomes an 'automatic factor' within the psyche of the next generation which makes them especially vulnerable to *"fall into that state into which it has already become without fail habitual for them to fall during these processes ...."* Such misguided youths can be whipped into a frenzy or patriotic fervour most simply.

The second concrete step that might be taken towards the eradication of warfare would be,

> "... the abolition even of one of their illustrious 'sciences' from among their many *Hasnamussian sciences,'* invented by certain pimpled begins among them, in which it is nonchalantly proved that the periodic reciprocal destruction on the Earth is very, very necessary, and that if it did not exist an intolerable overpopulation would result on the Earth, and such economic horrors would ensure that men-beings would begin to eat one another. (p. 1072)

According to Beelzebub, this is just one of *"those idiotic ideas ... constantly arising there"* which is passed from generation to generation as something 'lawful' and 'indubitable.' The sum of such idiotic ideas engenders in those strange three-brained beings *"even 'doubt in the existence of Divinity....''* (p. 1072) The consequence of such strange notions, invented Hasnamussian philosophies and sciences, results in such beings no longer attaining to the *"'instinctual sensing' of those certain cosmic truths."*

Of course, Beelzebub's description of the Hasnamussian sciences seems most bizarre and ridiculous, and yet this is only a parody of what actually occurs within the life of humanity.[11]

Beelzebub then launches into a long exposition about the varied 'intelligentsia' and the 'crats'—many

---

[11] The Rockefeller family has been one of the prime promoters of 'eugenics' and 'population control' in modern times. Adolph Hitler had received funding for his race theories and eugenics programs from the Rockefellers and allied financial and aristocratic interests. Bertrand Russell, one of the prime British intellectuals serving the plutocrats, theocrats and aristocrats with their desire for a 'new world order,' wrote:

> "At present the population of the world is increasing... If a Black Death could be spread throughout the world once in every generation, survivors could procreate freely without making the world too full... the state of affairs might be somewhat unpleasant, but what of it? Really high-minded people are indifferent to suffering, especially that of others.... Gradually, by selective breeding, the congenital differences between rulers and ruled will increase until they become almost different species. A revolt of the plebs would become as unthinkable as an organized insurrection of sheep against the practice of eating mutton." (*The Impact of Science on Society.*)

Bertrand Russell is a prime example of the pimpled intellectual depicted by Beelzebub, likely controlled by the same three principle motives ascribed by Beelzebub to the 'aristocrats' and the 'zevocrates:' *"The first concerns the question of food; the second consists of the recollections associated with the former functionings of the sexual organs; and the third relates to the memories of their first nurse."* (p. 1088)

Another author explains some of the current Hasnamussian objectives and plans being advanced under the euphemism of 'global government' or the 'new world order:'

> "The Rockefeller Foundation has the SAME agenda as the Illuminati and the Gates Foundation. David Rockefeller, a member of the Illuminati, is a founder and member of several organizations such as the Trilateral Commission, the Bilderbergers and the Club of Rome, whose purpose is to a) set up a One World Government, b) control ALL business throughout the world and, c) dramatically and rapidly reducing the population of the world from 6 billion to 500 million, by war, disease and famine." (Dr. L. Day, 2008)

The Hasnamussian science is thriving in modern times. Even the United Nations proposes in Agenda 21 that the ideal population for a sustainable earth would be 500 million. This is the figure carved in stone onto the Georgia Guide Stones erected in the state of Georgia, USA, by some Hasnamuss member of some 'special' and secret society. A message consisting of a set of ten guidelines or principles is engraved on the Georgia Guidestones in eight different languages, with the statement: "Let these be guidestones to an age of reason." The first of these reads:

of whom are candidates for Hasnamusses. Beelzebub explains firstly to Hassein that the true meaning of the word 'intelligentsia' would imply *"force-in-oneself"* and the capacity for objective reason. However, among your favourites, those called by this name are actually those beings *"who are the exact opposite of what this word denotes"* (p. 1080), in fact are the 'unintelligent' and should really be called the *"mechanogentsia."* Beelzebub explains that these mechanogentsia can *"give absolutely no direction at all to their being-functions,"* and are animated only by *"external shocks"* acting upon corresponding automatic perceptions, so many as imposed through their maleficent education. Most importantly, Beelzebub explains the lack within the so-called intelligentsia:

> "But never do their outer manifestations in general nor those inner-being-impulses of theirs, which ought to be under the directive of their being-'I,' proceed according to their own wish resulting from the whole of their entire presence. (p. 1082)

However, these intelligentsia are especially those with that *"'psycho-organic-need' of theirs to 'teach others sense' and to put them on the right road,"* and who *"always have at least one 'victim' for their teachings."*

Beelzebub views the so-called 'intelligentsia' as particularly affected by their superficial education and socialization:

> "These freaks lose, so to say, that outer mask which thanks to the same maleficent means existing there, called 'education,' most of them little by little learned to wear from their childhood and thanks to which they can very well conceal their genuine inner and outer trifling significance from others, and in consequence they automatically become slaves of others to the degree of humiliation; or, as they themselves say there, they fall as regards all their inner experience, under somebody's 'thumb'; for instance, under the

Maintain humanity under 500,000,000 in perpetual balance with nature.

This is the Hasnamussian science alive and well in modern times, supported by a plethora of other invented sciences. Humankind, in modern times, has never known life apart from the hidden influences of these terrestrial nullities, as Beelzebub describes.

A recent news item (October, 2010) entitled: *The Green Agenda Is About Getting Rid Of As Many Humans As Possible,* reads:

> The truth is that there are a growing number of environmental activists (including some very, very famous people) who are publicly advocating the end of our freedoms, the establishment of a Big Brother style world government and the systematic eradication of at least 90% of humanity all for the good of the environment. Unfortunately, this is not a joke and it is not an exaggeration. ... To these eco-fascists, climate change is the number one threat to the earth, and in order to eliminate that threat "democracy must be put on hold", an authoritarian world government must be established and we need to start getting rid of as many humans as possible. In a video, Gates describes how the number of people might be reduced.... *"The world today has 6.8 billion people... that's headed up to about 9 billion. Now if we do a really great job on new vaccines, health care, reproductive health services, we could lower that by perhaps 10 or 15 percent."*

Certainly, this is the Hasnamussian science of the day, along with quack sciences espousing inoculations, global warming due to human carbon emissions, genetically modified foods, chemtrail poisons—all *"invented by certain pimpled beings"* to prove *"nonchalantly"* the need for diseases, poisons and wars to maintain population control and for the infamous 'stock jugglers.'

The Hasnamusses are also very intent to squash within the populace any last semblance of a belief or feeling of the Divinity in life. A rash of recent publications are geared towards this end: Richard Dawkins, *The God Delusion*, 2006; Sam Harris, *The End Of Faith: Religion, Terror, And The Future Of Reason*, 2004; Carl Sagan, *The Varieties Of Scientific Experience: A Personal view Of the Search For God*, 2006; Daniel Dennett, *Breaking The Spell: Religion As A Natural Phenomenon*, 2006; Christopher Hitchens, *God Is Not Great: How Religion Poisons Everything*, 2007; Victor Stegner, *God: The Failed Hypothesis--How Science Shows That God Does Not Exist*, 2007.

'thumb' of 'wife' or 'mistress,' or of such another who by some means has ferreted out the inner insignificance of the given terrestrial being, and thus the latter ceases to have for them this artificial mask. (pp. 1077-8)

Beelzebub explains that it is just such 'freaks' who write various 'manuals' for the guidance and education of others. For example, a contemporary being "whose heart as they say always 'sinks into his boots' from fright when, for instance, a mouse runs past him," writes a book on "what must not be done on meeting a tiger;" or such a terrestrial being "under somebody's thumb" writes a book on "what must be done for the good 'government' of others." (p. 1078) Beelzebub portrays the intelligentsia as striving always to conceal from others their inner insignificance or 'terrestrial nullity.'

Beelzebub then explains to Hassein, that many of these intelligentsia also go by other names, particularly by those Greek names ending in the term 'crat:' These include the Bureaucrats, the Plutocrats, the Theocrats, Democrats, Zevrocrats and the Aristocrats. The suffix crat is derived from the Greek and means 'to keep' or 'to hold,' according to Beelzebub, who then characterizes each of these types. The Bureaucrats are those intelligentsia who look after the chancellery and who are completely controlled by their *"automatic associations"* to shocks coming from without, and who manifest without the participation of *"any separate spiritualized being-part whatsoever of their common presence."*

The 'plutocrats' are the intelligentsia described by Beelzebub as *"scoundrels of the deepest dye"* and *"saturated by every kind of Hasnamussness to the marrow of their bones."* (p. 1084) These plutocrats are those who:

> "... were able very artistically to get all the honest, that is 'naïve,' fellow countrymen of theirs they came across, into their toils, thanks to which they became the owners of a great quantity of what is called there 'money' and 'slaves.'

> "Here, bear in mind that it is just from these terrestrial types that most Hasnamuss-individuals arise. (p. 1083)

Beelzebub explains that when it was necessary to find some "very 'forceful' word" to denote them, the suffix 'plut' was borrowed from Russian, which means 'rogue.' These *"terrestrial parasites"* were quite content with such a title, not knowing its hidden significance, and *"out of swagger, they go about in top hats, even on weekdays"* and at other times, they *"strut like turkey cocks."* Beelzebub notes the influences of these "terrestrial monsters:'

> "... these terrestrial types, thanks to what is called 'ill-gotten' gains, had already then acquired 'force and power' far greater perhaps than that of their kings. (p. 1084)

The Theocrats are then described as those 'intelligentsia' in who we find almost *"the same 'perturbation' as in those who become plutocrats."* However, whereas the plutocrats *"act upon their surroundings for the satisfaction of their Hasnamussian needs through that function which is called among them 'trust,'"* the Theocrats pursue the satisfaction of their Hasnamussian needs based on "faith." And thus, humankind has come to 'trust' the bankers and the power elites, and to have 'faith' in their crooked Hasnamussian priests and perverted religious figures. Appropriately, Mullah Nassr Eddin is quoted as having remarked: *"Isn't it all one to the poor flies how they are killed? By a kick of the hooves of horned devils, or by a stoke of the beautiful wings of divine angels?"* (p. 1086)

The Democrats do not tend to come from the *'hereditary intelligentsics'* but were simple, ordinary terrestrial beings who became intelligentsia and only afterwards did the sacred function of 'Conscience' degenerate in them. However, when such Democrats become 'power-possessing beings,' *"they have in themselves no inherited aptitudes at all for instinctually being able to direct others and in consequence are quite unable to direct the existence of beings who happen to be in their power."* (p. 1086)

The last two types, the Zevrocrats and the Aristocrats are distinguished by the names given to them, such as 'emir,' 'count,' 'khan,' 'prince' and so on, which titles always elicit 'vanity' in such beings, *"up to their very death."* These two types are very similar but one comes from a 'republican state organization,' while the other is from a 'monarchic state organization.' Beelzebub describes both of these types as *'jokes of nature'* and *'misconceptions,'* and he depicts their basic motivational patterns:

> "All the experiencings, however, of these aristocrats and zevrocrats there, according to my observation, can be reduced to only three series.
>
> "The first concerns the question of food; the second consists of the recollections associated with the former functionings of the sexual organs; and the third relates to the memories of their first nurse." (p. 1088)

Beelzebub was quite astonished and puzzled by how such beings, such 'jokes of nature,' with only these three areas of experiencing, could have as lengthy an existence as the other beings there. Beelzebub describes 'your favourites,' the strange three-brained beings on plant Earth, as delighting in having their zevrocrats and aristocrats take part in staging their *'puppet shows,'* despite their being *"quite vacuous and consequently feeble."*

These are some of the various forms of Hasnamusses, Intelligentsia and 'crats,' that dominate the world stage, as the power possessing and important beings on that ill-fated planet. Beelzebub often refers to that *'certain something'* in the Hasnamuss-individual, which is not simply put into words but is detected more in its blending with the spectrum of the abnormal impulses they manifest. Beelzebub explains that this 'certain something' will eventually cause *"what are called 'serious-retributing-suffering-consequences' for these individuals themselves"* in afterlife, but meanwhile, they have a greater effect on those around them and lead others to imitate and manifest the same undesirable qualities and impulses.

The Hasnamuss individuals, like the aristocratic, corporate, financial and religious elites, do not experience the impulses of *"being-self-shame"* or of Objective Conscience. The current crisis in the life of humankind attests to the horrors, suffering and desolation caused by these *"terrestrial nullities."* The pseudo-illuminate are such Hasnamusses, willing to spray you and your children with chemtrails, while poisoning your food, water and air, sickening you through genetically modified poisons and additives, infesting you with inoculations and confusing your hearts and minds through all the lies and deceits of the corporate media and their Hasnamussian sciences.

The Hasnamuss are controlled by the three lower possibilities of money, sex and power, and do not attain to the awakening of the heart, nor to the possibilities inherent to the higher life of the soul. They are the product of lunacy and delusion. They feel such self-satisfaction from leading you astray, engaging in every kind of depravity and they indeed have such *"irresistible inclinations to destroy the existence of other breathing creatures."* Such types came to rule the human race, all part of the *new world psychiatric disorder*. This is the scum that rose to the top of the waters of life and their crimes are the blood streaks through human history.

> "As a rule, in consequence of the fact that these power-possessing or important beings there do not use the time foreseen by Great Nature for preparing themselves to become worthy responsible beings—owing chiefly to which during their responsible existence, even in their waking state, all kinds of associations in their common presences almost always flow automatically—therefore they themselves without any individual intentions and at times even half-intentionally try to do everything in such a way that the next process of reciprocal destruction should occur sooner, and they even hope that this next process should proceed on as large a scale as possible.

> "Such a monstrous need arises in their abnormal psyche because they expect certain egoistic profits from these processes, either personally for themselves or for their nearest, and with their degenerated mentation they even hope that the greater the scale of the next process, the greater the extent of the profits to be obtained, either personally for themselves or for their nearest. (p. 1062)

The pseudo-illuminate Hasnamusses are not so illumined and their false consciousness system and inner nullity has prevented the human race from attaining to higher consciousness and being-existence. Further, they have distorted and obscured the messages and teachings of all of the Sacred Messengers as described by Beelzebub, to such an extent, that the strange three-brained beings doubt even that they are a part of Divinity. Meanwhile, the archcriminal wars of the Hasnamusses stain the fabric of human history crimson red and their new Hasnamussian inventions provide new contrivances for their Hasnamussian impulses.

And so, humankind came to be ruled by Hasnamusses, 'crats' and 'intelligentsia' of varied types. However, as noted by Mullah Nassr Eddin: *"And that is just as it is everywhere on Earth: donkeys are alike, they are only differently called."* (p. 1090)

Hasnamusses, Intelligentsia & Crats

12. A Portrait of "Man" in Quotation Marks

For Gurdjieff, a *real man* has attained "real I." A *man in quotation marks* is a person asleep, governed by a multiplicity of i's, lost in self-love and vanity, in negative emotions and imagination. A man in quotation marks, a slug, is always lost in the world, unaware of what they are sensing, doing, thinking and feeling. They are lived out by life in a state of passive awareness and mechanical reactions, controlled by external influences, false personality and conditioning. A human asleep knows only pseudo-i and does not know the real world. In contrast, a real human can *"instinctually sense cosmic truths"* and *"know self."*

At the conclusion of *Beelzebub's Tales*, after Beelzebub's horns have grown and branched five times–indicative of his attainments, Gurdjieff includes a selection of writing, entitled *"From the Author."* It is there, that he draws a vivid portrait of what he labels *"a man in quotation marks."*

> "... the difference between a real man and a pseudo man ... is ... between one who has his own "I" and one who has not ...." (p. 1192)

Gurdjieff goes on to portray the automatic functioning of a typical human being. From the outside, this person seems to embody the virtues of life and success, but if we see into his inner life, we realize that he is essentially asleep, conditioned by the pushes and pulls of external and inner stimuli, the itches and wanderings of the nerves and sex organs. In the following passage, Gurdjieff portrays a person's "inner world"–a portrait which is both entertaining and horrifying. Mr. G. begins by depicting the outward appearances and then he delves into the hidden inner dynamics:

> "You have plenty of money, luxurious conditions of existence, and universal esteem and respect. At the head of your well-established concerns are people absolutely reliable and devoted to you; in a word, your life is a bed of roses.
>
> "You dispose of your time as you please, you are a patron of the arts, you settle world questions over a cup of coffee, and you are even interested in the development of the latent spiritual forces of man. You are not unfamiliar with the needs of the spirit, and are well versed in philosophical matters. You are well educated and widely read. Having a great deal of learning on all kinds of questions, you are reputed to be a clever man, being at home in a variety of fields. You are a model of culture.
>
> "All who know you regard you as a man of great will and most of them even attribute all your advantages to the results of the manifestation of this will of yours.
>
> "In short, from every point of view, you are fully deserving of imitation, and a man to be envied." (pp. 1024-5)

We certainly seem to have an intelligent and cultured "man" in our midst. From the outside, this slug presents as clever and successful, interested even in the spiritual nature of humanity. Gurdjieff then goes on to depict a typical morning of this gentleman and the processes of his inner life. Here, Mr. Gurdjieff provides a humorous peek into the inner world of *"a man in quotation marks:"*

II / The Strange Psyche & the Psychopathology of "Your Favorites"

"IN THE MORNING you wake up under the impression of some oppressive dream. Your slightly depressed state, that dispersed on awakening, has nevertheless left its mark. A certain languidness and hesitancy in your movements.

"You go to the mirror to comb your hair and carelessly drop the brush; you have only just picked it up, when you drop it again. You then pick it up with a shade of impatience, and, in consequence, you drop it a third time; you try to catch it as it is falling, but ... from an unlucky blow of your hand, the brush makes for the mirror; in vain you rush to save it, crack ... there is a star of cracks on that antique mirror of which you were so proud.

"Damn! Devil take it! And you experience a need to vent your fresh annoyance on some one or other, and not finding the newspaper beside your morning coffee, the servant having forgotten to put it there, the cup of your patience overflows and you decide that you cannot stand the fellow any longer in the house.

"It is time for you to go out. The weather being pleasant, and not having far to go, you decide to walk. Behind you glides your new automobile of the latest model.

"The bright sunshine somewhat calms you, and a crowd which has collected at the corner attracts your attention.

"You go nearer, and in the middle of the crowd you see a man lying unconscious on the pavement. A policeman, with the help of some of the, as they are called, 'idlers' who have collected, puts the man into a 'taxi' to take him to the hospital.

"Thanks merely to the likeness, which has just struck you, between the face of the chauffeur and the face of the drunkard you bumped into last year when you were returning somewhat tipsy yourself from a rowdy birthday party, you notice that the accident on the street-corner is unaccountably connected in your associations with a meringue you ate at that party.

"Ah, what a meringue that was!

"That servant of yours, forgetting your newspaper today, spoiled your morning coffee. Why not make up for it at once?

"Here is a fashionable café where you sometimes go with your friends.

"But why did you recall the servant? Had you not almost entirely forgotten the morning's annoyances? But now ... how very good this meringue tastes with the coffee.

"Look! There are two ladies at the next table. What a charming blonde!

"You hear her whispering to her companion, glancing at you: 'Now he is the sort of man I like!'

"Do you deny that from these words about you, accidentally overheard and perhaps intentionally said aloud, the whole of you, as is said, 'inwardly rejoices'?

"Suppose that at this moment you were asked whether it had been worth while getting fussed and losing your temper over the morning's annoyances, you would of course answer in the negative and promise yourself that nothing of the kind should ever occur again.

"Need you be told how your mood has transformed while you were making the acquaintance of the blonde in whom you were interested and who was interested in you, and its state during all the time you spent with her?

"You return home humming some air, and even the sight of the broken mirror only elicits a smile from you. But how about the business on which you had gone out this morning. ... You only just remembered it. Clever . . . well, never mind, you can telephone.

"You go to the phone and the girl connects you with the wrong number.

"You ring again, and get the same number. Some man informs you that you are bothering him, you tell him it is not your fault, and what with one word and another, you learn to your surprise that you are a scoundrel and an idiot and that if you ring him up again . . . then . . .

"A rug slipping under your feet provides a storm of indignation, and you should hear the tone of voice in which you rebuke the servant who is handing you a letter.

"The letter is from a man you esteem and whose good opinion you value highly.

"The contents of the letter are so flattering to you, that as you read, your irritation gradually passes and changes to the 'pleasant embarrassment' of a man listening to a eulogy of himself. You finish reading the letter in the happiest of moods.

"I could continue this picture of your day - you free man!

"Perhaps you think I am overdrawing?

"No, it is a photographically exact snapshot from nature." (pp. 1204-7)

This portrait of a 'man in quotation marks' depicts the inner world of a well respected, cultured and spiritual man about town. This is a typical "man-being" or slug. There is certainly a great gulf between the superficial outer appearances and the underlying reality. On the one hand, there is that which we imagine ourselves to be, clever and talented men and women about town, capable of solving life's mysteries over coffee and cigarettes. And then there is the inner man or woman, angry when we cannot find our slippers, when our self love or vanity is offended, controlled by the intestines and sex organs, and consumed by negative emotions. A person is absorbed moment to moment by every little thing that happens in the world around, each bringing about different i's in him or her. There is a great gap between what we imagine "man" to be and what the masses of humanity are in their being. This is the great lie, how man in quotation marks goes by the name "man," when we are what Beelzebub describes as *"terrestrial nullities."* In mechanical life, few people realize the terror of the situation.

In one *Tale*, Beelzebub humorously depicts humans as having *"four sources of action"* or motivation– *"existing there under the names of 'mother-in-law,' 'digestion,' 'John Thomas,' and 'cash'."* (p. 343) In

G.'s period, the term *"John Thomas"* signified the penis. In the portrait of a man in quotation marks, the most significant motives are those of the stomach, sex organs, cash and the ego.

Gurdjieff explains how such men in quotation marks are produced in life:

> "A man comes into the world like a clean sheet of paper, which immediately all around him begin vying with each other to dirty and fill up with education, morality, the information we call knowledge, and with all kinds of feelings of duty, honour, conscience, and so on and so forth.
>
> "And each and all claim immutability and infallibility for the methods they employ for grafting these branches onto the main trunk, called man's personality.
>
> "The sheet of paper gradually becomes dirty, and the dirtier it becomes, that is to say, the more a man is stuffed with ephemeral information and those notions of duty, honor, and so on which are dinned into him or suggested to him by others, the 'cleverer' and worthier is he considered by those around him.
>
> "And seeing that people look upon his 'dirt' as a merit, he himself inevitably comes to regard this same dirtied sheet of paper in the same light.
>
> "And so you have a model of what we call a man, to which frequently are added such words as 'talent' and 'genius.'
>
> "And the temper of our 'talent' when it wakes up in the morning, is spoiled for the whole day if it does not find its slippers beside the bed.
>
> "The ordinary man is not free in his manifestations, in his life, in his moods.
>
> "He cannot be what he would like to be; and what he considers himself to be, he is not that.
>
> "Man–how mighty it sounds! The very name 'man' means 'the acme of Creation;' but... how does his title fit contemporary man?" (p. 1208)

Gurdjieff draws a dismal view of a human asleep, a "man in quotation marks"--a "slug" breeding on planet Earth.

13. Being-Partkdolg-Duty: On Conscious Labours and Intentional Suffering

In *Beelzebub's Tales to His Grandson*, Gurdjieff places particular emphasis on the necessity for an individual to fulfill their *being-partkdolg-duty*. Such duties consist of *"conscious labours"* and *"intentional suffering."* These are described as *"the sole possible means for the assimilation of the cosmic substances required for the coating and perfecting of the higher being-bodies...."* (p.792)

Unfortunately, the three-brained beings on earth established such *"abnormal conditions of external ordinary being-existence"* that they no longer fulfill their *being-Partkdolg-duty*. Much of strangeness of the human psyche is attributed to this failure of *"your favourites"* and the role that this plays in the *involution* or *evolution* of the sacred sexual substances.

It is not easy to define exactly what such *being-partkdolg-duty* involves and the different meanings of this term as intended by Beelzebub—or Gurdjieff. One approach is to consider Beelzebub's life and visits to the earth—as a character in a life drama. Beelzebub exemplifies what conscious labours and intentional suffering might involve. Beelzebub undertakes varied tasks on Earth under conditions foreign to his nature and plays a role in the service of other Sacred Individuals and High Commissions, on behalf of Our ENDLESSNESS. At the end of the book, Beelzebub, because of his meritorious work, acquires additional forks in his horns—signifying that he had attained higher levels of Divine Reason and coated his higher being-bodies. Beelzebub's stories also describe other sacred messengers and individuals actualized from above who undertook such conscious labours and intentional suffering through their efforts on earth to help humankind and to restore cosmic harmony. Gurdjieff himself throughout his life similarly undertook such conscious labours and intentional suffering—in his searches for ancient wisdom, in his efforts to awaken, in his work with and for others, in his labour and suffering to complete *Beelzebub's Tales*, for the future of humankind.

Conscious labours include efforts to observe and remember oneself—making conscious efforts in the inner struggle towards self perfection and self-remembering. Conscious labours can also be in relationship to others in the work, in service to humankind or as required by nature or in service of Our ENDLESSNESS. With reference to *intentional suffering*, Beelzebub explains that Lord Buddha taught *"... the greatest intentional-suffering can be obtained in your presences if you compel yourself to be able to endure the displeasing-manifestations-of-others-towards-yourselves."* (pp. 241-2) Such an attitude towards others is in dramatic contrast to what Beelzebub describes as the property of *your favourites "to always grow indignant at the defects of others around them."*

Beelzebub also discusses conscious labours and intentional suffering in terms of the struggle within an individual between the processes of the planetary body and those of the higher being-bodies within the planetary body. The struggle between these two natures concerns the predominance of either "desires" or "non-desires." Beelzebub explains:

> "... only he, who consciously assists the process of this inner struggle and consciously assists the "non-desires" to predominate over the desires, behaves just in accordance with the essence of our COMMON FATHER CREATOR HIMSELF; whereas he who with his consciousness assists the contrary, only increases HIS sorrow." (p. 373)

This struggle is particularly relevant in terms of the involution or evolution of the sexual substances within the individual. According to Beelzebub, three main substances or being-foods are taken in and refined within the human organism. The final product of the evolution of the food octaves is sperm in men and other comparable sexual substances in the ovaries of women. Although the three-brained beings know of the *"being-Exioehary,"* they squander it whenever possible–the *"chief vice of contemporary three-brained beings."* Further, because *your favourites* do not actualize their 'being-Partdolg-duty,' these substances, if not wasted, begin to *"involve back ... towards those crystallisations from which their evolution began."* This involution of the sexual substances tends to *"'deperfect' their previously established essence-individuality,"* leading to innumerable "illnesses" and diminishing the *"thirst for Being."* (pp. 793-794)

Beelzebub explains how, under the right circumstance, the sacred substance Exioehary can:

> "... transform completely into new higher substances and in order to acquire vibrations corresponding to the vibrations of the next higher vivifyingness ... it inevitably requires just that foreign help which is actualized only in the presences of the three-brained beings exclusively owing to those factors mentioned by me more than once and which are manifested in the 'being-Partkdolg-duty,' ... which factors until now serve as the sole possible means for the assimilation of the cosmic substances required for the coating and perfecting of the higher being-bodies and which we at the present time call 'conscious labours' and 'intentional suffering.'" (p. 792)

Unfortunately, those strange three-brained beings strive only for their own welfare and the *"free gratification of the multitudinous vices and multiform vices fixed in their essences."* (p. 794) Thus, the sexual substances within the body are not refined so as to produce the substances required for the higher being-bodies, but are instead squandered in the multiform sexual vices and the desires predominate over the non-desires, only increasing the Sorrow of our ENDLESSNESS.

Beelzebub also explains how the development of the Reason-of-Understanding, in contrast to the Reason-of-Knowing, requires that the individual actualize his being-Partkdolg-duty. This involves maintaining active being-awareness at the registration of psychological impressions. He describes this as the *"persevering actualizing of the striving towards the manifestation of one's own individuality."* (p. 1167)[12] The striving towards perfection and the manifestation of one's real 'I' require that one actively maintain being-awareness–part of one's conscious labours in the striving towards self-perfection.

---

[12] In the Ouspensky version of the fourth way, this is related to the practice of *"self-remembering."*

14. Remembering, Forgetting & the Inevitability of Death

"... every man should strive to have his own "I" ..." **G. I. Gurdjieff** (1950, p.1201)

Humankind is in a terrible state, asleep to the realities of life, unable to perceive the real world, passively conditioned by the pleasuring of the stomach and sex organs, governed by a false consciousness system, and bound only to serve local cosmic purposes–feeding the earth and moon. Humans' psychological illusions blind them to the horror of the situation and of themselves. Most central are the illusions of being properly conscious, of having real will and of knowing "I." Beyond these, humans hold the illusion that they all have eternal souls, about to experience the pleasures of paradise and heaven or live innumerable lives until they get it right, and once again know God–Mr. God himself, with his comb sticking out of his vest pocket.

Gurdjieff presents a dismal view of the reality and horror of the situation:

> Nature takes all measures to ensure that we shall live without seeing the terror, and that we should not hang ourselves, but live long; and then, when we are required, She slaughters us. (p. 1226)

Humans in quotation marks are slugs who can end up as only fertilizer. Humans do not have a soul, as such, but only the potential for achieving one. They must produce the necessary being efforts through work on self, the struggle to awaken, conscious labours and intentional suffering, and the fulfilling of their being obligations, in order for this potential to be realized. In this view, the only thing that is serious is the possibility of attaining "I," real I. Gurdjieff explains by the title of Book III of his *"All and Everything"* series, that *The World is Real only then, when 'I AM.'* The I Am refers to the Particle, established in its own nature. Elsewhere, G. is quoted by Nicoll: *"Behind Real I lies God."* (1975, p. 1388)

Gurdjieff, as recalled by Ouspensky, always asked what is serious to a human in prison who is condemned to death, and then answered–to escape–to escape from the general law and to be free. In the light of the fourth way teaching, it is clearly evident that people normally turn around in circles of insignificant interest and insignificant aims, with no idea of what they are missing. Humans do not even realize that they are imprisoned, as slaves and slugs to Great Nature. At least, for one who encounters *the Work*, or *Beelzebub's Tales to His Grandson*, he or she can cultivate a more conscious attitude towards his or her slavery. This can initiate processes of self-study and self-remembering, experiences of the sacred being-impulses and the instinctual sensing of cosmic truths. The aim is to remember to be aware of the totality of ourselves within the present moment, within the depths of our being. Normally, humans are lost in forgetfulness and need to remember Self–as an emanation of the sorrow of the Common Father and as a particle of the Divine. Unfortunately, all of mechanical life puts the slugs to sleep, amusing them with pleasures and imagination, until they are fit food for the moon. Humans need to remember themselves always and everywhere, until they attain real I.

At the very end of his tales to his grandson, in a chapter entitled, *"The Inevitable Results of Impartial Mentation,"* Beelzebub explains one remaining route of escape for "your favorites:"

> "The sole means now for the saving of the beings of the planet Earth would be to implant again into their presences a new organ, an organ like Kundabuffer, but this time of such properties that every one of these unfortunates during the process of existence should constantly sense and be cognizant of the inevitability of his own death as well as of the death of everyone upon whom his eyes or attention rests.
>
> "Only such a sensation and such a cognizance can now destroy the egoism completely crystallized in them that has swallowed up the whole of their Essence and also that tendency to hate others which flows from it ..." (p.1183)

Beelzebub explains that only such an organ would break down the egoism crystallized in humankind and reveal the insignificance of *"all his favourite things."* Of course, Beelzebub notes that the organ Kundabuffer and human's psychological illusions prevent such cognition of *"these genuine terrors."* Humans have sown little and so shall they reap. Without the desire and struggle to remember self, a human does not attain real I and realize the larger possibilities for immortality, consciousness, genuine love and self perfection. The slugs can even serve higher cosmic purposes and blend again with the Most Most Holy Sun Absolute, although it may take a long time. Beelzebub's views and teachings on the nature of those unfortunate three-brained beings on planet Earth are as inspiring as they are horrifying.

"... every kind of what your favorites call 'knowledge' ... has absolutely nothing in common with what is called 'Objective Knowledge.'"

- 1950, p. 1169 -

"It is necessary to notice that in the Great Universe all phenomena in general, without exception wherever they arise and manifest, are simply successively law-conformable 'Fractions' of some whole phenomenon which has its prime arising on the Most Holy Sun Absolute."

- p. 123 -

III /
"Objective Science"

1. The Sacred Fundamental Cosmic Laws of World-Creation and World-Maintenance

As part of his education of his grandson, Beelzebub repeatedly returns to explanations of the fundamental cosmic laws. Most importantly, there are the *"first-degree"* Sacred Cosmic Laws of World-Creation and World-Maintenance. In *The Tales*, these are the sacred laws of Triamazikamno and Heptaparaparshinokh. In the Ouspensky version of Gurdjieff's teaching, these are referred to simply as the Law of Three and the Law of Seven—also referred to as the Law of the Octave. According to Beelzebub and Gurdjieff, these two sacred cosmic laws are embodied throughout the Universe in all phenomena in any world and throughout all time.[13]

Everything is some type of *"law conformable 'Fraction'"* of the original unity and these sacred principles of the threefold and sevenfold nature of the World depict the processes by which the multitude of things is created out of an original unity. The student Nicoll explains: *"God is ... first One and then Three and then Seven."* (1975, p. 1386) Just as white light is reflected through a three sided prism to yield a spectrum of seven colours; so also, these sacred principles state that all of life and creation is based on such patterns. In fact, these Sacred Cosmic Laws are even inherent in the primary Source, even before creation occurs. For Beelzebub, no education of his grandson Hassein could possibly be complete without attempting to articulate these archaic teachings of *"Objective Science."* Of course, "the slugs" have no memory of such principles and can no longer *"instinctually sense cosmic truths"*–given the degradation of the human psyche.

1a. The Sacred Triamazikamno

The Sacred Triamazikamno manifests, *"in everything, without exception, and everywhere in the Universe, in three separate independent aspects."* (p. 138) At different points, Beelzebub uses various terms to differentiate these three principles and to describe how they interrelate within some phenomena or process. The three forces are the *"Holy-Affirming," "Holy-Denying"* and the *"Holy Reconciling"*–or more simply, the active, passive and neutralizing principles. Whereas the "scientists of new formation" tend to conceive of all things in a dualistic manner, Objective Science is founded on an understanding of this ancient principle of the Threefoldness of all cosmic manifestations–within any cosmos on any order of scale.

In the *Tales*, Beelzebub explains the actions of this principle:

> "A law which always flows into a consequence and becomes the cause of subsequent consequences, and always functions by three independent and quite opposite characteristic manifestations, latent within it, in properties neither seen nor sensed." (p. 139)

---

[13] In addition to these Fundamental Cosmic Laws, there are also various "second" and "third degree" cosmic laws, but these flow from the effects of the threefoldness and sevenfoldness inherent in all processes.

Processes proceed through three forces in interaction, which give rise to a fourth effect, which then partakes in subsequent interactions. In occult teachings, this is illustrated by the magical principle of creation–by which fire acts upon water, is neutralized by air and results in the element earth. The three forces come together as one, and the resultant becomes a cause of subsequent phenomena, again participating in a threefold manner. Beelzebub elaborates: *"... the higher blends with the lower in order to actualize the middle and thus become either higher for the preceding lower, or lower for the succeeding higher..."* (p. 751)

Also evident in Beelzebub's explanation is the fact that the three separate forces are *"neither seen nor sensed"*–as they are blended together. It is the effects which might be seen or sensed, after different generations of causes and consequences. In discussions with Ouspensky, Gurdjieff explains that two forces can never produce a phenomenon, but require a third which is not directly visible, but is latent within the medium within which the interaction occurs. Gurdjieff states:

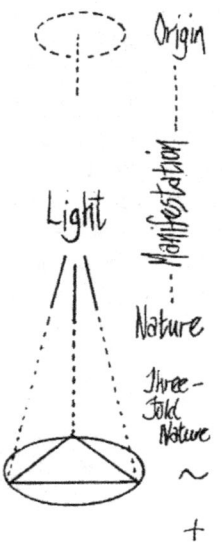

"The teaching of the three forces is at the root of all ancient systems. The first force may be called active or positive; the second, passive or negative; the third, neutralizing. But these are merely names, for in reality all three forces are equally active and appear as active, passive, and neutralizing, only at their meeting points, that is to say, only in relation to one another at a given moment. The first two forces are more or less comprehensible to man and the third may sometimes be discovered either at the point of application of the forces, or in the 'medium,' or in the 'result.' But, speaking in general, the third force is not easily accessible to direct observation and understanding. The reason for this is to be found in the fundamental limitations of man's ordinary psychological activity.... People cannot perceive and observe the third force directly any more than they can spatially perceive the 'fourth dimension.' ... people cannot observe phenomena as manifestations of three forces because we cannot observe the objective world in our subjective states of consciousness. ... If we could see the manifestation of three forces in every action, we should then see the world as it is (things in themselves). ... The third force is a property of the real world." (Ouspensky, 1949, pp. 77-8)

The third force is latent within the medium within which the opposing forces operate, acting as the neutralizing or reconciling force which mediates the interaction of the opposites. The third force is latent within the hidden dimensions of space/time. Occult teachings maintain that all things embody such a trinity of forces, which enter into endless combinations and permutations on different planes of creation.

Beelzebub uses other terms and descriptors to depict the three forces: these include the terms *'Surp-Otheos,' 'Surp-Skiros'* and *'Surp-Athanotos.'* These are also referred to successively as the *'Affirming-force,'* or *'Pushing-force'* or *'Force-plus;'* the *'Denying-force,'* or *'Resisting-force'* or *'Force-minus;'* and thirdly, the *'Reconciling-force,'* 'Equilibrating-Force' or the *'Neutralizing-force.'* Further, Beelzebub relates the three forces to the *"Holy Trinity"* of *'God-the-father,'* the affirming force, *'God-the-Son,'* the denying force, and *'God-the-Holy-Ghost,'* the reconciling force.

The meaning of the term Triamazikamno is apparently derived from the Greek language, and according to J. Bennett, it means *"I put three together."* For Beelzebub and Gurdjieff, all things consist in three aspects.

1b. Heptaparaparshinokh

The second of the first-degree, fundamental and Sacred Cosmic Laws, is that of Heptaparaparshinokh—or the *"Law of the Sevenfoldness."* Beelzebub elaborates:

> "The Law of Sevenfoldness exists on the Earth and will exist forever and in everything

> "For instance, in accordance with this Law, there are in the white ray seven independent colors; in every definite sound there are seven different independent tones; in every state of man, seven different independent sensations; further, every definite form can be made up of only seven different dimensions; every weight remains at rest on the Earth only thanks to seven 'reciprocal thrusts,' and so on." (p. 461)

In *Beelzebub's Tales*, the sevenfoldness of all things is described in relationship to the realms of nature, all the way up to the Prime Source. Beelzebub explains:

> ".. 'seven-classes-of-vibrations' of those cosmic sources, the arising and further action of each of which also arise and depend on seven others, which in their turn arise and depend on seven further ones, and so on right up to the first most holy 'unique-seven-propertied-vibration' issuing from the Most Holy Prime Source ... ." (p. 470)

A unique sevenfold vibration issues form the original unity of the Most Holy Prime Source and subsequently all patterns of creation embody this pattern. Both the Threefoldness and Sevenfoldness are inherent even within the Most Holy Prime Source, and then manifest within all phenomena on all planes of existence. This is an ancient teaching, a key to the mysteries of creation, embodied within Beelzebub's tales—as it is throughout the esoteric teachings of Objective Science.

Beelzebub explains that the Sacred Laws have been known throughout human history within small circles of Initiates as part of Objective Science. He traces this teaching back to the times of Atlantis and the period of Babylon, but unfortunately for the slugs, of this ancient knowledge *"absolutely nothing has reached the beings of contemporary civilization ... apart from a few 'empty words' without any inner content."* (p. 492) However, this archaic knowledge is preserved in subtle ways and resonates still with something deep within the human subconscious and inner essence. The division of white light into a spectrum of seven colors, like the seven rows of the periodic table of chemistry, the division of the week into seven days, the structures of the musical octaves explored by Pythagoras, and the myth of Genesis with seven days of creation—all illustrate this ancient teaching.

According to Beelzebub, the sacred Heptaparaparshinokh is formulated in objective cosmic science, most simply:

> "'The-line-of-the-flow-of-forces-constantly-deflecting-according-to-law-and-uniting-again-at-its-ends.'

> "This sacred primordial cosmic law has seven 'centers of gravity' and the distance between each two of these deflections or 'centers of gravity' is called a "Stopinder-of-the-sacred-Heptaparaparshinokh.'

> "This law, passing through everything newly arising and everything existing, always makes its completing processes with seven Stopinders." (p. 750)

The Stopinders are the intervals or distances between the centers of gravity.

These descriptions are illustrated by the music scale. A descending octave, or devolving octave, begins at Do and passes through the first interval or Stopinder into si, and then down through la-sol-fa-mi-re to a low do. The high Do, the eighth note, is the completion of the whole seven notes. Hence the Law of Sevenfoldness is also labelled as the "Law of the Octave"–as octave means eightfold. An ascending octave, an evolutionary octave, begins at a low do and passes through the first interval to re-mi-fa-sol-la-si to the high Do. Thus we can speak of both evolving and devolving octaves. The eighth note of the Octave is the Whole in contrast to its Fractions.[14]

Beelzebub, like Gurdjieff, maintains that this sacred principle of cosmic design is manifested in all phenomena and even within the prime source substance existent before creation is initiated. The seven notes are the seven gravity-centers within the grand scale of being, while the seven "stopinders" are the distances between these notes. Whereas modern scientists of "new format" talk only of "evolution" and speak of the "evolution" of life on Earth, the Solar System and the Universe, Beelzebub explains that there are both involutionary and evolutionary exchanges of cosmic substances within all planes of being. Creation, in the beginning, is an involutionary process.

These are the primary principles elaborated by Beelzebub in his explorations of "objective science." All things are created and maintained according to two fundamental primordial Sacred Laws. The study of these fundamental cosmic laws is very subtle and complex, but essential to understanding the nature of reality and how everything works. All phenomena are simply *"law-conformable 'Fractions' of some whole phenomena ...."*

The *"scientists of new formation"* may scoff at the claims of cosmic laws in numbers, or in principles of design and creation. In fact, they are conditioned to take the ephemeral for the real, to *"see only unreality"* and to *"wiseacre"* endless over things they know nothing about. From the perspective of Beelzebub, all of the rubbish accumulated through the ages in human mentation is simply the *"pouring-from-the-empty-into-the-void."* In the light of Objective Science, the men-being slugs no longer instinctively sense reality or cosmic truths–although they might.

---

[14] Similarly in Vedic teachings of ancient India, material nature is called Prakriti: which consists of one "fundamental" and "seven relative" classes of Prakriti. Vedic teachings regards all of nature as composed of the generations of causes and effects generated through the "three modes of nature"– of tamas, rajas and sattva—related to matter, energy and intelligence. In the same vein, Tibetan Buddhism construes reality as composed of forty-nine planes of existence, seven planes, each with seven sub-planes. So also, the Kabbalist Tree of Life is composed of three supernal spheres above the abyss, and seven created realms below the abyss, and the Tree is constituted of three pillars.

2. The Autocratic and the Trogoautoegocratic Systems

According to Beelzebub, in the beginning, before the creation of the Universe, or the Megalacosmos, the Most Most Holy Sun Absolute existed alone in empty space, and the UNI-BEING-CREATOR existed alone on the Most Holy Sun Absolute. Otherwise, only the prime source substance of Etherokrilno was present throughout the empty space.

However, this UNI-BEING-CREATOR then ascertained that the Sun Absolute was gradually diminishing in volume, and that this was due to the Heropass—or the flow of Time. Our ENDLESSNESS in HIS DIVINE deliberations, realized that sooner or latter this flow of Time could *"ultimately bring about the complete destruction of this sole place of HIS Being."* (p. 749) These factors led to the need to create the existing Megalocosmos or World—in order to prevent the further diminishing of the Most Most Holy Sun Absolute.

The CREATOR-OMNIPOTENT, upon ascertaining the diminishing of the Sun Absolute, undertook to review the laws which maintained this cosmic concentration: the primordial sacred laws of Triamazikamno and Heptaparaparshinokh.

Before the beginning of relative time and the creation of the Universe, these sacred laws operated on a different principle than they do within the created Universe—the Megalocosmos. Beelzebub elaborates upon how and why creation was brought about by explaining how the functioning of the sacred laws of these sacred laws was changed. This occurred before the creation process unfolded and the world came to be governed by the modified versions of these principles. Whereas the original system was based on the *"Autoegocratic"* principle, the change in the functioning of these laws created a system based on the *"Trogoautoegocratic"* principle.

Beelzebub enlightens Hassein as to the nature of the Autoegocratic principle which existed within the Most Holy Sun Absolute.

> "... the Most Most Holy Sun Absolute was maintained and existed on the basis of the system called 'Autoegocrat,' i.e., on that principle according to which the inner forces which maintained the existence of this cosmic concentration had an independent functioning, not depending on any forces proceeding from outside, and which were based also on those two fundamental cosmic sacred laws by which at the present time also, the whole of our present Megalocosmos is maintained ...." (p. 750)

In the Most Holy Sun Absolute, the sacred cosmic laws function independently, not relying on *"any forces whatsoever coming from outside ...."* (p. 752) The preface "auto," of autoegocrat, implies inherent and self-contained, individual and not dependent upon external forces. When the fundamental sacred laws were changed, their functioning was made to be dependent on forces coming from outside—hence, not self-sustaining.

The Trogoautoegocratic system rules within the whole of the created Universe—the *"Megalocosmos with all the cosmoses of different scales and relatively independent cosmic formations present in it*

....." (p. 752) Thus no cosmos or life form is self-sufficient but exchanges substances and forces with other cosmoses and the surroundings outside of themselves. Beelzebub explains that in the Trogoautoegocratic system, *"everything eats, and everything is eaten"*–in the grand cosmic exchanges of substances:

> "... everything in the Universe ... exists and in maintained exclusively on the basis of what is called the 'common-cosmic Trogoautoegocratic process.' ... This system, which maintains everything arisen and existing, was actualized by our ENDLESS CREATOR in order that what is called the 'exchange of substances' or the 'Reciprocal-feeding' of everything that exists, might proceed in the Universe." (pp. 136-137)

Thus, human *"men-beings"* feed on material food and water, the air and atmospheres, the influences of the planets and moon, radiations of the Sun and even the emanations of the Sun Absolute. A slug is sustained by three being-foods and forces from outside of themselves. In turn, a man-being will feed the earth with his planetary body upon his death, the moon with Askokin vibrations, and the planets and Sun with other elements or substances within his nature. Men-being eat and are eaten in the grand exchange of cosmic elements–all under the Trogoautoegocratic system.

The changing of the functioning of the two fundamental cosmic laws–especially the changing of the law of Sevenfoldness, is particularly important to understand as esoteric principles of objective science and as the foundation for Beelzebub's science of the soul.

Beelzebub explains to Hassein the basic changes in the law of seven which were introduced as the Autoegocratic principle was turned into the Trogoautoegocratic principle:

> "These changes in the functioning of the sacred Heptaparaparshinokh consisted in this, that in three of its Stopinders HE altered the what are called 'subjective actions' which had been until then in the Stopinders, in this respect, that in one HE lengthened the law-conformable successiveness; shortened it in another; and in a third, disharmonized it. (p. 753)

Beelzebub explains three changes in the functioning of the Law of Sevenfoldness–having to do with altering the intervals (or Stopinders) between the seven different *'centers of gravity.'* Beelzebub also provides a few terms and phrases descriptive of these altered Mdnel-Ins.

The interval lengthened is that between the third and fourth *"deflections,"* or 'centers of gravity,' which would correspond to the mi-fa interval in the octave. The lengthening of this Stopinder enables the *"automatic affluence of all forces which are near"* to fill this interval. This is labelled as the *'mechano-coinciding-Mdnel-In'* as its passage occurs automatically, without conscious effort. The Mdnel-In which is shortened is *"between its last deflection and the beginning of a new cycle of its completing process,"* the si-do interval. This shortening facilitates the completion of one cycle and the commencement of a new cycle.   Beelzebub explains that the functioning of this Stopinder was thus predetermined to *"be dependent only upon the affluence of forces, obtained from outside through that Stopinder from the results of the action of that cosmic concentration itself in which the completing process of this primordial fundamental sacred law flows."* (p.754) Somehow, the cosmos involved itself plays a role in bringing about the forces required to fill this Stopinder, hence it is called the *'intentionally-actualized-Mdnel-In.'*

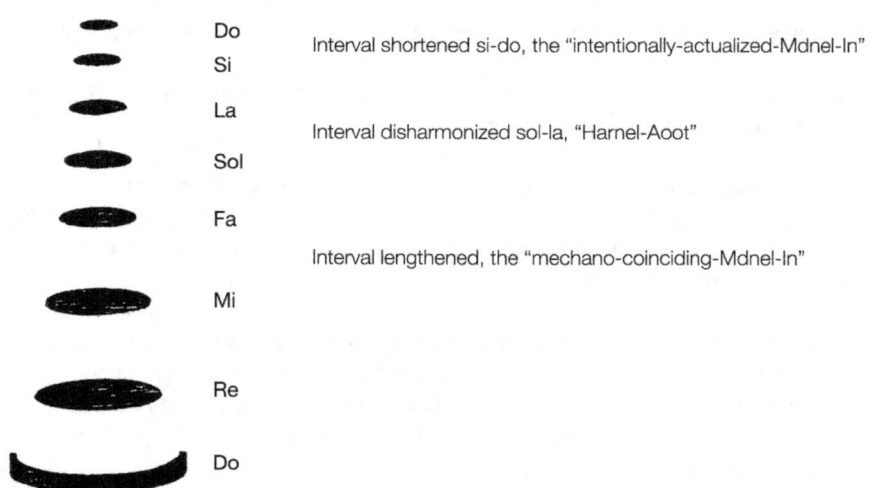

The third Stopinder to be changed in its *"subjective action"* is the fifth—between sol and la in the octave, which is given the special name of *'Harnel-Aoot.'* Beelzebub describes the disharmony in this Mdnel-In as flowing by itself from the change of the two other Stopinders, or from its *"asymmetry ... in relation to the whole completing process ...."* Because of the disharmony produced in this Stopinder, it can produce quite opposite result. Beelzebub explains:

> "If the completing process of this sacred law flows in conditions, where during its process that are many 'extraneously-caused-vibrations,' then all its functioning gives only external results."

> "But if this same process proceeds in absolute quiet without any external 'extraneously-caused-vibrations' whatsoever, then all the results of the action of its functioning remain within that concentration in which it completes its process, and for the outside, these results only become evident on direct and immediate contact with it." (p. 754)

Beelzebub explains that these two extreme conditions do not usually apply, as instead the actions of the process tend to be divided into both external and internal results. This quality of the Fifth Stopinder is essentially important to understand in order to grasp how life forms arose within the Universe through the processes of creation—to be addressed shortly; and to understanding the esoteric science of the soul elaborated by Beelzebub.

These seemingly obscure details of the Law of Sevenfoldness articulated by Beelzebub are of profound importance. All of these processes described apply both to the Megalocosmos and to the Tetartocosmos, the individual men-being, or to any other cosmos. For any slug—who would like to acquire his or her own "I" and crystallize the higher being-bodies—these alterations to the Law of Sevenfoldness have profound implications for the inner alchemy of being. This disharmonized

Stopinder has direct implications in terms of the evolution of the individual man-being, whether only internal or external results will be obtained, and whether or not the individual might attaining real "I." [15/16]

Beelzebub explains, to Hassein on one occasion, what it would mean if the intervals in the Sacred Heptaparaparshinokh had not been changed. In this case:

> "... the cosmic substances ... entering into such 'apparatus-cosmoses' for the local purpose of evolution, would accomplish their ascent up to their completing transmutation into other higher definite active elements without any obstacle and without any help coming from outside ... ." (p.789)

All slugs would thus attain the highest levels of evolution, through no conscious labors and intentional suffering, no striving for self-perfection, and so on. If the Law of Seven had not been modified, evolution would all be automatic and everything would just flow back into its completed results. Similarly, if the law of Heptaparaparshinokh was not altered, the created 'worlds' or Megalocosmos would automatically resolve back into the prime sources substance.

There are very deep meanings to these remarkable teachings which are not simply conveyed. According to Beelzebub, the Megalocosmos was created according to the modified law of sevenfoldness, as this retards the resolution of the created world back into the prime source substances.

Further, under this new Trogoautoegocratic process, the Most Holy Sun Absolute itself requires input from outside—from the completed results within the Megalocosmos. Beelzebub explains: *"there were required outside of the Sun Absolute corresponding sources in which such forces could arise and from they could flow into the presence of the Most Most Holy Sun Absolute."* Certain completed results are thus required from within the Megalacosmos, or from individual cosmoses, to flow back *"into the presence"* of the Most Holy Sun Absolute. All of this serves to prevent the action of the Heropass, or Time, in diminishing the Most Most Holy Sun Absolute.

These are actually the most remarkable concepts, ideas and model of creation, elaborated by Beelzebub, unlike anything conceived by those 'sorry-scientists' on planet Earth, but having remarkable applications to the studies of life and creation.

---

[15] In comparison to Ouspensky's explanations of Gurdjieff's teachings, Beelzebub adds new twists, turns and terminology in his explanations of the sacred Heptaparaparshinokh. In Ouspensky's writings there are two intervals in the octave where there are "missing semi-tones" –"discontinuities" in the development of vibrations through the law of the octave. Ouspensky does not mention a third "disharmonized" Stopinder. These "missing semi-tones" are between the notes mi-fa and si-do. It is at these points, where 'shocks' or outside forces are required in order for a process of evolution and involution to occur. Ouspensky uses the terms the "first mechanical shock" to describe how the mi-fa interval is breached, as of "conscious shocks" produced by an individual required to fill the other interval within the octave.

[16] In Section IV, Science of the Soul, these principles are used to explain the involution and evolution of the being-foods within human beings, and how the processes necessary for the crystallization of the higher being-bodies come about. At this point, the focus is on the creation of the Megalocosmos.

3. In the Beginning ...

Before creation occurred, *"nothing yet existed"* and the whole of the Universe was *"empty endless space."* The UNI-BEING CREATOR existed alone within the Most Most Holy Sun Absolute, but otherwise, the empty space was filled with the prime source cosmic substance of *"Etherokrilno."* Beelzebub defines the *'etherokrilno'* as that *"prime-source substance with which the whole Universe is filled, and which is the basis for the arising and maintenance of everything existing."* (p. 137)

Beelzebub explains then what happened, in the beginning:

> "And so, my dear boy, our COMMON FATHER CREATOR ALMIGHTY, having then in the beginning changed the functioning of both these primordial sacred laws, directed the action of their forces from within the Most Holy Sun Absolute into the space of the Universe, whereupon there was obtained the what is called 'Emanation-of-the-Sun-Absolute' and now called, 'Theomertmalogos' or 'Word-God." (p. 756)

The impetus for creation is an *"emanation"* of the Most Holy Sun Absolute. This is the Word of God and an act of the *"Divine Will Power of our ENDLESSNESS,"* according to Beelzebub. This is similar to the Book of Genesis, wherein the earth was empty and void, and then *"God said,"* or willed, that there be light. This emanation initiates the beginning of the creation of the varied world orders, which are sequentially formed through the operation of the laws of Triamazikamno and Heptaparaparshinokh operating within the primordial substance of the Etherokrilno.

This act of Divine Will *"participated only at the beginning"* in the process of creation of the world-orders. The subsequent creation proceeded automatically because of the changes introduced into the primordial cosmic laws. This act of *"Divine Will Power"* fills the *"intentionally-actualized-Mdnel-In"*–the Do-si interval of the cosmic octave, instigating a series of subsequent processes.

In the beginning, emanations issue from the Most Holy Sun Absolute. Beelzebub continues:

> "Thanks to the new particularity of the fifth Stopinder of the sacred Heptaparaparshinokh, these emanations issuing from the Sun Absolute began to act at certain definite points of the space of the Universe upon the prime source substance Etherokrilno from which, owing to the totality of the former and the new particularities of the sacred primordial laws, certain definite concentrations began to be concentrated. (pp. 756-757)

Notice that Beelzebub describes the emanations as acting upon *"certain definite points"* which arise within the prime source etheric substance.[17]

---

[17] In modern science, the Universe is conceived to have been created from such a "certain definite point,' a "singularity," out of the ether of the quantum vacuum (and the zero-point fields). Modern concepts of "singularities" and "vacuum genesis," are quite in keeping with Beelzebub's descriptions–at least in parts. The Etherokrilno might be described as a seeming void which is also the plenum, full of all the forces and particles of physics in a latent, unmanifest realm. In fact, modern physicist also conceive of a seven-dimensional hyperspace underlying and sustaining material reality, as depicted by Beelzebub when he describes the primordial sacred laws operating within the Etherokrilno. Although modern scientists conceive of ethers and higher dimensions, there is no concept of "Emanation," as a principle which might underlying life and pervade space, and which is distinct from the more familiar radiations. In Book II, Microcosm/Macrocosm (2010) of the Within-Without from Zero Points series, Dr. Holmes elaborates extensively upon the concept of "certain definite points" arising within the aether–drawing from a wide range of esoteric mystical and scientific sources.

At *"certain definite points," "certain definite concentrations"* begin to be concentrated. The Laws of Heptaparaparshinokh and Triamazikamno arise at these points and within these concentrations, and this leads to the crystallization of different elements within Second-order Suns. These Suns are second order relative to the first order of the Sun Absolute.[18] Further, these begin to influence one another and form a large concentration of *"Second-order Suns."* Beelzebub continues to depict the unfolding of creation:

> "When these newly arisen Suns had been completely actualized and their own functionings of both the fundamental laws had been finally established in them, then in them also, similarly to the Most Most Holy Sun Absolute, their own result began to be transformed and to be radiated, which, together with the emanations issuing from the Most Most Holy Sun Absolute into the space of the Universe, became the factors for the actualization of the common-cosmic fundamental process of the sacred law of Triamazikamno." (p. 757)

Notice that the influences of the Second Order Suns are "radiations" in contrast to the "emanations" of the Sun Absolute. Beelzebub emphasizes to Hassein that there are profoundly important differences between such *"emanations"* and the more familiar *"radiations:"*

> "... not once has the thought entered the head of a single one of them there (your favorites) that between these two cosmic phenomena which they call 'emanation' and 'radiation' there is any difference whatsoever.
>
> "Not a single one of those 'sorry-scientists' has ever thought that the difference between these two cosmic processes is just about the same as that which the highly esteemed Mullah Nassr Eddin once expressed in the following words:
>
> "They are as much alike as the beard of the famous English Shakespeare and the no less famous French Armagnac." (p. 142)[19]

This passage emphasis Beelzebub's point that emanations and radiations are very different indeed, although none of the *"scientists of new formation," "the learned"* and the *"sorry-scientists"* have any idea of what that difference is—beyond having their "empty" words to refer to it. Unfortunately, Beelzebub does not elaborate upon the differences himself, although there are various selections of the *Tales* relevant to such distinctions.

Radiations can be taken to describe electro-magnetic influences, which are labeled as *electromagnetic radiation* in science, and this influence propagates at the speed of light. Further, electromagnetic radiation loses force as it propagates through space. In contrast, emanations permeate space in an alternate way—not limited by the speed of light or diminishing through

---

[18] The terms the Most Most Holy Sun Absolute, or the Holy Sun Absolute, or simply the Sun Absolute are used interchangeable.

[19] In explanation: Mullah Nassr Eddin is a character whose pithy comments and absurd lines are used often by Beelzebub to emphasize or illustrate a point he is making. The Mullah often has an appropriate statement of some sort for any occasion. French Armagnac is a liquor—Mr. Gurdjieff's favorite.

propagation. Further, whereas radiation operates exclusively in and with matter, emanations similarly operate in and with matter, but also without it. One source suggests that *"Emanation is under the Law of Three. Radiation is under the Law of Seven."* [20]

The *"common cosmic sacred Triamazikamno"* is then *"established in the space of the Universe."* This includes the emanations of the Sun Absolute as a holy neutralizing force; while a particular Second-order-Sun assumes the role as the holy active force; and the mass of the other Second-order Suns acting in relation to the particular Sun, functions as the holy passive force. This sacred Triamazikamno underlies all further manifestations. A new generation of crystallizations of a different density is then formed around the Second-order-Suns, again out of the Etherokrilno. These Third order Suns are the planets, which group around the newly arisen Suns.

Beelzebub explains that after the formation of the planets in the *"first outer cycle"* of the fundamental sacred Heptaparaparshinokh, the *"initially given momentum for the fundamental completing process"* had lost half of the *"force of its vivifyingness."* This had been taken up by the initial creation processes. Again, due to the modification of the Fifth Stopinder, the creation impetus began in its further functioning to have *"only half of the manifestation of its action outside itself, and the other half for itself, ... the consequence of which ... there began to arise what are called, 'similarities-to-the-already-arisen.'"* (p. 758)

After this, the outer cycle of the sacred Heptaparaparshinokh ceased altogether, and all of its action entered into *"the results already manifested by it."* This then establishes the *"inherent permanent processes of transformation"*–of the involution and evolution of different substances and elements according to the sacred Heptaparaparshinokh–proceeded within the existing cosmoses and within the 'similarities-to-the-already-arisen.' This led to the crystallization and decrystallization of *"all kinds of definite cosmic substances,"* each with their own subjective properties. The involution and evolution of these active elements thus actualizes the Trogoautoegocratic process–the reciprocal feeding and maintenance of all cosmoses through the *"common-cosmic exchange of substances."*

Beelzebub introduces various terms to depict the different 'cosmoses' within the created universe. Firstly, he defines the term 'cosmos' in general as referring to any *"relatively independent concentration."* The Sun Absolute is referred to as the "Protocosmos;" the Second-order Suns are the "Defterocosmos;" and the Third-order-Suns, the planets, are referred to "Tritocosmos." The term "microcosm" is then used to describe the *"smallest relative independent formations,"* which arise on the planets due to the new inherency of the fifth Stopinder. The microcosms are living cells, which then mutually attract similar microcosmoses, to form and concentrate *"Tetartocosmoses"*–multicellular organisms. Beelzebub defines a Tetartocosmos as any *"relatively-independent-formation-of-the-aggregation-of-microcosmoses."* (p. 762) Finally, all of the Cosmoses together compose the World–or the Megalocosmos.

Overall, the World, or the *Megalocosmos*, is composed of the emanations of Sun Absolute, and six primary classes of radiations. Beelzebub lists these:

---

[20] This source was a letter to the Gurdjieff discussion group at chick@valley.net This idea is very interesting, suggestive and worthy of consideration. Beelzebub does explain that "the prime emanation of our Most Holy Sun Absolute, acquires just this same lawfulness (of Triamazikamno) at its prime arising; and, during its further actualizations, gives results in accordance with it." (p. 139) However, radiations also have a threefold nature in addition to their sevenfoldness. This distinction also relates to Kabbalist teachings in that the first three sephirot in the Tree of Life are described as the supernal triad, hence emanating, whereas the manifested worlds are the seven sephirot below, characterized by radiations.

"1. The emanation of the Most Most Holy Sun Absolute Itself ... 'Theomertmalogos' or 'Word-God.'

And the radiations of:

2. ... each separate Second-order-Sun, Mentekithzoin.'
3. ... each planet separately ... 'Dynamoumzoin.'
4. ... the Micocosmoses ... 'Photoinzoin.'
5. ... the 'Tetartocosmoses'... 'Hanbledzoin.'
6. ... all the planets together of any solar system ... 'Astroluolucizoin.'
7. ... all the 'Newly-arisen-second-order-Suns' taken together ... 'Polorotheoparl.'"
(pp. 760-1)

Beelzebub explains that all of these emanations and radiations *"penetrate everywhere throughout the Universe."* However, their influences are concentrated most freely within the atmospheres of the planets, which allows for such exchanges of these cosmic influences. The whole system taken together, Beelzebub labels as the *"common-cosmic Ansanbaluiazar,"* and he gives *"the formula"* of *"objective science:"*

"Everything issuing from everything, and again entering into everything."
(p. 761)

Beelzebub offers a profound model of creation with Emanations of the Sun Absolute and six primary classes of radiations penetrating everywhere, and everything issuing from everything, and entering into everything. This whole structure then gives rise to all kinds of *"temporarily independent crystallizations"* which arise within different cosmoses due to the *"evolutionary and involutionary processes of these fundamental sacred laws."* (p. 761)

We will return to the subsequent evolution of the Tetartocosmoses–among which, "your favorites," the slugs, or humanity on planet Earth, would count. Beelzebub offers profound descriptions of how the sacred laws were modified, how things emerge out of the Etherokrilno, and how life forms emerged through the alteration of the Fifth Stopinder, causing *"similarities-to-the-already-arisen"* to be formed. Beelzebub certainly deserved the horns which he grows at the end of his Tales, for expounding such an "ultrafantastic" model or myth of creation. All such processes eventually came to produce those strange three-centered beings on planet Earth, the men-beings–who Hassein happened to call *"the slugs."*

4. The Etherokrilno & the Omnipresent Okidanokh

In order to understand the processes of creation, or of the involution and evolution of any cosmic substance or cosmos, it is essential to grasp the nature of the Etherokrilno. This is the prime source substance which fills the Universe and is the basis for the arising and maintenance of everything existing. The sacred laws of Triamazikamno and Heptaparaparshinokh are latent within the Etherokrilno, which thus has an unmanifest threefold and sevenfold nature.

Some portion of "unblended" Etherokrilno enters into all cosmic formations, in order to connect the active elements in these cosmoses. Further, when cosmoses or elements dissipate, the elements are transformed back into the Etherokrilno. Beelzebub explains that on one occasion, an 'explosion' was so powerful, that *"everything without any exception was transformed into Etherokrilno."* (p. 731)

In modern science, the Etherokrilno would be most comparable to modern concepts of the quantum vacuum, the seeming nothingness, which is also the pleroma—containing all the forces and particles of nature in an unmanifest or latent state. All cosmic phenomena proceed only during the transformation of this fundamental cosmic substance; just as in science, all phenomena of nature involve processes underlying them within the zero point fields of the quantum vacuum.

A second cosmic substance, related to that of the Etherokrilno, is the *"Omnipresent Okidanokh."* Although this cosmic substance is 'crystallized' out of the Etherokrilno, it actually obtains its prime arising from the three Holy sources of the emanation of the Sun Absolute. Beelzebub explains that the prime emanation of the Sun Absolute embodies the principle of Triamazikamno, and always produces effects in accordance with this principle of its threefold nature. Thus, the Omnipresent Okidanokh always manifests a three-fold nature.

Like the Etherokrilno, the Okidanokh is present everywhere throughout space, thus omnipresent, and plays a role in all cosmic phenomena. Its effects and roles are particularly evident within the atmospheres—in producing daylight and night. However, it is the also the *"fundamental cause"* of cosmic phenomena—in its role embodying always the active principle. It is the active principle latent within the Etherokrilno. Beelzebub provides varied discussions of the Okidanokh and descriptions of elucidating experiments he witnessed, which illustrate its subtle nature.

The Okidanokh does not arise in the Sun Absolute itself, but from the spaces outside of the Sun Absolute. However, it arises from the blending of the three Holy forces embodied in the emanations of the Sun Absolute. Further, during the 'involution' of the Okidanokh, its *"Vivifyingness of Vibrations"* is changed as it passes through the seven 'gravity centers' and Stopinders—according to the sacred Heptaparaparshinokh.[21]

---

[21] Whereas the Etherokrilno might be compared to the quantum vacuum of modern science, there is no concept articulated in physics comparable to the role ascribed by Beelzebub to the Omnipresent Okidanokh—as the active principle latent within the ether and embodying forces from the 'emanations' of a supreme source. Of course, this must be so, as scientists do not consider even the difference between 'emanations' and 'radiations,' and have dismissed the idea of God or a conscious Creator in the world.

The Omnipresent-Okidanokh participates in the formation and processes of all cosmoses, and cosmic substances as an *Active Force*. Beelzebub describes it as a *"common-cosmic Unique Crystallization"* and *"Active Element."* As a substance, it has unique properties, which Beelzebub describes fairly extensively though his *Tales*, as he witnesses various elucidating experiments carried out by a particular cosmic individual–Gornahoor Harharkh, who *"devoted the whole of his existence to the study of the cosmic Omnipresent-Okidanokh."* (p. 1146)

Beelzebub, in his esoteric teaching of cosmic origins, articulates one of the "particularities" of the Omnipresent Okidanokh:

> "... when a new cosmic unit is being concentrated, then the 'Omnipresent-Active-Element' does not blend, as a whole, with such a new arising, nor is it transformed as a whole in any definite corresponding place–as happens with every other cosmic crystallization in all the said cosmic formations–but immediately on entering as a whole into any cosmic unit, there immediately occurs in it what is called 'Djartklom,' that is to say, it is dispersed into the three fundamental sources from which it obtained its prime arising, and only then do these sources, each separately, give the beginning for an independent concentration of three separate corresponding formations within the given cosmic unit. And in this way, this 'Omnipresent-Active-Element' actualizes at the outset, in every such new arising, the sources for the possible manifestation of its own sacred law of Triamazikamno." (pp. 139-40)

The process of 'Djartklom' involves the dispersion of the three active elements present within the Okidanokh, when it enters into any particular cosmic unit.

Beelzebub particularly stresses how important it is to understand this substance and its properties, in order to understand the phenomena produced within the atmospheres. However, it is also important to understand it in order to understand the nature of the three being-foods, the three being-centers or brains of human beings, and the three being-bodies which can be formed for the life of the soul. All things have a triune nature, as this is ultimately established by the Okidanokh, which divides into three active forces as it enters into any particular cosmic unit. It never blends as a whole.

The second particularity of this Unique Substance, as outlined by Beelzebub, is that when any cosmic unit is destroyed, then these three holy active sources "reblend" and are transformed back into Okidanokh. However, when these three forces reblend, they now have *"another quality of Vivifyingness of Vibrations"*–in accordance with the Law of Heptaparaparshinokh. The process of Djartklom, or the dispersal of the three holy sources into a cosmic unit, is ultimately followed by that of the "reblending" of the three holy forces. Beelzebub states: *"... this Active-Element is dispersed into its three prime parts which then exist almost independently, and when the said direct action ceases, these parts blend again and then continue to exist as a whole."* (p. 140) Further, this whole sequence thus produce a different *"Vivifyingness of Vibrations."* These are quite remarkable teachings of Beelzebub and of Objective Science.

During his *Tales to his Grandson*, Beelzebub elaborates upon some of the apparatuses and experiments conducted by his essence friend–Gornahoor Harharkh concerning the nature of the Okidanokh. Some of the components of the appliances used for these elucidating experiments are described as similar to an electric light, a dynamo, a vacuum pump, generators and accumulators. In brief, by means of Gornahoor's apparatus, it was possible to obtain all three fundamental parts of the

Okidanokh from any kind of sur-planetary or intraplanetary process; to store them separately so that the properties of each part could be studied; and, then to artificially blend them again into a whole. Normally, none of these processes occurring within the Okidanokh could be perceived or sensed by beings directly, although we perceive the results of such processes.

Beelzebub explains that two of the three components of the Omnipresent-Okidanokh are named in modern science–as Anodnatious and Cathodnatious, or the anode-cathode distinction of positive and negative electric forces or charges. Beelzebub explains that scientists name the *"blending and mutual destruction of two parts"* of the Okidanokh as 'Electricity.' (p.1159) However, scientists are unaware of the third component of "Parijrahatnatioose," the holy reconciling force. If all three forces are blended together, then noting can be perceived by beings. However, when the anodnatious and cathodnatious are artificially blended together, while the third force is excluded, then we have *"the-result-of-the-process-of-the-reciprocal-destruction-of-two-opposite-forces,"* which becomes *"the-cause-of-artificial-light."*

Another experiment is conducted on the substance of 'red copper.' If all three components of the Okidanokh were admitted to the red copper, no change in its condition was noted. However, if either of the flows of Anodnatious or Cathodnatious were increased to the red copper, it would either evolve or involve to produce other substances–other metals of a higher or lower degree of vivifyingness. This demonstrates the types of creative processes which produce all the different elements crystallized within different cosmoses, from different admixtures of the components of this omnipresent active element–the Okidanokh.

Imagine that, that a sacred individual spent almost his whole life studying such a unique cosmic substance! Beelzebub explains that the study of such World-laws remain, for your contemporary men-being, some of the *"great-inscrutable-mysteries-of-Nature."* (p. 162)

5. The Law of Falling & the Law-of-Catching-Up

> "Everything existing in the World falls to the bottom. And the bottom for any part of the Universe is its nearest "stability," and this said 'stability' is the place or the point upon which all the lines of force arriving from all directions converge." (Gurdjieff, 1950, p. 66)

Saint Venoma formulated the Law of Falling. Everything falls to the bottom–its nearest point or place of stability. Beelzebub elaborates:

> "The centers of all the suns and of all the planets of our Universe are just such points of stability. They are the lowest points of those regions of space upon which forces from all directions of the given part of the Universe definitely tend and where they are concentrated. In these points there is also concentrated the equilibrium which enable suns and planets to maintain their position." (p.66)

The Law of Falling provides an interesting view of the nature of gravity and of the curvature of the space-time complex. Everything existing in space will tend to fall into one or another Sun or planet depending upon which *"the given part of space belongs."*

The Suns emerge out of the Etherokrilno from *"certain definite points,"* as explained in our earlier creation studies. So also, the Earth has a lowest point of space, wherein is *"concentrated its equilibrium."* Objects on Earth thus fall towards the center of the planet, their lowest point of stability, where all the forces converge; just as the Earth will tend to fall into the stability of the center of the Solar system–the Sun.

In his stories to his grandson, Beelzebub explains how the early spaceships used the principle of the "Law of Falling" for locomotion between the spaces of the Universe. Beelzebub also uses this principle when describing what happened after a comet *"Kondoor"* stuck the Earth, breaking of the Moon and another fragment, which were ejected out into space. Beelzebub recounts:

> "The broken-off fragments of the planet Earth ... lost the momentum they received from the shock before they had reached the limit of that part of space which is the sphere of this planet, and hence, according to the "Law of Falling," these fragments had begun to fall back towards their fundamental piece." (p.83)

In modern science, the phenomena explained by gravity would be explained according to the Law of Falling. When the moons were rejected from the earth, their momentum was not great enough to escape from that part of space which is the sphere of the Earth. Thus, the moons begin to fall back towards the center of the Earth.

Beelzebub then elaborates a second principle, called the *"Law-of-Catching-Up:"*

> "But they could no longer fall upon their fundamental piece, because in the meanwhile they had come under the cosmic law called "Law-of-Catching-Up" and were entirely

> subject to its influence, and they would therefore now make regular elliptic orbits around their fundamental piece, just as the fundamental piece, namely, the planet Earth, made and makes its orbit around its sun "Ors." (p. 83)

The Moon had in a sense caught up to its own center of gravity and would subsequently tend to maintain its pull away from the Earth. If an object were now dropped in the space of the Moon, it would fall towards its primary center of gravity, within the Moon itself.

When this calamity happened, a whole commission of Angels and Archangels, *"specialists in the work of World-creation and World-maintenance,"* were immediately sent out from the Most Holy Sun Absolute to our Solar system Ors. They visited the planet Mars, where Beelzebub was living, to conduct their investigations. Although they concluded that it was unlikely that another such major catastrophe would occur, still there could be further *"Tastartoonarian-displacements,"* which could further disrupt the *"harmonious general-system movement."* The High Commission thus took the measure of having the Earth constantly send the sacred Askokin vibrations to the moons. This is how life on planet Earth, and even human life, came to be so intertwined with that of the moon.

However, the Law of Falling is not the only formulation of *gravity* within *Beelzebub's Tales*. Beelzebub talks of various *"gravity centers"*–ranging from the *"seven Stopinders or gravity-centers of the Heptaparaparshinokh,"* (p. 139) and of the *"seven temporarily independent center-of-gravity active elements crystallized in the presences of Tetartocosmoses"* (p. 761), the *"seven-gravity-center-vibrations-of-sound or whole notes of an octave"* (p.848), the seven *"gravity-center vibrations of the white ray"* (p. 468) and the *"three gravity-center-localizations in the common presence of man."* (p. 1190) A much broader conception of gravity is being implied here, as all cosmic substances have different places or points to which they fall, or gravitate.

An example of this, concerns the afterlife processes which occur as the Kesdjan body (or astral body) actually rises from the planet Earth upon the death of the planetary body. According to the Law of Gravity, it rises into the atmospheres. Beelzebub explains:

> "... in consequence of the fact that the body Kesdjan of the being is coated with those substances which in their totality make this cosmic formation much lighter than that mass of cosmic substances which surrounds the planets and is called the planetary atmosphere, then as soon as the body Kesdjan of the being is separated from the planetary body of the being, it at once rises according to the cosmic law called 'Tenikdoa,' or as it is sometimes called the 'law of gravity,' to that sphere in which it finds the weight proper to it equally balanced and which is therefore the corresponding place of such cosmic arisings ...." (p. 728)

In this case, it is due to the *'law of gravity,'* or Tenikdoa, that the Kesdjan body rises into the atmospheres surrounding the planet–to that sphere which corresponds to its own nature. The center of gravity of the astral body is different from that of the planetary body, which would fall to the Earth, or the Askokin vibrations which would 'feed the moon.'

The law of gravity within Beelzebub's cosmos is much more complicated than the scientists would usually define it–as they consider matter only in its material nature and not in terms of any underlying cosmic processes.

6. Time:
The 'Ideally-Unique-Subjective-Phenomena'

"But as in general, my boy, you do not yet know of the exceptional peculiarity of this cosmic phenomenon Time, you must first be told that genuine Objective Science formulates this cosmic phenomenon thus:

"Time in itself does not exist; there is only the totality of the results ensuing from all the cosmic phenomena present in a given place.

"Time itself, no being can either understand by reason or by outer or inner being-function. It cannot even be sensed by any gradation of instinct which arises and is present in every more or less independent cosmic concentration.

"It is possible to judge Time only if one compares real cosmic phenomena which proceed in the same place and under the same conditions, where Time is being constated and considered." (p. 123)

This is a profound description of the phenomena of Time, which Beelzebub labels as that *'Ideally-Unique-Subjective-Phenomena.'* Time in itself does not exist and cannot be sensed directly in any way. What is referred to as the experience of Time is really simply the experiencing of all the results from events happening within a given place–all the cosmic phenomena ensuing from the totality of the laws of world-creation and world-maintenance. Beelzebub states: *"Time ... does not issue from anything but blends always with everything ...."* (p124)

In order to explain the nature of Time on different scales, or within different World orders, Beelzebub provides this description of the nature of the Universe:

> "It is necessary to notice that in the Great Universe all phenomena in general, without exception wherever they arise and manifest, are simply successively law-conformable 'Fractions' of some whole phenomenon which has its prime arising on the Most Holy Sun Absolute.
>
> "And in consequence, all cosmic phenomena, wherever they proceed, have a sense of 'objectivity.'
>
> "And these successively law-conformable 'Fractions' are actualized in every respect, and even in the sense of their involution and evolution, owing to the chief cosmic law, the sacred "Heptaparaparshinokh.' (p. 123)

Everything is a *"law-conformable 'Fraction' of some whole phenomena."* Everything ultimately issued from the One, the Most Holy Sun Absolute, and is created and maintained by the laws of three and seven, which propagate forces through different generations of causes and effects.

Thus there are different *"cosmic arisings of various scales"* and with *"diverse -tempos."* Within any Cosmos–from that of the Universe as a whole, the Megalocosmos, to the life of a sun or planet, or a cell, atom, or a human being–all these cosmoses on different scales of being will have their own time scale and sense of time, according to what kind of 'Fraction' they are. Cosmoses exist on different orders of magnitude but everything is simply some law-conformable 'Fraction' of the whole!

To illustrate his explanations to his grandson Hassein, Beelzebub considers how the flow of time would proceed within a drop of water in a decanter standing on the table. Beelzebub points out that every drop of water is *"in itself a whole independent world, a world of 'Microcosmoses,"* and that relatively independent *"infinitesimal 'individuals' or 'beings'"* exist within it. These beings, like those beings of *"other 'scales,'"* have their own durations of time as required for their perceptions and manifestations. All beings are born, grow up, breath, move about, *"unite and separate for what are called 'sex-results,'"* and have other cycles of activity and manifestation. Yet in all cases, beings *"sense the flow of Time by the comparison of the duration of the phenomena around them."* (p. 125) This is why time is such an *'Ideally-unique-subjective-phenomena.'*

However, Beelzebub explains that in *"Objective Science,"* there is a *"standard unit of time"* that can be used to compare cosmic substances or cosmoses within every sphere of the Universe:

> "And for the definition of Time this standard unit has from long ago been the moment of what is called the sacred 'Egokoolnatsnarnian-sensation' which always appears in the Most Holy Cosmic Individuals dwelling of the Most Holy Sun Absolute whenever the vision of our UNI-BEING ENDLESSNESS is directed into space and directly touches their presences." (p. 124)

This standard unit can be used to define and compare the subjective experiences of individual beings with their "diverse tempos"–within different worlds on different scales of being. The briefest instance of time is defined as this sensation occurring within these Cosmic Individuals whenever the vision of his ENDLESSNESS touches their presences!

Beelzebub then explains to Hassein, that for the three-brained beings on their own planet of Karatas, and originally also for the men-beings on planet Earth, *"the process of the flow of Time ... flows forty-nine times more quickly than on the Sun-Absolute ...."* (p. 128) This makes sense as every world is a law-conformable 'Fraction' of some whole, and the Universe is created according to the sacred primordial law of Heptaparaparshinokh. Seven worlds were created, each of which has a further sevenfold nature–giving a factor of forty-nine.

Thus ends our foray into the creation myth and 'objective science' of Beelzebub–as recounted to Hassein, in Gurdjieff's ultra-fantastic book. Beelzebub explains the fundamental sacred cosmic laws, the creation of the world orders, the manner in which cosmoses arise on all different planes of being from the Etherokrilno–all as law-conformable Fractions of the Whole. Of course, these materials are anything but easy to grasp, but with time and active being deliberations, an understanding of the fundamental principles of World-creation and World-Maintenance can be trans-substantiated within a three-brained being, who represents "in miniature" the same laws and processes as which operate within the Megalocosmos. We can turn then to the esoteric science of the soul inherent to Beelzebub's teachings, and consider the nature of human beings in the light of these fundamental principles of 'objective science.'

"This Most Great Foundation of the All-embracing of everything that exists constantly emanates throughout the whole of the Universe and coats itself from its particles upon planets—in certain three-centered beings who attain in their common presences the capacity to

have their own functioning
of both fundamental
cosmic laws of the sacred
Heptaparaparshinokh and the
sacred Triamazikamno—into
a definite unit in which alone
Objective Divine Reason
acquires the possibility of
becoming concentrated
and fixed."

Beelzebub recounting the teaching of Lord Buddha - 1950, p. 244 -

IV /
Science of the Soul

1. An Impartial Perspective on "All the Rubbish Accumulated through the Ages in Human Mentation"

It is most important for us to understand the nature of three-brained human beings on planet Earth, as this includes ourselves–you, the reader, and I, the author. Where do we come from as human beings and what experiences are possible for us–in life and after-death? Gurdjieff provides a profoundly alternative model of reality–including explanations concerning the creation of the Universe and the primordial cosmic laws, a perspective on complementary processes of 'involution' and 'evolution,' and a profound model of human psychology–including descriptions of the subtle make-up or composition of a human being-one's various brains and being-bodies. Beelzebub's elaborations upon these questions of the 'science of the soul' are totally different from anything otherwise available in contemporary psychology, philosophy and science, or within the educational system. Beelzebub labels his teachings as *"objective Science"* and this includes an esoteric *"science of the soul."*

Gurdjieff describes influences during his youth which formed in him:

> "... an "irrepressible striving" to understand clearly the precise significance, in general, of the life process on earth of all the outward forms of breathing creatures and, in particular, of the aim of human life in the light of this interpretation." (1933, p.13)

Beelzebub thus articulates Gurdjieff's profound insights and realizations as to the true origins of breathing creatures and the aim of human life. It all has to do with this ancient science of the soul, which Beelzebub articulates through his ultrafantastic *Tales*.

Gurdjieff expressed the aim of *"All and Everything"*–the First Series, the full title of which is *Beelzebub's Tales to his Grandson: An objectively impartial criticism of the life of man*:

> "To destroy, mercilessly, without any compromises whatsoever, in the mentation and feelings of the reader, the beliefs and views, by centuries rooted in him, about everything existing in the world."

To understand the profound nature of the reality expounded by Beelzebub, it is very useful to contrast his views with those of contemporary psychology and science. This is a litmus test–to discern what is real and what is ephemeral and imaginary: what is wisdom and what is 'rubbish.'

Unfortunately, among your contemporary favorites, the *"scientists of new format"* –as Beelzebub would derisively label contemporary science practitioners and dispensers of invented theories– dismissed the idea of the existence of the human soul towards the close of the 1800s. Science adopted the views of Darwin and other Neo-Darwinian evolutionists, that human beings are simply higher primates evolved from lower life forms through purely material processes and 'random' genetic changes. In this view, human beings have no soul, nor spiritual and divine nature, and are strictly material, biological beings originating from non-sentient matter.

In reference to the most puzzling issue in contemporary science concerning the nature of the inner "consciousness" of human beings, scientists generally accept the view that the material brain processes in the head somehow produce consciousness–and our inner awareness of being.

(See Roth, P., *The Quest to find Consciousness. Scientific American*, MIND, 2004) Unfortunately, the scientists and psychologists do not understand how or where this happens, nor what this consciousness is. Instead, it is simply assumed that 'the brain' and 'the mind' are in the head, and that they must somehow manufacture human *consciousness* or our *awareness-of-being*.

Nobel laureate, Francis Crick, a prominent 'consciousness' theorist or *'wiseacre'*–according to Beelzebub, articulates *"the head doctrine"* of modern times. In his book, *The Astonishing Hypothesis: The Scientific Search for the Soul* (1995), Crick doesn't search for a soul at all and in fact dismisses it without even investigating such possibilities. He then explains his "astonishing hypothesis" –which is anything but "astonishing:"

> The Astonishing Hypothesis is that "You," your joys and your sorrows, your memories and your ambitions, your sense of personal identity and free will, are in fact no more than the behaviour of a vast assemble of nerve cells and their associated molecules. ... "You're nothing but a pack of neurons." This hypothesis is so alien to the ideas of most people alive today that it can truly be called astonishing. (p. 3)

Crick is merely restating the common belief and most basic assumption that has been the cornerstone of modern psychology and science for the past century: A human being is regarded as a material, biological and neurological being–a pack of neurons–but not as having a soul or a spiritual and divine nature. The modern view of human consciousness is that it is simply the end product of brain processes within the head. Crick's point is that this hypothesis is astonishing when contrasted with the popular belief in spirit and the existence of the soul.

In the *'sciences of new format,'* life must end at death because consciousness dies with the cessation of neurological activity within the brain. Popular science writer, Isaac Asimov, explains the modern so-called 'scientific' conception of human life:

> "The molecules of my body, after my conception, added other molecules and arranged the whole into more and more complex forms, and in a unique fashion, not quite like the arrangement in any other living thing that ever lived. In the process, I developed, little by little, into a conscious something I call "I" that exists only as the arrangement. When the arrangement is lost forever, as it will be when I die, the 'I' will be lost forever, too." (Asimov, 1981, p. 158)

This is the gist of modern psychology and science. Human beings are purely material beings who live and die with their functioning brains. When the molecules or neurons are destroyed, consciousness is no more and so life ends at death and the "I" is lost forever.

In the same vein, Carl Sagan elaborates such a theist viewpoint in a 1995 *Psychology Today* interview. Sagan states:

> ...the mind is merely what the brain does. There's nothing else, there's no soul or psyche that's not made out of matter, that isn't a function of 10 to the 14th synapses in the brain. (p. 65)

In this view, human beings are nothing more than the fortunate arrangements of molecules within the brain which generate the experience of consciousness and "I" for a limited period of time until they degenerate and come to an end.

The original meaning of the word "psychology" suggested a science (or logos) of the soul (or psyche). However, the term *"psyche"* which meant soul in Greek, was reinterpreted by *'the sorry scientists'* to mean 'mind' and then it was assumed that there is only 'mind,' centred in the head-brain. Psychology in modern times is defined as *"the science of behaviour and the mind,"* and an understanding of the true nature of human life has been completely lost. The "head doctrine" remains the main theory of human nature and human consciousness offered by those *"sorry-scientists."* Unfortunately for *"your favorites,"* such *"twaddle"* and *"rubbish"* still dominates modern thought and the educational system.

From the times of ancient Babylon, the twaddle and rubbish of intellectuals and popular thinkers, 'wiseacres,' has led to the dismissal of the soul and the imaginary idea that the substances of the brain produce their famous 'mind' and 'consciousness.' The "sorry scientists" even imagine that they have, as their own cherished possession, "a conscious mind." Beelzebub's psychology is far deeper than the superficial assumptions and perspectives offered within the *'sciences of new format'* as to the nature and purpose of human life.

Furthermore, *'scientist of new format'* consider all changes in cosmic or biological processes as constituting "evolution" and have no understanding of how complementary process of *"involution"* and *"evolution"* occur within all cosmoses. In modern thought, life only comes from below through evolution from non-sentient matter; whereas Gurdjieff, or Beelzebub, suggests that life is *'actualized from Above'* through 'involution.' "Involutionary processes" in the beginning set the stage for 'evolutionary processes' to follow. Creation was actualized in such a manner as to allow for the possible involution and evolution of cosmic substances–including consciousness and higher being-bodies for the life of the soul.

Modern scientists generally would agree with the statement of one such contemporary favorite science philosopher, Carl Sagan, when he declares: *"As we learn more and more about the universe, there seems less and less for God to do."* (1979, p.286) However, in reality, this viewpoint is simply rubbish and can be turned on its head–'topsy-turvy' perhaps. Really, the more science has advanced, the more awesome the universe appears and always new mysteries and enigmas emerge within every department of human knowledge. Furthermore, there are profound enigmas posed by the huge masses of evidences–scientific and anecdotal–documenting all kinds of paranormal phenomena and occurrences which cannot be explained within the existing paradigm of modern science. There are evidences for out-of-body experiences, ESP, psychokinesis, telepathy, remote viewing, near death experiences, ghosts and haunting, reincarnation, and much more. None of this can be explained within the existing paradigm of so-called 'scientific' psychology and the natural sciences. The three brained-beings have not seriously begun to understand the deep origins and nature of human beings, nor the underlying processes generating and sustaining the phenomena of life. Life is far more interconnected and multi-dimensional than all the 'sorry scientists' of new format could ever imagine.

In comparison with modern viewpoints, Beelzebub offers ultra-fantastic ideas concerning how creation entails the embodiment of certain primordial Sacred Cosmic Laws and their modifications, all manifesting out of a Divine Realm of Being. These processes produce generations of causes and effects upon different planes of being, through the formation or crystallization of diverse elements. These processes also turn partly inwards to produced *'similarities-of-the-whole,'* which are then capable of further evolution. Most importantly, the primordial Sacred Laws are actualized within the inner dimensions of human beings–in the same patterns of design as dictated by the Laws of Triamazikamno and Heptaparaparshinokh. Beelzebub actually describes how all these things happen and how your favorites involve and evolve upon planet Earth.

Beelzebub does not consider all human beings to "have a soul" and to be insured of everlasting life in heaven with Mr. God. Instead, he describes most human beings as living and dying according to the principle of *Itoklanoz*, which governs the life of one and two brained beings. Thus, they serve the purposes of Nature and then the 'I' will disappear forever.

However, Beelzebub explains that there is a whole other science of psychology—of the soul—and that indeed a human being might ultimately merge again with the Most, Most Holy Sun Absolute. Beelzebub offers a way of comprehending in an objective and impartial manner, what all such things might entail. The esoteric teachings offered provide a profoundly alternative view of *"All and Everything,"* and help to destroy all the rubbish accumulated within human mentation through the centuries.

2. The Sacred Triamazikamno and the Three Being-Brains

> "...each three-brained being arisen on this planet of yours represents in himself also, in all respects ... an exact similarity of the whole Megalocosmos ... but of course in miniature ... ." (p.775)

In elaborating upon the secrets of his esoteric cosmology, Beelzebub explains that all things manifest a three-fold nature in accord with the Law of the Sacred Triamazikamno—which forces are subsequently actualized through the law of Heptaparaparshinokh through successive generations of causes and effects. A particularly important role is ascribed in creation processes to the "Omnipresent-Okidanokh"—which embodies the three-fold nature of the Emanations of the Holy Sun Absolute. This Okidanokh is present everywhere within space or the Etherokrilno.

Recall that the Okidanokh is described as "the fundamental cause" of cosmic phenomena and that it always embodies an 'active principle' in all its subsequent effects. Further, it never enters as a whole into anything, but always undergoes dispersion into three components—the process of 'Djartklom.' Beelzebub explains that it is through the process of Djartklom, that the Omnipresent-Okidanokh gives rise to the crystallizations which form the three brains within a human being:

> "... when a new cosmic unit is being concentrated, then the 'Omnipresent-Active-Element' does not blend, as a whole, with such a new arising, nor is it transformed as a whole in any definite corresponding place—as happens with every other cosmic crystallization in all the said cosmic formations—but immediately on entering as a whole into any cosmic unit ... it is dispersed into the three fundamental sources from which it obtained its prime arising, and only then do these sources, each separately, give the beginning for an independent concentration of three separate corresponding formations within the given cosmic unit. And in this way, this 'Omnipresent-Active-Element' actualizes at the outset, in every such new arising, the sources for the possible manifestation of its own sacred law of Triamazikamno." (pp. 139-40)

Beelzebub explains that *each brain* or 'spiritualized being-part' of a human being is actualized by one of the three forces of the Okidanokh—each of which assumes a role as an active principle in this formative process. Beelzebub elaborates:

> "Know first that, in general, every such cosmic formation called 'brain' receives its formation from those crystallizations the affirming source for whose arising, according to the sacred Triamazikamno, is one or another of the corresponding holy forces of the fundamental sacred Triamazikamno, localized in the Omnipresent-Okidanokh. And the further actualizings of the same holy forces proceed by means of the presences of the beings, just through those localizations." (p. 143)

Thus, a human being has *"three independent localizations"* or *"three being-brains."*

Beelzebub explains the localization of these three being-brains. The brain, actualizing the first Holy force, the affirming or active principle is *"localized and found in the head."* (p. 146) This is the thinking or intellectual center for the being. The second brain, transforming the second Holy force or denying principle, is located *"along the whole of their back in what is called the 'spinal column.'"* The second brain is the moving-motor, or moving-instinctual brain. The third brain embodies the third force of the Holy Reconciling and is related to the functions of feelings and emotions. However, its localization is not so clearly established. Recall Beelzebub's explanations:

> "... in the beginning these three-brained beings of the planet Earth ... had this third concentration, similar to us, in the form of an independent brain localized in the region of their what is called 'breast.' But from the time when the process of their ordinary being-existence began particularly sharply to change for the worst, then Nature ... was compelled, without destroying the functioning itself of this brain of theirs, to change the system of its localization.

> "That is to say, she gradually dispersed the localization of this organ ... into small localizations over the whole of their common presence, but chiefly in the region of what is called the 'pit of the stomach.' The totality of these small localizations in this region they themselves at the present time call the solar plexus or the 'complex of the nodes of the sympathetic nervous system.' (p. 780)

Beelzebub is describing the third being-brain as centered, in your favorites, in the autonomic nervous system. However, in the *"primordial three brained-beings there, this said brain was localized in the same part of their planetary body as in us"*–namely, in an independent brain in the region of the *'breast;'"* (p. 146)

This passage suggests–at least to the author–that the original emotional center was within 'the heart'–the independent brain in the region of the 'breast.' This is still the case for the primordial three brained-beings and for Beelzebub, Hassein and their kinsmen, but not for those three-brained beings on planet Earth. For such slugs, because of their unnatural conditions of being-existence and the other cosmic factors explained, Nature had to *"regenerate this brain and to give it the form which it now has in the contemporary beings."* (p. 146)

A human being can thus experience and function–mentally, emotionally, and physically–and each of these being-centers is localized within different areas of his/her planetary body being. In contrast, modern psychology considers a human being to have only one mind in the head, which is attached to a second component, the body. That is why psychology is defined as the "science of mind and behavior," because a human being is thought to have only a dual nature—with no heart or soul. Oh, those 'sorry scientists!'

Another important concept in Beelzebub's psychology concerns how each of the three brains in a human being bears relationships to the three fundamental orders established with the Megalocosmos. Beelzebub explains that in the sacred cosmic Triamazikamno, the Emanations of the Sun Absolute, or the Protocosmos, act as the positive or affirming source. All of the newly arisen Second order Suns then act as *"various shades of denial,"* relative to this affirming principle. Lastly, *"the totality of everything newly arisen in the Megalocosmos is the neutralizing principle ...."* (p. 780)

Beelzebub explains the three being-brains within the human anatomy bear similar relationships:

> "... there is localized in the head of each one of them ... a concentration of corresponding cosmic substances, all the functioning of which exactly corresponds to all those functions and purposes which our Most Most Holy Protocosmos has, and fulfills, for the whole of the Megalocosmos. ...
>
> "... in the 'spinal marrow,' in which there are precisely those what are called denying sources, which actualize in their functionings in relation to parts of the head-brain just such fulfillments as the 'second-order newly arisen Suns' of the Megalocosmos actualize in relation to the Most Most Holy Protocosmos. ...
>
> "And in those nervous nodes scattered over the whole of the planetary body (of the sympathetic nervous system), there are accumulated at the present time all the results obtained from the affirming and denying manifestations of their head-brain and spinal marrow, and these results, having become fixed in these 'nervous nodes' ... are later such a neutralizing principle, in the further process of 'affirmation and denial' between the head-brain and spinal marrow, just as the totality of everything arising in the Megalocosmos is the neutralizing force in the process of the affirmation of the Protocosmos and various shades of denial of all the newly arisen Suns." (pp. 777-80)

The importance of these inter-relationships will become more evident once we have considered the various types of beings which evolved in the Universe, particularly on Earth, and have explored in more detail the nature of the *"three being-foods"* and the *"three being-bodies,"* elaborated by Beelzebub. *The Tales* offers a complex teaching concerning how cosmic forces and sacred laws bring about the actualizations of our three independent being-brains. The three factors within the Omnipresent Okidanokh lead to the formation of three brains, three independent minds, three spiritualized parts, which represent 'in miniature' the cosmic forces manifest in the whole Megalocosmos. This is one basis upon which a human being is a microcosm of the macrocosm, or a "similitudes-of-the-already-arisen."

We can end then with a verse from one of Beelzebub's sacred prayers.

> "Holy Affirming, Holy Denying, Holy-Reconciling, Transubstantiate in me For my Being." (p.752)

Unfortunately, these slugs have become such *"lopsided beings,"* that the three being-localizations are seldom *"spiritualized in their presence."* (p. 1172)

3. The Origin and Nature of the Tetartocosmoses, & the Higher Being-Bodies

Beelzebub describes *"your favorites"* as *"apparatuses of the Most Great common-cosmic Trogoautoegocrat."* Every cosmos or living being is actualized as some Fraction of the Whole produced through the effects of the primordial cosmic laws of the Sacred Triamazikamno and Heptarparaparshinokh manifested through generations of causes and effects. Thus, within us–'men-beings'–as in all three-brained beings, the involution and evolution of substances within the planetary body and higher being-bodies all proceed according to the Laws of Three and Seven. Beelzebub explains that human beings take in three major *"being-foods,"* each of which can be refined through a sevenfold process within three *"being-bodies."* This produces the various substances required for the physical, psychological and spiritual life–and for the planetary body, the Kesdjan (or astral) body, and the *"highest being-body."* The evolution of a human being depends upon the inner "coating" of the higher being-bodies for the life of the soul.

In order to understand these possibilities, we can follow Beelzebub's explanations of how life forms arose on planets throughout the universe. In brief, evolution proceeded through a sequence of stages– from *Microcosmoses* to *Tetartocosmoses*, to two-natured *'beings'* with Kesdjan bodies, to *"'three-in-one' formations"* –with a planetary body, a Kesdjan body and a higher being-body. In turn, these *"three-in-one"* formations can attain the highest faculties of Divine Reason and even return again to the Source–to blend again with the Holy Sun Absolute! This would involve the completion of the Sacred Heptaparaparshinokh within the living being.

Unfortunately, other unforeseen things happened after the original plans of HIS ENDLESSNESS, which led to changes such that the three-brained beings could no longer so attain such degrees of self-perfection. It is a subtle and complex story which Beelzebub has to recount but well worth active deliberation in all of its details. Essentially, Beelzebub, as part of the education of his grandson, and of us as the readers, offers a framework of esoteric secrets concerning how everything came about, the stages of evolution, the nature of the soul and our afterlife possibilities.

Beelzebub explains that after the formation of the planets in the *"first outer cycle"* of the fundamental sacred Heptaparaparshinokh, the *"initially given momentum for the fundamental completing process"* had lost half of the *"force of its vivifyingness,"* as it was taken up by the initial creation processes. Again, due to the modification of the Fifth Stopinder, the creation impetus began in its further functioning to have *"only half of the manifestation of it action outside itself, and the other half for itself, ... the consequences of which ... there began to arise what are called, 'similarities-to-the-already-arisen'"* upon the planets. (p. 758) These *"similarities-to-the-already-arisen"* are the *Microcosmoses*. Subsequently, the outer cycle of the sacred Heptaparaparshinokh ceased and all of its action entered into *"the results already manifested by it."* Thus, the *"inherent permanent processes of transformation"*–of the involution and evolution of different substances and elements according to the sacred Heptaparaparshinokh, proceeded within the *'similarities-to-the-already-arisen,'* the microcosmoses.

A second-grade cosmic law served to bring about the next phase of the cosmic evolution of life forms. Beelzebub labels this *"second-degree cosmic law"* as *"Litsvrtsi,'* and defines it a involving the *"aggregation of the homogeneous."* Thus, the *'relatively independent'* new formations, the microcosms or the smallest 'similarities-to-the-already-arisen,' began through mutual attraction to form new *'relatively independent formations'*–the Tetartocosmoses. Beelzebub defines a Tetartocosmos as a *"relatively-independent-formation-of-the-aggregation-of-microcosmoses."* (p. 762) In this vein, we might take the microcosms to refer to cells, which join together to create the different life forms–the multi-cellular organisms, or Tetartocosmoses. Once again, thanks to the sacred law of Heptaparaparshinokh, with its inherent processes of involution and evolution, there began "to crystallize" and "decrystallize" different substances within the Tetartocosmoses. These are the "active elements" which constitute the life form and are required for its processes.

Among the Tetartocosmoses, the possibility then arose of *"independent automatic moving"* upon the face of the planets. Thereupon, the COMMON FATHER ENDLESSNESS had the Divine Idea of using these independently moving Tetartocosmoses to help HIM in the *"administration of the enlarging World."* (p. 762) The Common Father thus began to actualize everything in these cosmoses so that there might be transformed and crystallized in them, substances not only for the common-cosmic exchange of substances, but which might also serve to form *"new independent formations"* within themselves. These new independent formations within themselves are the higher being-bodies.

Beelzebub explains that the involution and evolution of elements through the Sacred Heptaparaparshinokh always involves seven *"'centers-of-gravity active elements'"*–whether we are dealing with the Universe, the Megalocosmos, or with the nature of the *"similarities-of-the-already-arisen."* He lists the names of these seven substances in the Tetartocosmoses–in beings such as 'your favorites:'

> (1) Protoehary
> (2) Defteroehary
> (3) Tritoehary
> (4) Tetartoehary
> (5) Piandjoehary
> (6) Exioehary
> (7) Resulzarion

When the Common Father wanted to allow "new independent formations" to arise in the living beings, he undertook a particular intervention in terms of adjusting the flow of forces through the Heptaparaparshinokh. Beelzebub explains what the Common Father did to effect this:

> "From that time on HE began to actualize everything further for these cosmoses in such a direction that the inevitable what is called, 'Okrualno'–i.e., the periodic repetition in them of the completing process of the sacred Heptaparaparshinokh–might be accomplished ... ." (p. 762)

This intervention of the Common Father enabled the *"periodic repetition in them of the completing process of the sacred Heptaparaparshinokh"*–namely the production and refinement of all these seven classes of substances, which might then produce more refined substances of a *"greater vivifyingness."* These more refined substances could then help to "coat" the formation of the next higher being-body. Beelzebub explains this intervention of the Father Creator in greater detail:

IV / Science of the Soul

> "And so, the further results of this Divine attention in respect of the mentioned Tetartocosmoses consisted in this, that during their serving as apparatuses for the most great cosmic Trogoautoegocrat, the possibility was obtained in them that from among the cosmic substances transformed through them ... and composed exclusively of cosmic crystallizations which are derived from the transformations of that planet itself ... such results began to be obtained in their common presences ... as proceed from cosmic sources of a higher order, and consequently composed of what are called vibrations of 'greater vivifyingness." (p. 763)

The enabling of the completion of the Heptaparaparshinokh within the Tetartocosmoses produces new substances—notes within a higher octave of vibrations with a greater degree of *"vivifyingness."* Note also that this Divine attention acted *"exclusively"* on those *"cosmic crystallizations which are derived from the planet itself."* Here, Beelzebub is referring to what he labels the *"first being-food."*

Beelzebub describes the *"first being-food"* as having *"evolved"* as substances with the *"aid of their own planet"* into *"definite higher corresponding surplanetary formations"*—such as fruits, grains, plant life—which are taken in as *"food"* and *"drink."* Physical foods from the planet are taken into the body as being-Protoehary, which are then refined to produce being-Defteroehary, and so on, up to being-Exioehary and Resulzarion—the finest substances produced through the refinement of the first being-food. The intervention of the Father Creator was to enable the completing of this process, so as to produce more substances of a higher order of "vivifyingness."

Beelzebub describes what happened next in the evolution of the Tetartocosmoses and the higher being-bodies:

> "Now from such cosmic results, exactly similar forms began to be coated in their common presences, at first from the cosmic substances Mentekithzoin, i.e., from the substances transformed by the sun and by other planets of that solar system ... which cosmic substances reach every planet through the radiations of the said cosmic concentrations.
>
> "In this way, the common presences of certain Tetartocosmoses began beforehand to be composed of two different independent formations arisen from two entirely different cosmic sources, and these began to have a joint existence, as if one were placed within the other." (p. 764)

Beelzebub explains that when this new *"coating"* was completed and functioning within the presences of the Tetartocosmoses, then they ceased to be called by that name and were instead called *"'beings,' which then meant 'two-natured.'"* These second coatings were called *"'bodies-Kesdjan."*

The Kesdjan body or astral body in more popular language and in Theosophical terminology—is *"at first"* coated by the *Mentekithzoin* cosmic substances. These are radiations from the second-order Suns, as well as from the planets. All such cosmic substances and influences permeate the atmospheres of our planet Earth and Beelzebub relates their energies to the second being-food—which is the *"'air,' by which they breathe."* Beelzebub explains that the air does not simply contain the material elements known to your favorites, but includes *"transformations of their own sun and of all the other planets of their solar system."*

The substances required for the coating of the Kesdjan body enter the atmosphere of Earth through radiation and are acquired through breathing and even through the pores of the skin. Substances within the being-food of *"air"* serve *"for the coating and maintenance of the existence of their second being-bodies."* (p. 781) Beelzebub refers to that *"totality of cosmic substances which your favourite call air"* which *"enter into the common presences of beings for the coating and feeding of their second being-bodies Kesdjan."* (p. 788)

Just as the first being-food of physical food enters the body as a substance being-Protoehary and is refined to produce being-Defteroehary and other substances; so also, the second being-food, Astralnomonian-Protoehary can be refined into Astralnomonian-Defteroehary and higher elements through its own Heptaparaparshinokh process. These Astralnomonian substances, of which there would be seven, compose the second-being body.

Once the Tetartocosmoses were transformed into two natured *"beings"* and the functions of such *"a cosmic arising"* are established, then these two centered beings underwent an additional stage of evolution. Beelzebub explains that they:

> "in their turn ... began to absorb and assimilate into themselves such cosmic substances as had their arising immediately from the Most Most Holy Theomertmalogos, and similarities of a third kind began to be coated in them which are the 'higher sacred-parts' of beings and which we now call 'higher being-bodies.'" (pp. 764-5)

The third being-food elaborated by Beelzebub is *"from the direct emanations of our Most Holy un Absolute"* and this serves *"for the coating of the highest being-body, which sacred being-part of theirs ... they call soul...."* (p. 569) These cosmic substances can be assimilated, Beelzebub explains, only through the process of *'Aiessirittoorassnian-contemplation'* which can be 'actualized' in *"the common presence by the cognized intention on the part of all their spiritualized independent parts."* (p. 570)

Again, there are seven centers of gravity within the *"highest being-body"*–in accord with the sacred Heptaparaparshinokh. Once the higher being-body is fully coated and its functioning established, then it *"became possible for the data for engendering the sacred function, named 'objective Reason,' to become crystallized in them ...."* (p. 765) This is the highest level of evolution attainable by those early Sacred Individuals who acquired their highest being-body and the faculties of objective or Divine Reason. This is what it means for an individual to 'acquire' their own soul through their own self-perfection, conscious labours and intentional suffering, and Aiessirittoorassnian-contemplation within a unified spiritual state.

Beelzebub describes this attainment of such sacred Individuals:

> "When each separate 'higher-perfected-being-body' becomes an independent Individual and acquires in itself its own law of Sacred Triamazikamno, it begins to emanate similarly to the Most Most Holy Sun Absolute but in miniature." (p. 798)

Thus, human beings might *"obtain in their common presences"* these substances or vibrations of a higher order involving a *"'greater vivifyingness,"* which coat the higher being-bodies and allow for the attaining of Divine Reason. At this point, these Sacred Individuals could be taken directly into service of the Endlessness or they might blend again with the Sun Absolute. However, these possibilities could only happen after death–or the Rascooarnos. Beelzebub explains:

> "... when what is called 'Rascooarno' occurred to these 'Tetartocosmoses' or 'beings,' i.e., the separation of these diverse-natured 'three-in-one' formations from each other, only then did this 'higher-being-part' receive the possibility of uniting itself with the Cause-of-Causes of everything now existing, i.e., with our Most Most Holy Sun Absolute, and began to fulfill the purpose on which OUR ALL-EMBRACING ENDLESSNESS had placed HIS hope." (p. 765)

Beelzebub explains that those individuals who perfect the highest being-body assume a role in relationship to the Sun Absolute similar to that played by "cells-of-the-head-brain" in a three centered-being:

> "... the 'cells-of-the-head-brain,' actualize for the whole presence of each of them exactly such a purpose as is fulfilled at the present time by the 'higher-perfected-bodies' of three-brained beings from the whole of our Great Universe, who have already united themselves with the Most Most Holy Sun Absolute ..." (pp. 777-8)

Such independent Holy Individuals can serve larger cosmic purposes. This was the original plan conceived by HIS COMMON FATHER ENDLESSNESS, when HE observed the 'relatively independent movement' among the Tetartocosmos and intervened so as to enable the formation of the higher being-bodies. And so, when this system was originally established and functioning, such Sacred Individuals would be taken into service of the Common Father.

However, this system functioned only until other unforeseen cosmic catastrophes and unfortunate events brought it about that such possibilities were no longer realized—especially for the decidedly strange 'men-beings' on planet Earth. After the removal of the organ Kundabuffer, the men-beings had lived and died according to the *Fulasnitamnian* principle, and the second-being-food was fully assimilated by their common presences. However, when Great Nature had to change their Fulasnitamnian-existence into a life under the *Itoklanoz principle*, as is common to one and two brained beings, then these substances were no longer crystallized for the coating and perfection of the Kesdjan body, *"ceased, owing to their abnormal being-existence."* (p. 571) Unfortunately, your favorites ended up—because of the abnormal conditions of being-existence, the organ Kundabuffer, their strange psyches and various cosmic catastrophes— living and dying more like slugs, according to the Itoklanoz principle—as govern one and two brain-beings. They no longer developed the higher being-body, the Kesdjan body, nor attain the "highest being-body" with its potential faculties for Divine Reason—as involved in such advanced levels of cosmic evolution.

The slugs on planet Earth are still created and maintained by the same laws of Triamazikamno and Heptaparaparshinokh as embodied within the larger cosmos. This is the basis upon which human beings could perfect their higher being-bodies and assume larger cosmic purposes:

> "... through each of them the cosmic substances arising in all seven Stopinders of the Sacred Heptaparaparshinokh could be transformed, and all of them ... besides serving as apparatuses for the Most Great cosmic Trogoautoegocrat, could have all possibilities for absorbing from those cosmic substances which are transformed through them what is corresponding for the coating and for the perfecting in them of both higher-being bodies; because each three-brained being arisen on this planet of yours represents in himself also, in all respects ... an exact similarity of the whole Megalocosmos ... but of course in miniature ... " (p.775)

At varied times, Beelzebub refers three-brained beings as potentially becoming *"a particle of all that exists,"* (p. 163) or *"a particle though an independent one, of everything existing in the Great Universe."* (p. 183) Elsewhere, he describes humans *"as beings having in their presences every possibility for becoming particles of a part of Divinity ...."* (p. 453)

In the context of describing Saint Buddha's teachings, Beelzebub explains the most profound secrets of human potential:

> "This Most Great Foundation of the All-embracing of everything that exists constantly emanates throughout the whole of the Universe and coats itself from its particles upon planets-in certain three-brained beings who attain in their common presences the capacity to have their own functioning of both fundamental cosmic laws of the sacred Heptaparaparshinokh and the sacred Triamazikamno-into a definite unit in which alone 'Objective Divine Reason' acquires the possibility of becoming concentrated and fixed. ... certain parts of the Great All-embracing, already spiritualised by Divine Reason, return and reblend with the great Prime Source of the All-embracing ..." (pp.244-5)

Beelzebub explains that after Buddha's talk, the people misunderstood his message and began to believe that they already were such *"parts of the Most Great Greatness"*–even without any striving for self-perfection or performance of their being-Partkdolg duty. Instead, they were *"convinced that they were already particles of Mister Prana himself."* (p. 246)

A soul is not given to a human being but must be acquired. Unfortunately, the cosmic catastrophes which occurred to the earth and the miscalculations around the organ Kundabuffer lead to the emergence of a strange breed on the planet, the slugs, who according to Beelzebub are willing to believe any old tale and who are dominated by a whole false consciousness system. Humans have missed the mark and do not establish their own inner triangle or sevenfold nature, to complete the inner octave and blend again with the Most Holy Sun Absolute or to assume other roles within the larger Cosmos.

Imagine that, human beings are similitudes of the whole, particles of the Great Universe, with deep hidden roots within higher dimensions of being and non-being. Most importantly, an individual might attain a higher Kesdjan body or a highest being-body, if it were not for their common psychopathologies. Behind essence is real I, behind real I, is God, or at least the Most Most Holy Sun Absolute.

4. The Evolution and Involution of Exioehary

Beelzebub explains in detail to Hassein the processes by which the first being-food is refined within the planetary body to produce seven different classes of substances. His descriptions illustrate the application of the Law of Heptaparaparshinokh.

Beelzebub mainly describes the evolution of substances within the planetary body from the intake of the first being-food. A similar refinement and evolution of substances occurs within the higher being-bodies–from the assimilation of the other two being-foods. Beelzebub states: *"... these higher cosmic substances in beings are transformed according to exactly the same principles as the substances of the first being-food."* (p. 790) To understand all of the physical-psychological-spiritual possibilities for a human being, we would ideally be able to detail all three Heptaparaparshinokh processes and their inter-relationships. However, in *The Tales*, Beelzebub more fully explicates only the processes that occur within the physical or planetary body. He states to Hassein that the same analysis might be applied to the other being-foods, but does not subsequently explain these processes.[22]

Recall that any involutionary-evolutionary process embodies the Heptaparaparshinokh and produces seven "centers-of-gravity active elements" in any Cosmos. Beelzebub lists these seven substances which constitute a Tetartocosmoses, like ourselves: (1) Protoehary (2) Defteroehary (3) Tritoehary (4) Tetartoehary (5) Piandjoehary (6) Exioehary and (7) Resulzarion. At other times, Beelzebub uses variations of these terms. Thus, in describing the evolution of the first being-food, Beelzebub uses the terms being-Protoehary, being-Defteroehary, being-Tritoehary and so on, with the preface 'being.' Beelzebub states that if we were talking of the evolution of the second being-food, air, we would use the terms Astralnomonian-Protoehary, Astralnomian-Defteroehary and so on. This same pattern might be extended to descriptions of the third being-food, although Beelzebub does not elaborate further on this.[23]

Beelzebub's model of the refinement of the being-foods within a human being provides a profound teaching concerning how a human three-brained being might become no longer a slug, but consciously participate in the formation and coating of their own higher being-bodies. Human beings feed on three primary substances which provide the elements necessary to nourish and sustain three being-bodies.

This is Beelzebub's account of the refinement of the first being-food within the body.[24]
Immediately that the first being-food enters the mouth, it begins to mix and fuse with other active elements which have already been evolved within the organism. Beelzebub calls this process "Harnelmiatznel" and it occurs at all levels of the refinement of the food substances, as the being foods interact with elements produced within the body which have a corresponding *"affinity of*

---

[22] Ouspensky presents (1950) Gurdjieff's teachings about the three foods and their development within the "food diagrams," and has other useful perspectives which supplement Beelzebub's explanations. (See Holmes, 2010)

[23] This background is important in order to explain varied 'inexactitudes' posed by Beelzebub's descriptions concerning the different use of the terms Exioehary and being-Exioehary.

[23] Beelzebub does not use the musical notes as references but I have added them to help clarify these processes, as they are used within the Ouspensky version of G.'s teachings.

vibrations." The first being-food in the stomach, after being transmuted by other active elements, is the substance being-Protoehary–the first note–do–of the food octave. This substance then evolves through the "intestinal track" and into the "duodenum" where it becomes "being-Defterochary"–the note re. A portion of these substances serve the planetary body in that form, while the other part continues to evolve, next to form "being-Tritoehary" in the "liver"–the note mi. At this point, the refinement of the food substances encounters the Stopinder, or interval, which has been lengthened in the functioning of the Heptaparaparshinokh and so the process comes to a standstill.

At this interval, a "shock" or "input" from outside of the organism is required in order to fill the gap, allowing the food substances to evolve further. Beelzebub explains: *"... this totality of substances named 'being-Tritoehary' can in the given case evolve further from this state only with the help of forces coming from outside."* Recall that this is how a Trogoautoegocratic system functions, requiring forces from outside, and is no longer self-sufficient or self contained.

This "shock point" or interval is filled by the intake of air–the second being-food. Air, enters as a side-octave and provides the extra force or influence to allow the progressive refinement of the first being-food. Beelzebub has a special name for this interval which is filled automatically and does not require any particular being-effort or participation. He calls this interval the *"mechano-coinciding-Mdnel-In."* In Gurdjieff's teachings, as outlined in Ouspensky, the input of the air octave is described as providing the first *"mechanical shock."* If no outside force intervenes, then the substances crystallized through the digestive system would *"involve back again into those definite cosmic crystallizations from which they began their evolution."* (p. 788)[24]

Of course, *"Great Nature"* adapted beings so that the second being-food required for the Kesdjan body, enters from outside and provides the shock which allows the further evolution of the substances of the first being-food. The air enters the "lungs" where it is transformed into Protoehary, but in this case "Astralnomonian-Protoehary." This enables the further development of the first being-food, which then produces "being-Tetartoehary," as the note fa. This substance has its center of localization within the *"hemispheres of their head-brain."* Part of this Tetartoehary will serve the planetary body but the remainder further evolves by mixing with other substances in the body. The next substances to be formed are the *"higher definite being-active-elements"* called "Piandjoehary," localized within *"the cerebellum,"* at the back of the brain in the head–sol in the scale. Again, part of this substance is used for the planetary body, while the rest passes *"in a particular way through the 'nerve nodes' of the spine and the breast"* and is then concentrated in the "testicles" or the "ovaries" –the note la. This is the *"being-Exioehary"*–sperm in men–which Beelzebub describes as *"for the beings themselves their most sacred possession."* (p. 791)

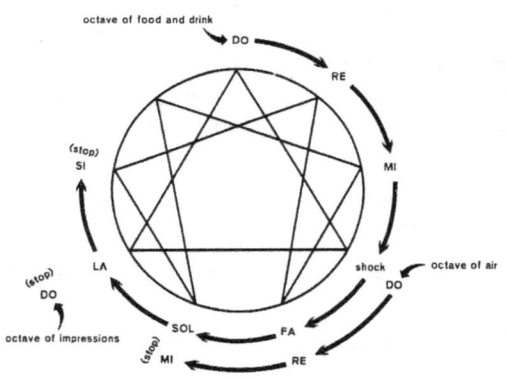

[24] This portrayal of the being-foods is drawn from the Ouspensky work, wherein the third being-food is "psychological impressions" rather than the "direct emanations of our Most Holy Sun Absolute" of Beelzebub. The diagram indicates how the second being-food air fills the shock point in the evolution of the first being-food octave.

IV / Science of the Soul

Beelzebub depicts then a final step:

> "Only after this are the cosmic substances which enter being-apparatuses for the purpose of evolution ... transformed into that definite totality of cosmic substances—which transformation is the lot of all beings in general and also of your contemporary three-brained beings who breed on the planet Earth in particular, for the automatic justification of the sense and aim of their existence, and this totality of cosmic substances is everywhere called Exioehary." (p. 790)

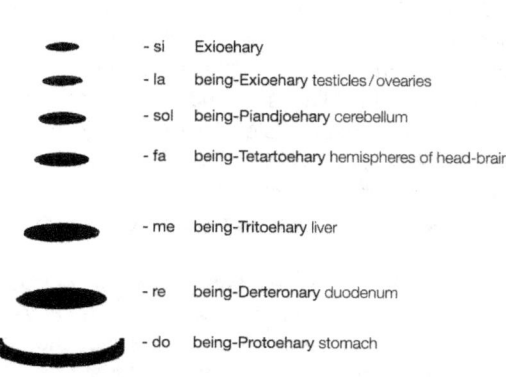

- si — Exioehary
- la — being-Exioehary testicles / ovearies
- sol — being-Piandjoehary cerebellum
- fa — being-Tetartoehary hemispheres of head-brain
- me — being-Tritoehary liver
- re — being-Derteronary duodenum
- do — being-Protoehary stomach

In this passage, there are certain "inexactitudes" in terms of the naming of these substances. Beelzebub describes being-Exioehary being formed in the testes or ovaries and then continues to say *"only after this"* is there produced Exioehary. Now, according to the seven names originally given for the seven gravity-center substances, the sixth was Exioehary and the seventh was Resulzarion. And so, we might have expected Beelzebub to use the term being-Resulzarion if this is the seventh element, but instead he seems to repeat Exioehary.[25] However, consider Beelzebub's next lines:

> "And so, my boy, this totality of their first being-food which results from the evolution in these being-apparatuses, corresponds with its vibrations to the last Stopinder of the being-Heptaparaparshinokh ...."

In Beelzebub's account, there is a seventh element, which brings the octave to the Last Stopinder. This might be taken as Exioehary or as being-Resulzarion.

The food octave has now passed to si in the octave structure and encounters another interval, which has been shortened. Beelzebub explains that this interval of si-do requires a *"higher intentionally-actualizing-Mdnel-In"* (or shock) in order for the Exioehary to evolve further. Beelzebub explains that, in this case, the Exioehary can:

> "... transform completely into new higher substances and in order to acquire vibrations corresponding to the vibrations of the next higher vivifyingness ... it inevitably requires just that foreign help which is actualized ... in the 'being-Partkdolg-duty,' ... which factors until now serve as the sole possible means for the assimilation of the cosmic substances required for the coating and perfecting of the higher being-bodies ...." (p. 792)

Being-Partkdolg duty, of conscious labours and intentional suffering, cannot "happen" accidentally but can only be the result of a certain being-effort and the striving of the individual towards his/her own self-perfection. This is why this interval is described as *"intentionally actualized."* In order to breach this highest interval, to produce a completed do on a new order of "vivifyingness" within the higher-

---

[25] I mention these points not fully understanding the issues here but having a particular way to interpreted this section of the Tales. Part of the solution lay in the fact that three octaves of being-foods need to be considered to have a fuller account of these dynamics; and that Exioehary as a substance is different from being-Exioehary, but its formation depends also on further processes within the other being-foods.

being bodies, the individual must participate in actualizing these higher possibilities. The processes of conscious labors and intentional suffering thus have actual effects on the inner alchemy of the human being in producing substances of a greater "vivifyingness and coating the higher being bodies.

Thus, Beelzebub describes the refinement of the first being-food through seven levels while explaining the nature of the Heptaparaparshinokh process—with its different intervals and centers of gravity. The substances of the other being-foods are developed in a similar fashion and so in the larger scheme, different mechanical and conscious shocks will be required to complete these inner octave processes.

Unfortunately, your favorites, know of none of this and do not actualize their 'being-Partkdolg-duty.' Subsequently, these sexual substances begin to *"involve back ... towards those crystallizations from which their evolution began."* This involution of the sexual substances tends to *"'deperfect' their previously established essence-individuality,"* leading to innumerable "illnesses" and diminishing the *"thirst for Being."* (pp. 793-794) And so, the slugs do not use the substances of the 'Exioehary' for their own self-perfection, to coat and perfect the higher being-bodies or even to consciously reproduce themselves. Without such an inner alchemy, the beings are described as *"strongly sensing the emptiness of their existence."* Beelzebub describes such creatures as being "terrestrial nullities." [26]

Although some of the three-brained beings do strive for self-perfection by *"abstaining from the ejection from oneself in the customary manner of these substances formed in them called sperm ...,"* (p. 807) they usually do not understand the necessity of fulfilling of their being-Partkdolg-duty if this abstinence is to have its desired effect—in terms of enabling them to attain a soul and quenching the thirst for being. Instead, they began "to imitate" the practices of the genuine initiates and to organize themselves in various groups and sects, putting this abstinence into effect. Thus, "monasteries" were established and various "monks" began to refrain from the ejection of sperm, but little was ever achieved as the brothers did not understand the importance of fulfilling one's being obligations or of *"intentionally absorbing"* the second and third being-foods.

These practices led to varied pathologies and perversions according to Beelzebub. The reason for this was that unless the substances pass through both "Mdnel-Ins" and discontinuities in their octave development, then these same substances begin to "involve" or degenerate into the earlier stages of their evolutionary development. And so, these sorry monks retain their semen but fail to transmute these substances through the final si-do interval and so the sexual substances degenerate within them.

Beelzebub offers shocking portraits of humankind, especially as concerns the misuse and squandering of the sacred sexual energies and the involution of these substances into poisons and perversions. The lack of being-partkdolg-duty and the striving towards self-perfection, and the failure to consciously absorb the three being-foods, all lead to various forms of degeneracy common among *"your favorites."*

---

[26] Mantak Chia (1984), a Taoist master, similarly explains that the cultivation of male or female sexual energy is essential to the alchemy of the soul. In the preface to Chia's work, Winn explains:

> "The Taoist teaching of physical immortality ... means that before (men) die they have the opportunity to cultivate a "solid" or substantial spiritual body, also known as the Immortal Body, the Solar Body, the Crystal Body, and other names. ... The Taoists insist each adept preserve his individual nature within a body (physical or spiritual) so he can oversee the growth of his soul until final union with "wu chi," the nothingness from which the oneness of the Tao emerges." (p. iii)

Chia explains that the sperm energy can be mixed with the chi, or vital energy of the organs, and then refined into shien, or spirit. Thus, the sexual energies link the biological body to the metaphysical identity–the animal nature to the divine.

Readers are recommended to Chia's teachings for practical techniques for the cultivation of non-ejaculatory sex, as practised by the Taoist masters. Chia references Gurdjieff's teachings as supportive of the Taoist philosophies and practices.

5. The Alchemy of the Blood

> "... the quality of the composition of the blood in the three-brained beings ... depends on the number of the being-bodies already 'completely formed.'" (p. 569)

In *Beelzebub's Tales* and within Mr. Gurdjieff's talks recorded by Ouspensky, there are profound teachings about the inner alchemy of being, the nature of the subtle being-bodies and the role of various bloods within the life of a man-being. The quality of the blood actually makes one man a slug and another *"immortal within the limits of the solar system."*

Recall that, according to Beelzebub, a dual consciousness system formed in those strange three-brained beings on planet Earth. The true consciousness in their essence has passed into the so-called "subconscious" and a false consciousness system—based on conditioning, education and outside influences—has become the so-called normal "waking consciousness." Further, the functioning of these two consciousness systems is related to differences in the blood flow within the human organism. Beelzebub explained this while recounting his work as a hypnotist while living on the Earth. In particular, he explained that the *"centre-of-gravity-of-the-blood-pressure"* in their presences will sometimes predominate within one part of the general system of blood vessels, and at other times within another part of the blood vessels. These differences are related to differences between the waking and sleeping states and used to explain the phenomena of hypnosis. Beelzebub functioned as a hypnotist putting humans into this state by altering the particularities of their blood flow. Largely, this was through the use of his own Handbledzoin (the blood of the Kesdjan or astral body), which he labels as "animal magnetism." However, Beelzebub explains that even the ordinary waking existence of humans flows under the influence of such a hypnotic state.

However, these dynamics are only part of the complex teachings which Beelzebub and Mr. Gurdjieff elaborate upon the nature of what your favorites and the 'sorry scientists' would simply call 'the blood.' Ouspensky (1949) recalls Gurdjieff's explanations of the alchemy of a human's possible evolution. The inner alchemical processes involve the accumulation of certain "hydrogens" (or substances) within the human factory, or what Beelzebub refers to as the human "being-apparatus." [27] According to Ouspensky's recollection of Gurdjieff's discourse on this subject, the human factory is capable of a whole series of complicated alchemical processes, which are involved in the process of self-perfection. The result is that:

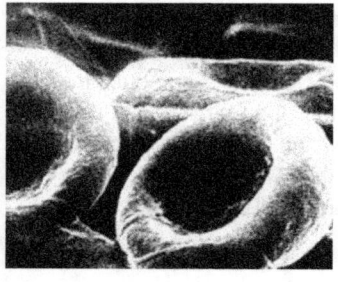

[27] In Mr. Gurdjieff's teaching as explained by Ouspensky and others, the term 'hydrogen' is used in a generic way to refer to any "substance" or element of different matter/energy/intelligence density. The Hydrogen diagrams in Ouspensky's work provide a complex and invaluable scheme for conceptualizing the nature of reality and all of the varied 'substances' composing the psyche, the Universe and the Absolute.

Figure 1.
Red blood cells magnified 20,000 times. They have a diameter of .007 to .008 mm and are 60% water. The cells contain Hemoglobin, and an iron element, which binds to oxygen and transport it throughout the planetary body.

> "...the tissues, all the cells ... become saturated with these fine 'hydrogens' which would gradually settle in them, crystallizing in a special way. This crystallization of the fine 'hydrogens' gradually brings the whole organism onto a higher level or plane of being. ... 'Learn to separate the fine from the coarse'–this principle from the 'Emerald Tablets of Hermes Trismegistus' ... creates ... the possibility of an inner growth ... the growth of the inner bodies of man, the astral, the mental, and so on, is a material process completely analogous to the growth of the physical body. (1949, pp. 179-80)

This is a valuable perspective on the alchemy of the higher being-bodies and the effects of the refinement of the three being-foods.

Higher states of consciousness and levels of Divine reason depend upon the accumulation of subtle substances through the refinement of the being-foods and psycho-spiritual processes. These things all effect the makeup of the blood. The development and refinement of the astral and mental bodies, which Beelzebub refers to as the "higher being-bodies," is a process "completely analogous" to the growth of the physical body. Further, each of these different bodies has its own forms of 'blood,' or vital substances.

Beelzebub explains that the substance which compose the blood arise through the transformation of *"three separate independent what are called 'general-cosmic-sources-of-actualizing.'"* (p. 569) The substances in the blood required for the planetary body are from those substances of the planet on which the beings are formed and exist. The substances required for the Kesdjan body (the astral/emotional body) are given the special name of "Hanbledzoin." These are derived from *"the transformation of elements of other planets and of the sun itself of that system ...."* These substances are those of the second being food–the air. Beelzebub defines this important term–Hanbledzoin, as:

> "... nothing else than the 'blood' of the Kesdjan body of the being, just as the cosmic substances called in totality blood serve for nourishing and renewing the planetary body of the being, so also Hanbledzoin serves in the same way for nourishing and perfecting the body Kesdjan." (p. 568)

The third set of substances is also given a special name by Beelzebub. This is called the *"sacred Aiesakhaldan"* and it serves *"the highest part of the being called the soul."* This is the part of the being-blood which is formed from the direct *"emanations of our Most Holy Sun Absolute."* (p. 569) Unfortunately, although this third being-food still "flows," it does so *"without their cognized intention"* and only for *"the purposes of the common-cosmic Trogoautoegocratic harmony"* and the *"automatic continuation of their species demanded by Nature."* So although the third being-food, the "emanations" of higher sources, are partially absorbed automatically to enable procreation and the needs of the local cosmic harmony, they are not accumulated for the coating of the highest being-body for the life of the soul. These sacred particles are described by Beelzebub as being absorbed when *"intense being-experiences"* and *"active deliberation"* proceed within them.

Each of the three being-foods is primarily related to one of the three being-bodies. Food sustains the planetary body; air the Kesdjan, or astral body; and the emanations of the Sun Absolute can nourish and sustain the higher being-body. Complex inner processes proceed within the various bodies, which allow for the evolution and involution of these substances within the men-being.
The three being-bloods are related to the three being-foods and to matter, radiations and

emanations—all related to different dimensions within the Cosmos. In this view, various refined subtle energies and influences of the larger cosmos circulate through the blood of the physical, astral and highest being bodies.

The accumulation of rarefied "hydrogens," the Hanbledzoin and Aiesakhaldan, allow for the crystallization of the subtle higher being-bodies and changes the alchemy of the blood. The objective in self-perfection described by Gurdjieff and as recounted by Ouspensky is to become *"immortal within the limits of the Solar System."* This comes about through the accumulation of finer energies (or hydrogens) within the blood. Similarly, Beelzebub describes the "coating" the higher being-bodies for the life of the soul as involving even *"the emanations of our Most Holy Sun Absolute."*

Whereas scientists conceive of blood simply in material terms, Gurdjieff explains that all things have a subtle nature–related to the subtle planes, energies and matters. Thus, in addition to material blood, there are various subtle bloods (or vital energies) related to the subtle bodies and dimensions. In this view, the alchemy and spiritualization of the blood involves not only the purification of the physical body, but also the refinement of subtle life energies and substances within the higher being-bodies.

Gurdjieff describes humans as "three-brained beings," who function physically, emotionally and mentally. The centers of these activities are interconnected through the blood of the physical body, as well as the blood of the subtle bodies:

> "... the body is connected to the feeling organization by the blood, and the feeling-organization is connected to the organization actualizing the functioning of mentation or consciousness by what is called Hanbledzoin (the blood of the astral/or Kesdjan body)." (p.1200)

The body and emotions are connected through the physical blood, while the emotions and mind are linked through the more subtle energies of the astral blood.

The three being-foods and the three bloods of the different being-bodies have complex relationships to the larger cosmos, but humans asleep do not assimilate the finer hydrogens necessary for the growth of the higher being-bodies. Beelzebub offers enigmatic teachings about the secret alchemy of being and the coating of the higher being-bodies!

6. Afterlife Processes

According to Beelzebub, a variety of afterlife fates might await those three-brained beings from planet Earth. Some will die like dog according to the Itoklanoz principle, *"as Nature actualizes one-brained and two-brained beings."* (p. 131) Their planetary bodies are returned to feed the Earth and Askokin vibrations feed the moon—but generally they serve only local cosmic purposes. Others may have formed a Kesdjan body and will be drawn into the corresponding spheres of such substances, at least for a limited time. Others might even be embodied as one or two-brained beings or suffer varied conditions of remorse, retribution and purgatory conditions. The highest possibility is to actualize those possibilities for which the three-brained beings were originally designed—of becoming Sacred Individuals worthy of assuming a role in the larger world order or of blending again into the Most Holy Sun Absolute. Beelzebub suggests that behind real "I" is God, not with a comb in his pocket, but as the Most Holy Sun Absolute. He depicts the ultimate possibility for human evolution, which is to be thought worthy *"... of uniting with the presence of our Most Most Holy Sun Absolute."* (pp. 765-6) This is quite a possibility for "a slug" and one that unfortunately is no longer realized.

6a. The Sacred Rascooarnos

In his *Tales*, Beelzebub defines the sacred Rascooarnos as *"... the separation of these diverse-natured 'three-in-one' formations from each other."* (p. 765) The Rascooarnos involve the separations of a human's different being-bodies—the planetary body, the Kesdjan body and the highest being-body, which occur at death and into afterlife realms.

Beelzebub explains what happens through the Sacred Rascooarnos:

> "Now it is necessary to explain to you in more detail in what successiveness the first sacred Rascooarno then occurred ... At first on the planet itself the 'second-being-body,' i.e., the body-Kesdjan, together with the 'third-being-body' separate themselves from the 'fundamental-planetary-body' and, leaving this planetary body on the planet, rise both together to that sphere where those cosmic substances—from the localizations of which the body-Kesdjan of a being arises-have their place of concentration.

> "And only there, at the end of a certain time, does the principle and final sacred Rascooarno occur to this two-natured arising, after which such a 'higher being-part' indeed becomes an independent individual with its own individual Reason." (p. 765)

The first Rascooarno is the separation of both higher being-bodies from the planetary body. These then rise to that 'sphere' corresponding to their own nature—or their center of gravity of being. The higher being-bodies thus rise into the atmospheres of the planet, which provide the medium in which the radiations of the Sun and planets most easily convey their influences.

Beelzebub explains this subtle process involving the Kesdjan body in afterlife states:

> "And so, in consequence of the fact that the body Kesdjan of the being is coated with those substances which in their totality make this cosmic formation much lighter than that mass of cosmic substances which surrounds the planets and is called the planetary atmosphere, then as soon as the body Kesdjan of the being is separated from the planetary body of the being (i.e., at death), it at once rises according to the cosmic law called 'Tenikdoa,' or as it is sometimes called the 'law of gravity,' to that sphere in which it finds the weight proper to it equally balanced and which is therefore the corresponding place of such cosmic arisings ..." (p. 728)

The Kesdjan body rises according to the 'law of gravity' to that sphere where *"it finds the weight proper to it equally balanced."* This broadens the familiar concept of gravity, as a force between material masses, to the concept of different substances having their own 'centers-of-gravity' –a place or realm to which they are naturally drawn, or to which they gravitate. The atmospheres are described as providing the ideal medium for planetary and solar emanations, radiations and influences; and the Kesdjan body is sustained by the second being-food, air, which contains the substances required for coating and maintaining it.

The Kesdjan, after the first sacred Rascooarno, rises into upper levels of the atmosphere or into other concentrations as related to the planetary sphere. An individual who has crystallized the Kesdjan body is thus granted further existence beyond the death of the material planetary body, although this existence is also time bound. Beelzebub explains that the body Kesdjan *"can exist in space only for a limited period, namely, only until the completion of the appointed movement of that planet, on which the given being had arisen, around its sun."* (p. 729)[28] This suggests that the Kesdjan body persists for only a year.

The Kesdjan body cannot exist long before it also decomposes and this is the second Rascooarno. As this time approaches, if the highest being body has not reached the required degree of Reason and is still dependent upon a Kesdjan body, it will search for a similar Kesdjan body to inhabit, in order to continue to exist for its further self-perfection. This *"Okipkhalevnian-exchange-of-the-external-part-of-the-soul"* or the *"exchange of the former being-body-Kesdjan"* is a process whereby incomplete beings maintain their existence through the second Rascooarno. Beelzebub comments on this strange phenomenon:

> "Here, you might as well be told that your favourites also have, as it were, a similar representation about the 'Okipkhalevian exchange' and they have even invented a very clever name for it, namely, 'metempsychosis' or 'reincarnation' ... According to this fantastic branch of this theory of their 'science,' now called spiritualism, they suppose among other things that each of them already has a higher being-part or, as they call it, a soul, and that a transmigration must be occurring the whole time to this soul, i.e., something of the kind of this same 'Okipkhalevnian exchange' ... those fantastic souls of theirs, (are) only the fruits of their idle fancy ... nothing else but ... 'twaddle.'" (pp. 767-8)

---

[28] Gurdjieff describes various processes by which individuals who have attained more advanced levels of the crystallization of their Kesdjan body can help to "materialize" the Kesdjan body of another being who has died, so that for a certain time period, the second individual is able to manifest some of the functions proper to the physical body. Mr. G. and Beelzebub describe how people might maintain a connection to an evolved teacher through having established a connection with his or her Handbledzoin (the blood of the astral body). In Beelzebub's Tales, "the sacred Almznoshinoo" is described in reference to the last supper of Christ, where the sharing of the body and blood of Christ with the disciples establishes a link between them which persists beyond physical death.

This strange process described by Beelzebub involves an individual inhabiting the Kesdjan body of another being in order to continue their existence—still within the sphere of the radiations of the sun and planets.

Beelzebub's descriptions of afterlife possibilities and phenomena of the okipkhalevnian exchange of the external part of the soul, of reincarnation and recurrence, are difficult to understand and elaborate, and raise many questions and issues. Such processes simply cannot be explained in words, "to slugs," who take the ephemeral for the real and imagine that they already know Mr. God himself with his comb in his vest pocket or sitting on his throne. Gurdjieff, in Ouspensky (1949), describes *"something like what people consider 'reincarnation' and 'recurrence'"* as occurring—particularly involving individuals with crystallized higher being-bodies returning to material existence.

Beelzebub explains that if the highest being-body has been formed but has not attained the required degree of reason and self-perfection required to return to the Sun Absolute, it will continue to live throughout the life of the solar system and will not decompose:

> "... the higher being-body itself, being formed of crystallizations received directly from the sacred Theomertmalogos into the solar system within the limits of which the being arises and where his existence proceeds, can never decompose; and this 'higher part' must exist in the given solar system as long as it does not perfect itself to the required Reason." (p. 768)

The highest being body is formed from the Emanations of the Sun Absolute, the Theomertmalogos or Word God, and is *immortal within the limits of the solar system*.

6b. 'Choot-God-litanical period'

Originally, the higher-being-bodies which evolved on various planets would pass through the Sacred Rascooarnos and blend again with the Most Holy Sun Absolute. However, this was all before *"that all-universal calamity, which we call the 'Choot-God-litanical period' occurred in our Great Universe ...."* This universal calamity made it so that the higher being-bodies which later arose *"cease to have the possibility of blending directly with our Most Most Holy Sun Absolute."* (p. 745) This obviously produced a major change for the higher being-bodies who arose after this period.

Beelzebub explains how this unfortunately condition came about. When the original beings attained their higher-being-bodies, their own law of Triamazikamno was established and they begin to "emanate" similarly to the Sun Absolute–although in miniature. However, when many of these Sacred Individuals had assembled on the Sun Absolute, then between their emanations and the atmospheres of the Sun Absolute, a *"Geneotriamazikamnian contact"* was established. This caused the emanations of the Sun Absolute to *"issue changed,"* partly contaminated through elements within these new sources of emanation, which were not as pure as the original Emanations. This effected the harmonious movement of the existing solar systems, *"the inner functioning of certain of their planets,"* and the purity of the higher being-bodies which later arose. (p. 798)

Beelzebub explains how this all happened:

> "This Geneotriamazikamnian contact occurred because, in the atmosphere itself of the Most Most Holy Sun Absolute, various-sourced unusual vibrations began, as I have already said, to issue from these higher-being-bodies and to unite with the emanations of the Most Most Holy Sun Absolute, and together with them also to penetrate everywhere in the Megalocosmos and to reach even to those planets on which higher being-bodies were continuing to arise in beings; and these unusual vibrations began to be transformed and crystallized together with the sacred Theomertmalogos and to take part in the coating of the 'higher-parts' in the beings. (p. 799)

After the Choot-God-litanical period, the higher being-bodies which subsequently arose had *"certain manifestations"* assimilated into them, which Beelzebub describes as related to *"sins-of-the-body-of-the-soul."* Thus, even those *"'independent-cosmic Sacred Individuals' perfected in Reason"* had lost the opportunity to be worthy enough to blend again with the Holy Sun Absolute. Thus, a fundamental change occurred in cosmic conditions for later three-brained beings.

6c. The Holy Planet "Purgatory"

> "Here, it is interesting to notice, that almost all three-brained beings arising on all the various planets of our Great Megalocosmos either know of or instinctively sense the holy planet Purgatory; it is only the three-brained beings arising on your planet who do not know of it ...." (p. 801)

> "... this same holy planet, which is called Purgatory, is for the whole of our Great Universe, as it were, the heart and place of concentration of all the completing results of the pulsation of everything that functions and exists in the Universe." (p. 745)

Beelzebub explains to Hassein that the holy planet Purgatory is the place where those unfortunate 'higher-being-bodies' reside who obtained their coating on various planets of the Great Universe, but who are no longer able to return directly to the Most Holy Sun Absolute.

The planet Purgatory was not created with its current function at the beginning of time along with the formation of the Megalocosmos and all the other cosmoses. It was after the calamity of the Choot-God-litanical period, that the necessity arose for such a planet to actualize the type of *"general-universal functioning"* which Purgatory now actualizes.

Beelzebub describes Purgatory as a remarkable planet—*"the best, richest, and most beautiful of all the planets of the Universe."* He describes springs of pure natural water, the most beautiful and best songbirds, in fact, *"almost the whole 'flora,' 'fauna,' and foscalia' from all the planets of our Great Universe."* (p. 746) Its atmospheres are pure like crystal and have a turquoise radiance. Beelzebub explains that the beings there sense everything external 'Iskoloonizinernly'–or *'blissfully-delightfully.'* Recall that the planet is the center for *"the concentration for the concentration of the results of the functioning of all that exists,"* and thus has the finest of all worlds.

The higher-being-bodies which exist there dwell in natural caves where there are no reasons for any *"essence-anxiety,"* in conditions both blissful and tranquil. These higher-being-bodies, through their own merits, have been deemed worth to come to the Holy planet Purgatory for their continued existence. Unfortunately, these beings *"suffer, maybe, as much as anybody in the whole of our Great Universe."* (p. 745) Although Purgatory is described, on one hand as a paradise, on the other hand, it is described as a "hell." Hell is the inner state experienced by the higher being-bodies dwelling there, who understand the reality of everything existing and are able to perceive the Common Father who is so near, but who are yet unable to blend again with the Most Holy Sun Absolute. Thus, these higher being-bodies experience *"constant anguish, grief and oppression."* (p. 804) This is because they have lost the possibility of again blending with the presence of the Most Holy Sun Absolute.

6d. The Fate of Hasnamuss-Individuals

The prospects for Hasnamuss individuals in afterlife states are not too promising. Recall that according to Beelzebub, Hasnamuss individuals are those who have not crystallized the Divine impulse of Objective Conscience. Further, they are subject to the seven *"Naloo-osnian-spectrum-of-impulses,"* which include such impulses as towards *"every kind of depravity,"* *"irresistible inclinations to destroy the existence of other breathing creatures,"* the *"feelings of self-satisfaction from leading others astray,"* and so on. (p. 406) Their pathological manifestations cause all kinds of grief and suffering for others and eventually the Hasnamusses will face what Beelzebub calls *"serious-retributive-suffering-consequences."* Some of these individuals consist of only a planetary body but others have at least partially coated the higher being-bodies.

Beelzebub distinguishes four types of Hasnamuss individuals and outlines their afterlife fates. All four types experience afterlife states as determined by the actual nature of their actions and their consequences and the responsibilities pre-established for these being. Beelzebub explains:

> "For these four kinds of Hasnamuss-individuals ... the mentioned retributive-suffering-consequences are various and correspond both to the nature of each kind as well as to what is called 'objective-responsibilities' ensuing from the primordial providence and hopes and expectations of our COMMON FATHER concerning these cosmic actualizations." (p. 407)

The first type is a person who consists of only a planetary body and has formed neither a Kesdjan body nor the highest being-body. During the Sacred Rascooarno, he will be *"destroyed forever such as he is."* (p. 406) His planetary body will devolve into its elements and return to the Earth and subtle vital energies, the Askokin vibrations, will feed the Moon.

Beelzebub explains that when this being dies, all of his impulses and sensations do not die at once, or simultaneously. Instead, he dies by thirds. Firstly, *"one of his brains"* or of the *"independent spiritualized 'locations'"* will die, then the second and third. One by one, the independent brains *"cease to participate in his common presence."*

Beelzebub also notes that after the final death, the *"disintegration-of-all-the-active-elements"* of the planetary body proceeds much more slowly than usual. As this occurs, there is an ongoing *"inextinguishable action ... of the mentioned 'sensed-impulses' he had during life."* This suggests a gradual repetition of impulses and sensations within the disintegrating psyche through the processes of death and the dissolution of the brains.

The second type of Hasnamuss-individual has formed a Kesdjan body, which has the property of *"Toorinoorino"*–defined as *"nondecomposition in any sphere of that planet on which he arose."* This type *"has to exist, by being formed again and again in a certain way,"* in order to eradicate a certain 'something' from his psyche and to continue to strive for self-perfection. He is unable to perfect himself without a planetary body and so he must be coated again and again in planetary bodies, even taking the forms of one and two-brained beings. This process will proceed until the Hasnamuss qualities have been eliminated from him. Beelzebub states: *"... he must constantly begin all over again in the form of another being of the planet ...."* (p. 409)

The third type has acquired a third being-body, which for Beelzebub, is what it means to have attained a soul. This is evident in his description:

> "The third kind of Hasnamuss-individual is the highest being-body or soul, during the coating of which is the common presence of a three-brained being this something arises and participates, but he also acquires the property of Toorinoorino, but this time proper to this highest being-body; that is to say, this arising is no longer subject to decomposition not only in the spheres of that planet on which he had his arising, but also in all other spheres of the Great Universe." (p. 407)

The "something" which participates in the arising of the third being-body or soul, is the undesirable properties and qualities formed in the Hasnamuss individual. This being has attained a *"degree-of-cognition-of-one's-own-individuality,"* but is unable to evolve further until *"a certain something is entirely eradicated from his common presence."* This being is not subject to decomposition during the existence of the Great Universe.

Beelzebub explains that compared with the second type, *"the matter is still more terrible"* for the third type. This is because this type *"according to the foreseeing FIRST-SOURCED-PRINCIPLE-OF-EVERYTHING-EXISTING was predetermined to serve the aim of helping the government of the whole increasing World ...,"* and had a certain responsibility for his manifestations. (p. 409) The certain 'something,' the Hassnamus tendencies, can now only be eliminated as a result of *"intentionally actualized Partkdolg-duty"*–of conscious labours and intentional suffering. However, the third type of individual *"never loses the possibility of freeing himself"* from that *"certain 'something,'"* which participated in the formation and coating of the third being-body.

Beelzebub states that certain HIGHER-SACRED-INDIVIDUALS have allotted three planets of the Universe, in remote corners, as a place for the *"suffering existence"* of this higher order of Hasnamuss-individuals. These planets exist under the names of 'Remorse-of-conscience,' 'Repentance' and 'Self-Reproach.' The Hasnamuss individual, Lentrohamsanin who spread his false doctrines and is described as *"the chief culprit in the destruction of all the very saintly labors of Ashiata Shiemash,"* is one of the few inhabitants of the planet 'Retribution.'

The fourth type is the *"Eternal-Hasnamuss-individual."* This individual faces varied *"retributive-suffering-consequences"*–without chance of attaining real I or of blending again with the Most Holy Sun Absolute. Whereas the third type of Hasnamuss individual can at least still possibly be *"cleansed from this something,"* those undesirable qualities, the fourth type has lost such possibilities forever. As a special place for the continued, eternal existence of the fourth type, the higher Sacred Individuals allotted the planet *"Eternal-Retribution."* Beelzebub depicts their eternal state:

> "The chief torture of the state of these 'highest being-bodies' is that they must always experience these terrifying sufferings fully conscious of the utter hopelessness of their cessation." (p. 410)

Certainly, this is a dismal fate with no end in sight until the dissolution of the Great Universe.

Beelzebub provides remarkable teachings about the subtle afterlife possibilities for the four types of Hasnamusses–from dying by thirds, to repeated material lives even in the forms of one and two-brained beings, to Eternal Retribution or suffering without cessation!

7. Gradients of being-Reason, Objective or Divine Reason

Beelzebub elaborates in varied ways throughout the *Tales* upon the different kinds and degrees of Reason that beings can attain. He introduces complex terms to depict these levels of reason and the processes of their attainment. The three-brained beings on planet Earth are potentially capable of attaining high degrees of Objective or Divine Reason. In fact, this was part of the original Divine Plan, that the *'three-in-one'* beings could coat their own higher being-bodies and have the data crystallized within them as required for higher levels of Reason. They could then assume roles in the maintenance of the growing Megalocosmos—like brain cells within the Mind of God. Alternatively, they might blend again with the Most Most Holy Sun Absolute.

In general, Beelzebub explains that the sacred *'Determinator-of-Reason'* concerns *'the-totality-of-self-awareness'* of the being. This is further related to the *'degree-of-justification-of-the-sense-and-aim-of-their-existence,'* and to the role they might assume *"in relation to everything existing in our great Megalocosmos."* (p. 769)

Beelzebub outlines three basic forms of *"being-mentation,"* or gradients of reason:

> "In every three-brained being in general, irrespective of the place of his arising and the form of his exterior coating, there can be crystallized data for three independent kinds of being-mentation, the totality of the engendered results of which expresses the gradation of his Reason. The first highest kind of being-Reason is the 'pure' or objective Reason which is proper only to the presences of a higher being-body or to the common presences of those three-brained beings in whom this higher part has already arisen and perfected itself, and then only when it is the, what is called, 'center-of-gravity-initiator-of-the-individual-functioning' of the whole presence of the being. The second being-Reason, which is named 'Okiartaaitokhsa,' can be in the presences of those three-brained beings, in whom their second-being-body-Kesdjan is already completely coated and functions independently. As regards the third kind of being-Reason, this is nothing else but only the action of the automatic functioning which proceeds in the common presences of all surplanetary definite formations, thanks to repeated shocks coming from outside, which evoke habitual reactions from the data crystallized in them corresponding to previously accidentally perceived impressions. (pp.769-70)

These three levels of being-reason depend upon what bodies—whether the planetary, Kesdjan or highest being body—are formed and coated, and can function independently. Beelzebub explains that it is *"the totality-of-self-awareness,"* which determines the degree of reason and this self-awareness can exist in relationship to the substances of all three bodies.

The lowest level of being-Reason—that of automatic functioning—is characteristic of the slugs, the pathological three brained-beings on planet Earth. They have become totally mechanized in their being, conditioned and controlled by everything around them, and the chance circumstances of their lives. They are controlled by "repeated shocks" from outside and the habits structures which these form within the planetary body, and they continually waste their sacred sexual substances.

The second degree of being-reason requires the crystallization of the Kesdjan body. However, this Kesdjan body has to be able to function completely independently of the planetary body in order to attain the 'Okiartaaitokhsa' level of reason. Although some individuals may have a Kesdjan body partially formed and coated, and interpenetrating their planetary body, they are not as likely to have crystallized this body to the extent to which they can function apart from the planetary body.

The third degree of reason is the 'pure' or "objective Reason" and this is only present with the completion of the highest being-body. Further, this body must be the individual's *"center-of-gravity-initiator-of-the-individual-functioning of the whole of the being."* In a sense, real "I" has been attained. Elsewhere, Beelzebub describes how this objective Reason can involve a state called 'Irankipaekh,' which he defines:

> "... such formations of the mentioned Most Most Sacred substances as can exist and be independent of Kesdjanian arisings and at the same time not be subject to what are called 'painful' influences from any external cosmic factors whatsoever." (p. 768)

Just as the attainment of the second degree of Reason, Okiartaaitokhsa, involves independence of the planetary body, so also, the third degree of Reason can exist independently of the Kesdjan body.

Beelzebub provides a fascinating description of what higher gradients of Objective Reason involve, when he describes what beings are considered "learned" elsewhere in the Universe, under normal conditions of being-existence. These are those who:

> "... acquire by their conscious labors and intentional sufferings the ability to contemplate the details of all that exists from the point of view of World-arising and World-existence, owing chiefly to which, they perfect their highest body to the corresponding gradation of the sacred measure of Objective Reason in order that they might later sense as much about cosmic truths as their higher being-body is perfected." (p. 322)

Imagine this! That we as human beings might be able to actually *"sense cosmic truths"* and *"contemplate the details of all that exist."* Further, these faculties might be developed to the degree that the higher being-bodies is fully perfected! These are astonishing possibilities. Beelzebub notes that this is a very different situation from that existent on planet Earth, where among contemporary beings, the men-beings considered "learned" are those who *"'learned-by-rote' as much vacuous information, such as old women love to relate about what was presumably said in olden times."* (p. 323) There is a world of difference between the automatic being functioning of a slug and the ultra-fantastic possibilities of such Sacred Individuals with objective Reason.

Beelzebub provides an interesting description of the teaching of Ashiata Shiemash, which illustrates how higher levels of being-reason might be able to dispel the illusions characteristic of the lowest level of automated being-reason:

> "... and he began enlightening their Reason by means of objectively true information, and guiding their being-impulses in such a way that they could sense these truths without the participation either of the abnormally crystallized factors already within their presences, or of the factors which might newly arise from the results of the external perceptions they obtained from the abnormally established form of ordinary being-existence." (pp. 367-368)

Just as Ashiata Shiemash enlightened the brothers of the order which he established, so also Gurdjieff, through the personage of Beelzebub, is attempting to enlighten the reader of *The Tales*. Gurdjieff is providing *"objectively true information"* which can allow one to *"sense these truths,"* while bypassing the usual crystallized patterns of the false consciousness system. However, just as the sacred being-impulses have atrophied in the three brained-beings on planet Earth, so also has their *"being-function called 'instinctually-to-sense-cosmic-truths'"* (p. 334)

In addition to these three degrees of Reason, Beelzebub also mentions the *"total absence of any Reason ... absolute 'firm-calm,'"* and, that Reason of our INCOMPARABLE CREATOR ENDLESSNESS, which he labels Absolute Reason. Certainly, this is quite a scale of levels of Reason—from absolute firm-calm, through automated consciousness, to the faculties of the higher being-bodies and then to Absolute Reason.

These are fascinating possibilities and even human beings can attain such higher levels of Reason. Beelzebub explains:

> "... always and up to the present time, at the arising and the beginning of the formation of each one of them, there is always in their presence the germs of all possibilities for the crystallization, during their completing formation into responsible beings, of corresponding being-data, which later during responsible existence could serve for the engendering and functioning of objective Reason, which should be in the common presences of three-brained beings of all natures and of all external forms, and which, in itself, is nothing else but, so to say, the 'representative-of-the-Very-Essence-of-Divinity.'" (p. 815)

Unfortunately, because of the abnormal forms of being-existence established on Earth and the maleficent so-called 'Education,' these higher possibilities for objective Reason are seldom realized. Oh yes, Beelzebub does mention one other type of reason—the *'bobtailed reason,'* so characteristic of humankind.

If fact, the process of obtaining and perfecting Objective Reason is given a special name by Beelzebub—the sacred 'Antkooano.' This sacred process was *"intentionally actualized"* by the COMMON ENDLESS FATHER in order that the three-in-ones might attain Objective or Divine Reason. Normally, this process occurs naturally simply from the *"flow of time"* and from the individual's conscious labors and intentional suffering—fulfilling their being-Partkdolg-duty. However, conditions of normal being-existence are also required. Beelzebub explains:

> "This sacred Antkooano can proceed only in those planets upon which in general all cosmic truths have become known to all the beings.
>
> "And all cosmic truths usually become known to all on these planets, thanks to the fact that the beings of the given planet who by their conscious labors learn some truth or other share it with other beings of their planet, and in this way all the cosmic truths gradually become known by all the beings of the given planet without any distinction." (p. 563)

On Earth, such cosmic truths are not currently known, although they were during the time of Atlantis and afterward within the Akhaldan society in ancient Egypt. However, the abnormal conditions of being-existence established on the Earth and the distortions of the teachings of Sacred Individuals sent from Above during the course of human history, led humans to take *"the 'ephemeral' for the Real"* and to perceive every new impression without being-Partkdolg-duty. Humans thus came to *"believe everything anybody says, and not solely that which they themselves have been able to recognize by their own sane deliberation."* (p. 103) Modern education is so destructive, as it fills the being-centers with so many *"artificial perceptions"* learned by rote.

At different times, Beelzebub uses different terms to define various levels of Objective or Divine Reason and individual attainment. One account occurs at the end of *The Tales*, when Beelzebub is being recognized for his meritorious behaviour and he has his horns restored. Recall that during his exile to the remote solar system Ors, Beelzebub had lost his horns and thus was able to pass among the men-beings without being noticed. However, at the end of *The Tales*, Beelzebub has received a pardon *"granted from Above,"* for his conscious labours and intentional suffering during the period of his banishment. At a sacred ceremony, Beelzebub has his horns restored:

> "As the virility and degree of Reason of beings of your nature are defined and manifested by the horns on your head, we must ... restore the horns lost by Beelzebub. ... During the solemn, sacred action, horns little by little began to grow upon the head of Beelzebub. ... everybody was agitated by the wish to learn how many forks would make their appearance on Beelzebub, since by their number the gradient of Reason to which Beelzebub had attained according to the sacred measure of Reason would be defined." (p. 1176)

First one fork appeared, then a second and third. A fourth fork appeared signifying that Beelzebub had attained the level of Reason corresponding to *"the sacred Ternoonald,"* and lastly a fifth, indicating that he had attained to the level of *"the sacred Podkoolad."*

At this point, all of the attendant beings and even an archangel prostrated themselves before Beelzebub—as such a degree of reason is very rarely attained in the Universe. This degree is the last gradation before the Reason of the sacred Anklad, the highest to which any being might attain, only the third in degree from Absolute Reason of "HIS ENDLESSNESS HIMSELF." Beelzebub had indeed *"become worthy with his essence to be one of the very rare Sacred Individuals of the whole of our Great Universe."* (p. 1178)

And further, the reader of *The Tales* is thus privileged to have had such a fine teacher as Beelzebub, who attained such a high level of objective or Divine Reason. Beelzebub has provided the essential teachings of Objective Science, an esoteric science of the soul, and an objectively impartial critique of the life of humankind. *The Tales* indeed are intended to enable the growth of Reason within those three-brained beings who fulfill their own being-Partkdolg-duty in actively deliberating its teachings.

8. Striving for Self-Perfection

> "When the abnormal conditions of ordinary being-existence were finally fixed there—in consequence of which there disappeared from their essence both the instinctive and the intentional striving for perfecting—there not only disappeared in them the need of conscious absorption of cosmic substances, but even also the very knowledge and understanding of the existence and significance of higher being-foods." (p. 782)

Throughout *The Tales*, Beelzebub provides numerous discussions relevant to the theme of striving towards one's self-perfection. Two of the five *'being-obligolnian-strivings'* outlined by Beelzebub are related to such strivings. This includes the second—*"to have a constant and unflagging instinctive need for self-perfection in the sense of being"* and the fifth—*"the striving always to assist the most rapid perfecting of other beings ... up to the degree of self-individuality."* (p.386) Beelzebub's complex teachings constitute an esoteric science of the soul—a framework for understanding what might be attained through such striving towards self-perfection and what this 'striving' entails.

The objective of the striving is to aid in the formation and coating of the higher being-bodies—thereby acquiring a soul and crystallizing the necessary data to obtain objective Reason. Further, from Beelzebub's discussions of afterlife processes, it is apparent that one's afterlife fate reflects the same tendencies and imperfections which we acquire through our life, and so the striving certainly must begin now if we are to have future opportunities before the sacred Rascooarnos take their toll. An individual faces different forms of remorse of conscience, self-reproach, suffering and retribution within afterlife conditions, or even eternally suffering with no chance of self-perfection. However, in afterlife conditions, the striving towards self-perfection persists, even if one is embodied again in different life forms. The importance of the striving towards self-perfection, in terms of being, is a fundamental teaching of the whole of Beelzebub's marvellous *Tales*.

Of course, there are many other ideas and practices presented within *The Tales* which can aid the sincere individual in such striving. This includes the profound teachings about the sacred being-impulses—of hope, faith and love—and the importance of awakening conscience; as concerns the struggles between the needs of the planetary body and those of the higher being-bodies—or between the 'desires' and 'non-desires;' teachings concerning the horror of the situation of humankind in their automated states of consciousness; and the teaching concerning the importance of remembering the inevitability of one's own death. At the very end of his tales to his grandson, Beelzebub explains this route of escape for "your favorites:"

> "The sole means now for the saving of the beings of the planet Earth would be to implant again into their presences a new organ, an organ like Kundabuffer, but this time of such properties that every one of these unfortunates during the process of existence should constantly sense and be cognizant of the inevitability of his own death as well as of the death of everyone upon whom his eyes or attention rests.
>
> "Only such a sensation and such a cognizance can now destroy the egoism completely crystallized in them that has swallowed up the whole of their Essence and also that tendency to hate others which flows from it ..." (p.1183)

Humankind need such an organ which would break down the 'egoism' crystallized in their presences and reveal the insignificance of *"all his favourite things."* The striving towards self-perfection is enabled by such a remembrance of death and by efforts to overcome such a dreadful 'egoism' as is common the slugs. Imagine this, that they, those strange slugs, would have such a tendency *"to hate others"* within their presences, while the sacred being-impulses have passed into their so-called 'unconscious.' Beelzebub explains that our *'spiritual parts'* have indeed passed into the unconscious, which should normally be the consciousness of a three-brained being. All of Beelzebub's profound teachings serve to awaken the individual to the realities of life and self.

However, in terms of striving towards self-perfection and the alchemical processes of the formation of the higher being-bodies, *Beelzebub's Tales* emphasis the importance of fulfilling one's being-Partkdolg-duty, perhaps more than any other factor. We must make a final attempt to understand the psycho-spiritual and metaphysical processes which Beelzebub explains as pertain to the being-Partkdolg-duty and its effects within the subtle dimensions of one's being. There are profound ideas here which are simply not easy to explicate or understand. This subject has to be approached from different angles within one's life.

Recall that in the refinement of first being-food substances, the completion of the process produces Exioehary, or being-Resulzarion, the seventh class of substances. These substances correspond in their vibrations with the last Stopinder of the 'being-Heptaparaparshinokh.' However, in order for these substances to be transformed and acquire a "vivifyingness" corresponding to the next higher order of substances, this last interval of the being-Heptaparaparshinokh must be breached. This interval is that which Beelzebub labels the *"intentionally-actualized-Mdnel-In."* This is a critical process in the formation and crystallization of the Kesdjan and higher being-bodies. It is exactly to fill this interval, that the necessity arises to perform one's being-Partkdolg-duties–of 'conscious labors' and 'intentional suffering.' Beelzebub states: *"these factors until now serve as the sole possible means for the assimilation of the cosmic substances required for the coating and perfecting of the higher being-bodies ...."* (p. 792)

Beelzebub elaborates other important dynamics related to the effects of conscious labors and intentional suffering on the processes of coating the higher-being-bodies. In particular, Beelzebub recounts his conversation with an Archangel Looisos, when it was explained to him that the Sacred Askokin vibrations as required for the maintenance of the moons, now exists *"in general in the Universe chiefly blended with the sacred substances 'Abrustdonis" and 'Helkdonis.'"* (p. 1106) These other sacred substances are in fact just those substances by which the higher being-bodies are formed and perfected. The Abrustdonis is required for the Kesdjan body and the Helkonis for the highest being-body. And how are these three elements separated? Once again, this requires being-partkdolg-duty.

Beelzebub emphasis the role that 'active mentation,' as part of the being-Partkdolg-duty, plays in this process of absorbing sacred substances for the formation of the higher being-bodies. In one instance, Beelzebub explains to Hassein, that his *Tales* and expositions are being recounted *"in order that from active mentation the proper elaborations in you of the sacred substances of Abrustonis and Helkdonis for the purpose of coating and perfecting both of your higher being-parts should proceed more intensively."* (p. 1166)[29] The being-partkdolg-duty involves a state of presence maintained through

---

[29] Recall that one of the principles causes of "war," or the horrific "process of reciprocal destruction," was that humans no longer strove to fulfill their being-Partkdolg-duty; and thus the Sacred Askokin was not being naturally released. Great Nature then has to extract this substance by other means.

'active mentation,' self-remembering and conscious labor. When one is in such a state, even the dynamics of the Triamazikamno forces proceed quite different.

Recall that the prime source substance of the Omnipresent-Okidanokh obtains its arising from the three aspects of the Emanation of the Sun Absolute and that these three forces are localized in the three being-brains. This is why we have the possibility of attaining self-perfection. Beelzebub explains the implication of this:

> "Just in this is the point, that the beings having this three-brained system can, by the conscious and intentional fulfilling of being-Partkdolg-duty, utilize from this process of Djartkom in the Omnipresent-Okidanokh, its three holy forces for their own presences and bring their presences to what is called the 'Sekronoolanzaknian-state'; that is to say, they can become such individuals as have their own sacred law of Triamazikamno and thereby the possibility of consciously taking in and coating in their common presence all that 'Holy' which, incidentally, also aids the actualizing of the functioning in these cosmic units of Objective or Divine Reason." (p. 145)

It is upon acquiring one's own sacred law of Triamazikamno that one begins to 'emanate' like the Holy Sun Absolute—although in miniature.

However, for this to be brought about, a certain state has to be achieved. This is described in a passage where Beelzebub explains the difference between the Reason-of-knowing and the Reason-of-understanding. Recall that the *'Reason of knowing,'* common among your favorites and their *'sorry scientists,'* involves the rote memorization or absorption of ideas or information from outside of oneself. Such 'knowledge' is "only a temporary part of the being" and not dependent upon active being mentation. It has to be repeated or 'refreshed' or else, it will *"entirely, so to say, 'evaporate' out of the common presence of the three-brained being."* (p. 1167) Beelzebub describes the Triamazikamno process involved in the Reason-of-knowing: *"the formerly perceived contradictory impressions crystallized in any one of the three localizations ... serve as the affirming and denying factors and the new impressions proceeding from without serve in this case as the third factor."* (p. 1167)

In contrast, the formation of the Reason-of-understanding requires *"being-contemplation of the totality of formerly perceived information,"* active deliberation and *"cognizance by the whole of their being."* The results of such a process become *"forever a part of his essence."* This state for the reception of impressions is a critical aspect of being-partkdolg-duty. Beelzebub then explains the flow of forces required for the development of the Reason-of-understanding. In this case:

> "... the first, that is the 'sacred-affirming,' is the newly perceived impressions of any localization which has at the given moment what is called 'the-center-of-gravity-functioning'; the second or 'sacred-denying' is the corresponding data present in another of his localizations; and the third factor is what is called the being-Autokolizikners,' or as they otherwise call it 'Hoodazbabognari,' the sense of which names signifies, 'the results of the persevering actualizing of the striving towards the manifestation of one's own individuality.'

> "By the way, you might as well hear still once more even if you do know it, that the said being-Autokolizikners are formed in the presences of three-brained beings in

general in all three localizations exclusively only from the results of the actualization of 'being-Partkdolg-duty,' that is to say, thanks to those factors which, from the very beginning of the arising of the three-brained beings, our UNIBEING COMMON FATHER designed to be the means for self-perfection." (pp. 1167-8)

This is a certainly a complex passage. For the formation of reason-of-understanding, the impressions are now the active force instead of embodying the neutralizing force. The denying force involves corresponding data in another center, while the reconciling force is provided by these strange 'being-Autokolizikners.' These are dependent upon *'the results of the persevering actualizing of the striving towards the manifestation of one's own individuality.'* Once again, these 'being-Autokolizikners' are only formed as a result of efforts to fulfill one's being-Partkdolg-duties and this special state is required for the development of the Reason of understanding, or Objective Reason.

In fact, the whole of Beelzebub's exposition and stories are intended to have just such effects upon the reader; destroying all the rubbish accumulated as artificial impressions and forcing a state of active deliberation and the striving towards the manifestation of one's individuality. The difficulty of the materials, the strange and awkward language introduced, and the manner in which cosmic secrets are interblended with comic humour, all force the reader to actively mentate and to transsubstantiate in their own being the significant principles of objective science being offered. Beelzebub does not offer new age pabulum, easy to digest and memorize, all in the *'bon ton'* language, but an understanding that requires conscious efforts and labors on the part of the reader in order to grasp the pearls of ancient wisdom.

The contents of *Beelzebub's Tales* are also most relevant to another of the five being-obligations: the third—*"the conscious striving to know ever more and more concerning the laws of World-creation and World-maintenance."* Beelzebub's descriptions of the fundamental sacred and primordial laws, the processes of creation, the alchemical process of the coating of the higher being-bodies, and so much more, are all part of such a study. He offers an 'Objective Science' and an esoteric science of the soul, which cannot simply be 'known' in the usual way, as three brained-beings are used to assimilating information and learning by rote. To understand such principles forces active deliberation, a state or degree of Self-Remembering requiring *"a cognizance by the whole of one's being,"* and a *'persevering actualizing of the striving towards the manifestation of one's own individuality.'*

One practical route to self-perfection is the reading, rereading and study of *Beelzebub's Tales*—a book that soars above anything produced by the *'sorry scientists,'* but which requires a whole new form of reason, that of understanding and eventually of Divine Reason. Fulfilling one's being-Partkdolg-duty, living in accord with one's *'being-obligolnian-strivings,'* striving to instinctually sense reality, experiencing the sacred being-impulses, consciously absorbing the three being-foods, remembering death, and the study of the Sacred Laws— can all contribute to this: That a three brained-being on planet Earth, such as those whom Hassein dared to call "slugs," might indeed become *"immortal within the limits of solar system,"* or *"within the limits of the Great Universe,"* or even unite again with the Most, Most Holy Sun Absolute.

Beelzebub offers a view of all and everything, which exposes all the rubbish accumulated through the ages in human mention, and which indicates a route towards one's own self-perfection–in terms of being. Unfortunately, Beelzebub explains the sorry state of humankind, where: *"... every kind of what your favorites call 'knowledge' ... has absolutely nothing in common with what is called 'Objective*

Knowledge.'" (p. 1169) Of course, the slugs can still serve higher cosmic purposes and blend again with the Most Holy Sun Absolute, although it may take a long time. Beelzebub's portrayals of the sad state of humankind and the possibilities of self-perfection and higher attainments are as inspiring as they are horrifying.

"To destroy, mercilessly, without any compromises whatsoever, in the mentation and feelings of the reader, the beliefs and views, by centuries rooted in him, about everything existing in the world."

Objective of the First Series - 1950 -

Gurdjieff

V /
"A Particle of All that Exists"

1. A Particle of All that Exists

Beelzebub's Tales to His Grandson is undoubtedly one of the most profound and mysterious books among the sacred literature of the world. The framework of ideas, claims and objective science offers a fundamentally alternative view of the miraculous nature of life–a perfectly coherent, intelligible and astounding account of *"All and Everything."* In the light of *The Tales*, all of modern thought and understanding is so much *'pouring-from-the-empty-into-the-void.'* The *'sorry scientists'* of *'new format'* have no conception of the great inscrutable mysteries of Nature and the subtle inner dimensions of human beings. The materialist science philosophy has led to the dismissal of the human soul and of views of the Cosmos as due to the actualization of Divine Laws or supernatural Beings. Of course, most of the scientists of new formation will dismiss *Beelzebub's Tales* as a work only of myth, allegory and fantasy, and not grasp the secrets of 'objective science' and the deep truths articulated. Of course, like all of the slugs, the sorry scientists and wiseacres are conditioned to take the ephemeral for the real and they no longer instinctually sense cosmic truths, as is natural to three centered beings with three spiritualized independent brains. As a higher type, Mr. Gurdjieff himself attained his horns through it all–his own conscious labours and intentional suffering.

Imagine that, human beings are potentially similitudes of the whole, particles of the Great Universe. In this way, everything is some Divine Fraction, a law conformable portion of the whole. Behind essence is real I, behind real I, is God, or at least the Most Most Holy Sun Absolute. Beelzebub provides strange and provocative tales for his grandson Hassein about the hidden dimensions of those strange three-brained beings on planet Earth, the principles of esoteric science, and the meaning and purpose of it all for living, breathing creatures.

The notion of a particle is very profound, like that of *"certain definite points,"* used by Beelzebub to describe the effects of the Emanations of the Sun Absolute, acting upon the etherokrilno of empty space to involve into Second-order Suns. Ouspensky recalls Gurdjieff's discussion of dimensions, which is suggestive as to how to conceive the nature of a point:

> "... seven cosmoses related to one another in the ratio of zero to infinity. ... The zero-dimension or the point is a limit. This means that we see something as a point, but we do not know what is concealed behind this point. It may actually be a point, that is, a body having no dimensions and it may also be a whole world, but a world so far removed from us or so small that it appears to us as a point." (1949, p.209)

The relation of "I" to "God" or the "Sun Absolute" is surely the relationship of the zero-dimension to the infinite and it is all tied up in seven dimensions.

The slugs on planet Earth are created and maintained by the same laws of Triamazikamno and Heptaparaparshinokh as embodied within the larger cosmos. This is the basis upon which human beings can perfect their higher being-bodies and assume larger cosmic purposes. Beelzebub explains firstly the triune nature of human beings and then the sevenfold:

> "When each separate 'higher-perfected-being-body' becomes an independent Individual and acquires in itself its own law of Sacred Triamazikamno, it begins to emanate similarly to the Most Most Holy Sun Absolute but in miniature." (p. 798)

> "... through each of them the cosmic substances arising in all seven Stopinders of the Sacred Heptaparaparshinokh could be transformed, and all of them ... besides serving as apparatuses for the Most Great Trogoautoegocrat, could have all possibilities for absorbing from those cosmic substances which are transformed through them what is corresponding for the coating and for the perfecting in each of them of both higher-being bodies; because each three-brained being arisen on this planet of yours represents in himself also, in all respects ... an exact similarity of the whole Megalocosmos ... but of course in miniature ... " (p.775)

At varied times, Beelzebub refers three-brained beings as potentially becoming *"a particle of all that exists;"* (p. 162) as *"a particle though an independent one, of everything existing in the Great Universe;"* (p. 183) and as, *"beings having in their presences every possibility for becoming particles of a part of Divinity ...."* (p. 452)

In the context of describing one of Saint Buddha's teachings, Beelzebub explains this profound secret of human potential:

> "This Most Great Foundation of the All-embracing of everything that exists constantly emanates throughout the whole of the Universe and coats itself from its particles upon planets-in certain three-brained beings who attain in their common presences the capacity to have their own functioning of both fundamental cosmic laws of the sacred Heptaparaparshinokh and the sacred Triamazikamno-into a definite unit in which alone 'Objective Divine Reason' acquires the possibility of becoming concentrated and fixed. ... certain parts of the Great All-embracing, already spiritualised by Divine Reason, return and reblend with the great Prime Source of the All-embracing ..." (pp.244-5)

Beelzebub explains that after Buddha's talk, the people misunderstood his message and began to believe that they already were such *"parts of the Most Great Greatness,"* even without performing any being-Partkdolg duty. They were *"convinced that they were already particles of Mister Prana himself."* (p. 246)

A soul is not given to a human being but must be acquired. Unfortunately, the cosmic catastrophes which occurred to the earth and the miscalculations around the organ Kundabuffer, lead to the emergence of a strange breed on the planet, slugs, who according to Beelzebub are willing to believe any old tale. Humans have missed the mark and do not establish their own inner triangle or sevenfold nature, completing the inner octave to blend again with the Most Holy Sun Absolute or to assume other roles in the larger Cosmos.

However, such independent Sacred Individuals can serve larger cosmic purposes—a role initially conceived also for those three brained-beings on planet Earth. Unfortunately, your favorites ended up—because of various cosmic catastrophes, the organ Kundabuffer, the abnormal conditions of being-existence, the Hasnamusses with their vile impulses, warfare and science —with very strange psyches, living and dying like slugs. Beelzebub provides strange and provocative talks for his grandson Hassein about the *strangeness* and *archcriminal* nature of those three-brained beings—the slugs—on planet Earth.

V / "A Particle of All that Exists"

About the Author
Christopher P. Holmes

Christopher P. Holmes was born in England, on October 7 1949, and raised in Ontario, Canada. He graduated with a B.A. from Carleton University, Ottawa in 1971 and a Ph.D. in clinical psychology from the University of Waterloo in 1978. He taught at York University, Downsview, Ontario over an eleven year period, amidst controversy over his investigations of mystical and spiritual psychology, science and psychic phenomena. He co-founded with Anita Mitra, three centers–the Institute for Mystical and Spiritual Science, Maple, Ontario, the Rainbow Centre in Toronto, and Zero Point in the Ottawa valley. Christopher has also worked for twelve years as a forensic psychologist with young offenders and adults within the Ontario Ministry of Corrections. He currently dedicates himself to furthering the aims of Zero Point-Institute for Mystical and Spiritual Science–currently in Kemptville, Ontario.

Dr. Holmes has studied widely in modern psychology and science, as well as in the mystical and spiritual traditions. In his view, the mainstream of modern thought is seriously misguided in dismissing the spiritual and soul nature of human beings, and in failing to explore the deep roots of human consciousness and the heart. Dr. Holmes explains that a science of soul and spirit must consider the physics, metaphysics and cosmology of consciousness. Most importantly, it involves self study and awakening through the alchemy of psycho-spiritual transformation.

Christopher was introduced to the Gurdjieff teaching while a graduate student in clinical psychology interested in the development of consciousness within psychotherapy and in the broader nature of human psychopathology. His early years of study were focused more on the Ouspensky version of the fourth way teaching, and it was only over the following twenty years that he began to fathom the depths of Gurdjieff's masterpiece *Beelzebub's Tales* and to apply the study of the sacred laws to the findings, theories and philosophy of modern science.

Bibliography

Anderson, M.
The Unknowable Gurdjieff. Weiser, New York, 1962.

Adi Da. (Da Love Ananda, Buddha Free John).
The Knee of Listening: The early-life ordeal and the radical spiritual realization of the divine world teacher.
Dawn Horse Press, California, 1995.

Anonymous.
Guide and Index to G. I. Gurdjieff's Beelzebub's Tales to His Grandson.
Traditional Studies Press, Toronto, 2003.

Asimov, I.
The Subtlest Difference.
In Abell,G. & Singer,B. eds.
Science and the Paranormal.
Scribner's Sons, New York, 1981.

Bennett, J.
Gurdjieff: Making a New World.
Harper & Row, New York, 1978

Commentary on Beelzebub's Tales to his Grandson.
Columbe Press, England. 1977.

Chia, M.
Taoist *Secrets of Love: Cultivating Male Sexual Energy.* Aurora Press, New York, 1984.

Crick, F.
The Astonishing Hypothesis: The Scientific Search for the Soul.
Touchstone Books,London, Great Britain, 1995.

Gurdjieff, G.
All and Everything: Beelzebub's Tales to His Grandson. Routledge & Kegan, London, (1959) 1950.

Cited by Ouspensky,
In Search of the Miraculous. 1949.

Life is Real only Then, When "I AM".
E. Dutton, New York, 1975.

Meetings with Remarkable Men.
Routeledge & Kegan, New York, 1974 (1963).

Views from the Real World.
Dutton & Co., New York, 1975.

The Herald of the Coming Good.
Weiser, New York, (1974) 1933.

Holmes, C.
Within-Without from Zero Points: Book I, *The Heart Doctrine: Mystical Views of the Origin and Nature of Human Consciousness.*
Zero Point Publications, Kemptville, Ontario, Canada 2010.

Within-Without from Zero Points. Book II, *Microcosm/Macrocosm: Towards a Metaphysics and Cosmology of Consciousness.*
Zero Point Publications, Kemptville, Ontario, Canada, 2010.

Psychological Illusions: Explorations of the G. I. Gurdjieff Fourth Way Teaching.
Zero Point Publications, Kemptville, Ontario, Canada, 2010.

Lee, C.
The Promised GOD-MAN is Here.
Ruchira Avatar Adi Da Samraj.
Dawn Horse Press, Middletown, California. 1998.

Nicoll, M.
Psychological Commentaries on the Teachings of G. I. Gurdjieff and P.D. Ouspensky.
Robinson & Watkins, London, 1975.

Nott, C.
Journey Through This World: Meetings with Gurdjieff and Ouspensky.
Weiser, New York, 1969.

Ouspensky, P.
In Search of the Miraculous: Fragments of an Unknown Teaching.
Harcourt, New York, 1949.

The Fourth Way.
Vintage, New York, 1957.

Patterson, W.
Struggle of the Magicians: Exploring the teacher-student relationship. Arete Communications, Fairfax California, 1998.

Peters, F.
Boyhood with Gurdjieff.
Penguin Books, Inc., Baltimore, 1964.

Roth, G.
The Quest to find Consciousness.
Scientific American, Special Edition, MIND. 2004.

Sagan, C.
Psychology Today interview.
Jan/Feb. 1996.

Broca's Brain: Reflections on the Romance of Science. Random House,
New York, 1979.

Zero Point Publications
Box 700, Kemptville, Ontario, Canada K0G-1J0

PSYCHOLOGICAL ILLUSIONS
Explorations of the Gurdjieff Fourth Way Teaching

Christopher P. Holmes

The central illusion of humankind is that we *"know self."* The components of this illusion concern the different powers or capabilities which men and women think that they possess but which in reality they do not. Four primary illusions or misunderstandings concern the faculties of consciousness, the unity of I, the possession of will (or the capacity to do) and the existence of the soul. The fourth way psychology begins with a study of humans as they are under the conditions of mechanical life and then describes the psychology of man's *possible evolution*. Humans can awaken and experience new states of consciousness, achieve a unity of "I" and real will, and thus attain the soul. Unfortunately, wrong ideas and convictions about the nature of consciousness, unity and will, are major obstacles to self knowledge. If we can begin to understand these illusions, then there is a chance of escape, of awakening and evolution.

According to Beelzebub, the central character in Gurdjieff's *Tales*, the three-brained beings on planet Earth are microcosmoses or *"similitudes of the Whole."* As such, they have the possibility of not only serving local cosmic purposes, feeding the earth and moon as part of organic life on earth, but also of experiencing sacred being-impulses, attaining varied levels of objective reason and individuality and even of *"blending again with the infinite."* (1950) As a microcosm of the macrocosm, a human being can potentially coat higher being-bodies for the life of the soul, instinctually sense cosmic truths and phenomena, and maintain existence within the subtle realms of being after death—achieving different levels of immortality. Unfortunately, humankind came to exist only in waking sleep states of automated consciousness, perceiving reality topsy-turvy, conditioned by pleasure and self love, and wasteful of their sacred sexual substances. Human beings no longer realize their deeper cosmic purposes and possibilities, or attain real "I."

Psychological Illusions explores the psychology, metaphysics and cosmology of the fourth way teaching. This includes material on the *Ray of Creation*, the fundamental cosmic laws, the alchemical crystallization of *higher being-bodies* for the life of the soul, and the miraculous possibilities existing for the evolution of the individual human being. The Gurdjieff fourth way teaching is a profound and coherent system of esoteric teaching about the horror of the situation for humanity asleep, living under their psychological illusions.

ISBN 978-0-9689435-2-6
www.zeropoint.ca

$24.95 Cdn

Zero Point Publications

GOD, SCIENCE & THE SECRET DOCTRINE
The Zero Point Metaphysics and Holographic Space of H. P. Blavatsky

Christopher P. Holmes, Ph.D. (Psych)

"... the Secret teachings ... must be contrasted with the speculations of modern science. ... To make of Science an integral whole necessitates, indeed, the study of spiritual and psychic, as well as physical Nature. ... Without metaphysics ... real science is inadmissible."

H. P. Blavatsky, 1888

H. P. Blavatsky's *The Secret Doctrine* was published in 1888 and is relatively unknown in modern times. As it happens in this strange universe, Madame Blavatsky over a century ago anticipated numerous modern concepts concerning the creation of the Universe and the mechanisms of the laws of nature, including the holographic paradigm in psychology and physics. Blavatsky articulated the concept of the zero point or singularity origin of the Cosmos and of Sons, and a profoundly alternative view of the nature of the Aether and higher Space dimensions.

Blavatsky states: *"... 'material points without extension' (zero-points) are ... the materials out of which the 'Gods' and other invisible powers clothe themselves in bodies ... the entire universe concentrating itself, as it were, in a single point."* Dr. Holmes has grasped the profound meanings of this claim and related these ancient mystical teachings to the newest ideas in physics and science, and to explorations of human consciousness, spirit and soul, and the mysteries of the Heart. *God, Science & The Secret Doctrine* raises the ultimate question of the existence or non-existence of God—and what we mean by this term.

ISBN 978-0-9689435-6-4

www.zeropoint.ca

$24.95 Cdn

Zero Point Publications

WITHIN-WITHOUT from ZERO POINTS I

THE HEART DOCTRINE
Mystical Views of the Origin and Nature of Human Consciousness

Christopher P. Holmes

" ... "material points without extension" are Leibnitz's monads, and at the same time the materials out of which the 'Gods' and other invisible powers clothe themselves in bodies.... the entire universe concentrating itself, as it were, in a single point."

H. P. Blavatsky, The Secret Doctrine, I. Cosmogenesis, 1888

Modern psychology and science have been dominated by "the head doctrine"–the assumption that the material brain produces consciousness. In contrast, mystics claim that the origins of consciousness and Self are related to the mystical dimensions of the Heart. We are individual "eyes" or "I"s of "THAT," the divine unity within which we live, move and have our being. Mystical experiences involve penetrating various veils of nature which allow for the awakening of consciousness and the Heart, the realization of higher Space dimensions, and experiences of the unity of things within the inner life. Most importantly, human beings have a zero point centre and this is the means by which higher dimensional influences bring life and consciousness into the living being. These are the deep mysteries explored by the fool at the zero point.

Within-Without from Zero Points is an extremely unusual and provocative series which juxtaposes the most advanced concepts in modern science with mystical and spiritual teachings. It provides a sweeping scope of inquiry into the ultimate mysteries of consciousness, life, creation and God.

"My mission is to help uncover the forgotten, deep heart teachings of Jesus. ... The information you have gathered on the zero point has been a powerful validation of my own inner meditation practice and intuitions. Hence it has greatly enhanced my faith and the effectiveness of my meditation. Thank you so very much for your labors." **John Francis, *The Mystic Way of Radiant Love: Alchemy for a New Creation.***

"... if Christopher Holmes' articulation of 'the heart doctrine' had been restricted to citing and commenting upon those awe-inspiring teachings, he would have accomplished a great deal by establishing the foundation of an alternative paradigm to that which dominates contemporary approaches to the study of consciousness. However, when he introduces the mysterious concept of "the zero point," his arguments take on a level of significance which is, in my opinion, unparalleled in modern consciousness research. ..." **James A. Moffatt**

ISBN 978-0-9689435-0-2
www.zeropoint.ca

$24.95 Cdn

UPCOMING

WITHIN-WITHOUT from ZERO POINTS III

TRIUNE MONADS IN SEVEN DIMENSIONAL HYPERSPACE
Scientific and Mystical Studies of the Multi-Dimensional Nature of Human Existence

Christopher P. Holmes

Monads draws from the teachings of Madame Blavatsky, Kabbalah and Judaism, Gurdjieff, and a wide range of mystical doctrine about the multidimensional nature of human existence. Esoteric teachings identify the abode of the 'I' as within the human heart, where a triune Monad element is established within a Seven Dimensional Eternal Parent Space which underlies and sustains our normal physical four-dimensional space-time complex. Such ideas from mystical sources bear profound relationships to theories in advanced physics as to the nature of Space itself, quantum interconnectedness and higher dimensional superstring elements at zero point levels. A triune and sevenfold Monadic Essence spins a Web of Spirit, Soul and Matter within a Seven Dimensional Virual Reality out of the Aethers of the void and plenum, the quantum vacuum. In order to illustrate the necessity for such an alternative understanding of reality, this work examines evidences for out-of-body experiences, Sheldrake's fields of extended mind, enigmas posed by heart transplant patients and twin studies, and an interpretation of other paranormal investigations.

Zero Point Publications

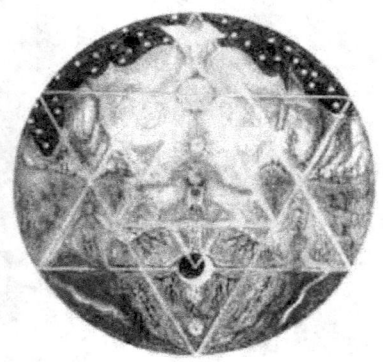

WITHIN-WITHOUT from ZERO POINTS II

MICROCOSM-MACROCOSM
Scientific and Mystical Views on the Origin of the Universe, the Nature of Matter & Human Consciousness

Christopher P. Holmes

" ... "material points without extension" are Leibnitz's monads, and at the same time the materials out of which the 'Gods' and other invisible powers clothe themselves in bodies.... the entire universe concentrating itself, as it were, in a single point." H. P. Blavatsky, The Secret Doctrine, I. Cosmogenesis, 1888

"... all the so-called Forces of Nature, Electricity, Magnetism, light, heat, etc., are in esse, i.e., in their ultimate constitution, the differentiated aspects of that Universal Motion. ... for formative or creative purposes, the Great Law modifies its perpetual motion on seven invisible points within the area of the manifest Universe." Madame H. P. Blavatsky, The Secret Doctrine, 1888

"It is necessary to notice that in the Great Universe all phenomena in general, without exception wherever they arise and manifest, are simply successively law-conformable 'Fractions' of some whole phenomenon which has its prime arising on the Most Holy Sun Absolute." G. I. Gurdjieff, 1950

Mystical accounts of states of Union, or unity with the world or universe on varied levels, attest to the fact that there is some kind of inner magic and alchemy going on within the inner cosmos of human consciousness—a metaphysics and physics to consciousness and the human heart.

Microcosm-Macrocosm explores the newest theories in physics and creation science—including materials on superstrings, higher dimensions, singularities, the quantum vacuum and the holographic principle. It also draws from ancient metaphysics—particularly The Secret Doctrine of H. P. Blavatsky (1888), esoteric Judaism and Kabbalah, and the cosmology and metaphysics of G. I. Gurdjieff. This is a challenging and provocative work with deep insights into the Divine Mystery teachings and a unique critique of modern science philosophy. It provides a shocking alternative view of the zero point origins of human consciousness and cosmos.

ISBN 978-0-9689435-1-9
www.zeropoint.ca

$30 Cdn

WITHIN-WITHOUT from ZERO POINTS IV

A FOOL AT THE ZERO POINT
An Autobiographic Tale about the Strange Case of Professor Z, the Mysteries of Love and Ecstasies of the Heart & the Horror of It All

Christopher P. Holmes

Christopher, by the grace of God, will provide an autobiographical account of his life experiences, his psychical and mystical experiences, his life struggles and relationships, and an account of awakening to the horror of it all. This work includes materials on Christopher's struggles for academic freedom at York University, his twelve years of work in correctional centres as a forensic psychologist, his life and loves, and his awakening to psychopathology of the world elites with their plans for committing genocide against the human race.

Zero Point Publications

ZERO POINT TEACHINGS
Selected Articles and Writings
of Mystical Psychologist & Scientist

Dr. Christopher P. Holmes

The zero point teachings are a portal of some sort to awaken you to a higher dimensional model of yourself and the structure of reality--to view the world in a magical and mystical way. The basic idea is that all living beings, including yourself, have a zero point centre within and this is the means by which "the Gods and other invisible powers clothe themselves in bodies"--as explained by mystic scholar Madame Blavatsky in The Secret Doctrine (1888). Just as the scientists conceive that the huge universe grew from an infinitesimal singularity out of the quantum vacuum, so also, I suggest that you also have such a hidden zero point or singularity source condition--a singular I within the Heart. Further, we ourselves emerge "out of nothingness" in some mysterious way unknown to modern science and contemporary understanding.

This selection of articles and writings is drawn from the www.zeropoint.ca web site and from Christopher's varied books. It also includes original socio-political writings briefly posted to the zero point web site but then withdrawn. This book includes materials on the origin and nature of human consciousness, the mystery teachings of the heart doctrine, Kabbalah and The Secret Doctrine, modern physics and quantum theory, a commentary on the psychopathology of humanity based on the teachings of G. I. Gurdjieff, book, movie and music critiques, and much more.

ISBN 978-0-9689435-7-1
www.zeropoint.ca

$30 Cdn

ZERO POINT RADIO
Live two hour Internet Radio Broadcasts

every second Saturday
www.bbsradio.com.

In North America- 4 to 6 pm Eastern Time, 1 to 3 pm Pacific, 10-12 pm GMT Dr Christopher P. Holmes hosts an online internet Radio Broadcast through **www.bbsradio.com.** Previous broadcasts are available for online listening at the Zero Point archive service. These include shows on the zero point hypotheses, the magical formula of 137, on consciousness and the heart doctrine, the metaphysics of H. P. Blavatsky's The Secret Doctrine, the insanity of humankind and the criminality of the elites. James A Moffatt serves as commentator and interviewer, with invited guests. Shows archived at **www.bbsradio.com.**

www.ingramcontent.com/pod-product-compliance
Lightning Source LLC
Chambersburg PA
CBHW080921180426
43192CB00040B/2609